About This Book

Why is this topic important?

This book is based on the premise that organization development (OD) should be more relevant today than ever before and the observation that, by and large, executives ignore OD or relegate it to the bowels of the organization. We believe that it is time to take a tough look at the field. OD still has much to offer, but to continue pretending that all is well guarantees that OD will continue to struggle to find its place and its identity in today's world.

What can you achieve with this book?

By collecting the contributions of leaders in the field of OD, we have provided you with tremendous food for thought about the current condition and future prospects for OD. We hope that this book will be an impetus to self-examination and then to true revitalization.

How is the book organized?

We asked a dozen leaders in the field to consider the discrepancy between OD's relevance for the current organizational climate and the fact that most leaders make little use of OD. What has resulted is a rich variety of thinking on the status of OD and its future. Bracketed between opening and closing chapters by the book's editors are chapters addressing such topics as contemporary challenges in OD; the principles of organizational performance; a discussion of the "morphing" of OD; a treatise on how current OD practitioners should be part anthropologist, part therapist; and a call to revitalize the field through a shift in its paradigm, among others.

About Pfeiffer

Pfeiffer serves the professional development and hands-on resource needs of training and human resource practitioners and gives them products to do their jobs better. We deliver proven ideas and solutions from experts in HR development and HR management, and we offer effective and customizable tools to improve workplace performance. From novice to seasoned professional, Pfeiffer is the source you can trust to make yourself and your organization more successful.

Essential Knowledge Pfeiffer produces insightful, practical, and comprehensive materials on topics that matter the most to training and HR professionals. Our Essential Knowledge resources translate the expertise of seasoned professionals into practical, how-to guidance on critical workplace issues and problems. These resources are supported by case studies, worksheets, and job aids and are frequently supplemented with CD-ROMs, websites, and other means of making the content easier to read, understand, and use.

Essential Tools Pfeiffer's Essential Tools resources save time and expense by offering proven, ready-to-use materials—including exercises, activities, games, instruments, and assessments—for use during a training or team-learning event. These resources are frequently offered in looseleaf or CD-ROM format to facilitate copying and customization of the material.

Pfeiffer also recognizes the remarkable power of new technologies in expanding the reach and effectiveness of training. While e-hype has often created whizbang solutions in search of a problem, we are dedicated to bringing convenience and enhancements to proven training solutions. All our e-tools comply with rigorous functionality standards. The most appropriate technology wrapped around essential content yields the perfect solution for today's on-the-go trainers and human resource professionals.

www.pfeiffer.com   *Essential resources for training and HR professionals*

Reinventing Organization Development

Practicing Organization Change and Development

The Change Agent Series for Groups and Organizations

MISSION STATEMENT

The books in this series are intended to offer leading-edge approaches to organization change and development. They are written for and by practitioners interested in new approaches to facilitating effective organization change. They are geared to providing both theory and advice on practical applications.

SERIES EDITORS

Kristine Quade
Roland Sullivan
William J. Rothwell

EDITORIAL BOARD

David L. Bradford
W. Warner Burke
Lenneal Henderson
Edith Whitfield Seashore
Christopher G. Worley

Other Practicing Organization Change and Development Titles

Practicing Organization Development: A Guide for Consultants, A Second Edition
William J. Rothwell and Roland L. Sullivan

*Finding Your Way in the Consulting Jungle: A Guidebook
for Organization Development Practitioners*
Arthur M. Freedman and Richard E. Zackrison

Facilitating Organization Change: Lessons from Complexity Science
Edwin E. Olson and Glenda H. Eoyang

Appreciative Inquiry: Change at the Speed of Imagination
Jane Magruder Watkins and Bernard J. Mohr

*Beyond Change Management: Advanced Strategies
for Today's Transformational Leaders*
Dean Anderson and Linda Ackerman Anderson

The Change Leader's Roadmap: How to Navigate Your Organization's Transformation
Linda Ackerman Anderson and Dean Anderson

Guiding Change Journeys: A Synergistic Approach to Organization Transformation
Rebecca Chan Allen

Balancing Individual and Organizational Values: Walking the Tightrope to Success
Ken Hultman with Bill Gellermann

The Conscious Consultant: Mastering Change from the Inside Out
Kristine Quade and Renée M. Brown

Organization Development and Consulting: Perspectives and Foundations
Fred Massarik and Marissa Pei-Carpenter

*Relationships That Enable Enterprise Change:
Leveraging the Client-Consultant Connection*
Ron A. Carucci, William A. Pasmore, and the Colleagues of Mercer Delta

*Rewiring Organizations for the Networked Economy: Organizing,
Managing, and Leading in the Information Age*
Stan Herman, Editor

The Innovation Equation: Building Creativity and Risk Taking in Your Organization
Jacqueline Byrd and Paul Lockwood Brown

*Consulting to Family Businesses: A Practical Guide
to Contracting, Assessment, and Implementation*
Jane Hilburt-Davis and W. Gibb Dyer, Jr.

*Organization Development at Work: Conversations
on the Values, Applications, and Future of OD*
Margaret Wheatley, Robert Tannenbaum, Paula Yardley Griffin,
Kristine Quade, and Organization Network

Enterprise-Wide Change: Superior Results Through Systems Thinking
Stephen Haines, Gail Aller-Stead, and Jim McKinlay

Reinventing Organization Development

New Approaches to Change in Organizations

David L. Bradford and
W. Warner Burke

EDITORS

Pfeiffer

A Wiley Imprint

www.pfeiffer.com

Published by Pfeiffer
An Imprint of Wiley
989 Market Street, San Francisco, CA 94103-1741
www.pfeiffer.com

Readers should be aware that Internet websites offered as citations and/or sources for further information may have changed or disappeared between the time this was written and when it is read.

For additional copies/bulk purchases of this book in the U.S. please contact 800-274-4434.

Pfeiffer books and products are available through most bookstores. To contact Pfeiffer directly call our Customer Care Department within the U.S. at 800-274-4434, outside the U.S. at 317-572-3985, fax 317-572-4002, or visit www.pfeiffer.com.

Pfeiffer also publishes its books in a variety of electronic formats. Some content that appears in print may not be available in electronic books.

ISBN: 0-7879-8118-4

Library of Congress Cataloging-in-Publication Data

Reinventing organization development : new approaches to change in organizations / David L. Bradford and W. Warner Burke, editors.— 1st ed.
      p. cm.
  Includes bibliographical references and index.
  ISBN 0-7879-8118-4 (alk. paper)
  1. Organizational change. 2. Reengineering (Management) I. Bradford, David L. II. Burke, W. Warner (Wyatt Warner), 1935-
  HD58.8.R45 2005
  658.4'06—dc22
                            2005011542

Acquiring Editor: Matthew Davis
Director of Development: Kathleen Dolan Davies
Developmental Editor: Susan Rachmeler
Production Editor: Justin Frahm
Editor: Thomas Finnegan
Manufacturing Supervisor: Becky Carreño
Illustrations: Justin Frahm

Printed in the United States of America

Printing   10   9   8   7   6   5   4   3   2   1

Contents

Introduction   1

1. The Crisis in OD   7
   W. Warner Burke and David L. Bradford

2. The Future of OD, or Why Don't They Take
   the Tubes out of Grandma?   15
   Jerry B. Harvey

3. Contemporary Challenges to the Philosophy
   and Practice of Organization Development   19
   Robert J. Marshak

4. A Historic View of the Future of OD:
   An Interview with Jerry I. Porras   43
   David L. Bradford and Jerry I. Porras

5. Organization Development: Requiem or Reveille?   65
   Tony Petrella

6. OD: Wanted More Alive Than Dead!   87
   Larry E. Greiner and Thomas G. Cummings

7. On the Demise of Organization Development   113
   Chris Argyris

8. Organization Development: A Wedding of
   Anthropology and Organizational Therapy   131
   Edgar H. Schein

9. A Paradigm for Professional Vitality   145
    Peter P. Vaill

10. Ideas in Currency and OD Practice:
    Has the Well Gone Dry?   163
    Barbara Benedict Bunker, Billie T. Alban,
    and Roy J. Lewicki

11. The Future of OD?   195
    David L. Bradford and W. Warner Burke

About the Editors   215
About the Contributors   217
Index   223
Pfeiffer Publications Guide   231

*To the pioneers, the first generation of OD practitioners,
who saw the potential—and to the present innovators
who strive to keep the field relevant*

Practicing Organization Change and Development Board Statement

On behalf of the advisory board, it is my pleasure to be a part of and to support the (re)launching of the Practicing Organization Change and Development Series. The series editors, the publishers, and the advisory board vigorously discussed and debated the series' purpose, positioning, and delivery. We challenged extant assumptions about the field of organization change, change management, and organization development; we argued about perspectives on relevance, theory, and practice; and we agreed that there's a story that needs to be told through a series of books about change. In this first board statement, I want to relate—as best as I can—our rationale for renaming the series, describe our purpose, and position this book in the series.

The most obvious change in this relaunching is the series title. We argued and agreed that it should be changed from "Practicing Organization Development: The Change Agent Series for Groups and Organizations" to the "Practicing Organization Change and Development Series." While that may be the most obvious change, it is certainly not the most significant one. Our discussion and debates led us to the firm belief that organization development (OD) was only one method of organization change, that OD was misunderstood by many to be synonymous with organization change and change management, that OD's reputation is at best fragmented, that the field could not be defined by tools and techniques but had to embrace the entirety of the social and behavioral sciences, and that the series we wanted should be of the highest quality in terms of both theory and practice. Ultimately, we agreed that the books in this series should redefine the field of organization change and development in the broadest sense and should describe the best of innovative approaches to organization change and development.

A good example of our intent to redefine the field is to compare and contrast OD and change management. While both are concerned with change, the labels do describe their intent and philosophy. Organization development is concerned with development, growth, learning, and effectiveness. It is based primarily in the behavioral sciences. Change management, on the other hand, is concerned with implementation, control, performance, and efficiency. It is borne out of reengineering and project management perspectives. Our view was that organization leaders would be best served by a series that embraced and integrated a variety of views on change. "Good" change in a global economy cannot be defined only by amounts and levels of participation, by costs (or people) reduced or profits achieved, or increases in organization size.

The first book in the series relaunching, *Practicing Organization Development, Second Edition,* is a good example of this purpose. It represents an initial step to define one boundary of the field of organization change and development. Written from the OD perspective, it proposes that good change is more often participatory than dictated, more concerned with learning and growth than performance, and more dependent on the behavioral sciences than on economics. To be sure, the field of organization change and development is broader than the perspective described here. However, this first installment in the series does represent a practical, state-of-the-art description of the OD perspective.

In addition to redefining the field, we believed that the series should be written for and by practitioners interested in facilitating effective organizational change. Books should be grounded but not constrained by theory and practice and geared to providing advice on the practical issues and applications facing organizations and their leaders. Again, *Reinventing Organization Development* reflects our intended purpose. It is written by some of the best scholar-practitioners in the field. The authors have the standing to describe best practice authoritatively. Finally, the chapters in this book are grounded in both theory and practice.

Our hope is that this series will raise the level of debate about organization change and development and that it will be of great assistance to change practitioners and organization leaders entrusted with growth, development, and performance of organizations. We hope you agree that this book is a good start.

Christopher G. Worley

March, 2005

Malibu, California

Introduction

This book is built around two observations:

1. Given the issues confronting today's leaders, OD should be highly relevant and central to an organization's operations.

2. But for the most part, leaders make little use of OD. Instead, OD, if it exists at all in organizations, is either relegated to the lower ranks in the hierarchy or brought in periodically to "clean up problems." Rarely does OD sit at the executive decision-making table as a partner in driving the organization.

Why is this? It is truly a troubling state of affairs for a field to be so marginalized when it started out fifty years ago with great promise. In this book, we have asked a dozen of the leading scholar-practitioners in the field (including several of its founders) to speak to these issues. What, in their view, has caused this discrepancy? What needs to be done to have OD play a central role as organizations face increasing change in moving more and more into the knowledge economy?

Chapter One, "The Crisis in OD," tees up the discussion by elaborating on these two observations—the contemporary need for OD and its marginal position. We then contrast the original role that OD played half a century ago with its present (peripheral) acceptance. We note the tension inherent in the question, Is the field truly based on "the applied behavioral sciences," or is it more driven by humanistic values?

"The Future of OD, or Why Don't They Take the Tubes out of Grandma?" (Chapter Two) is a provocative piece by Jerry B. Harvey, who uses a disturbing analogy to argue that the heyday of OD is past and we should abandon efforts to keep the field on life support. Instead, he argues, it's time to pull the plug and hold a decent burial.

In Chapter Three, "Contemporary Challenges to the Philosophy and Practice of Organization Development," Robert J. Marshak, an experienced organizational consultant, notes that in the past OD was in the forefront of organizational change, but now it has been eclipsed by the field of change management. He then explores five forces that account for this loss of centrality. If "Classical OD" is less relevant, Marshak explores the possibility of "Neoclassical" and "New OD" approaches.

In Chapter Four, "A Historic View of the Future of OD: An Interview with Jerry I. Porras," we have a personal account of the development of the field. Porras, one of the early scholars of OD who has done some of the best research on its effectiveness, traces the development of OD. He suggests how several of the early assumptions have limited the field's present effectiveness by placing undue emphasis on the individual and group (a point that Schein elaborates in Chapter Eight). Porras too wonders about the future relevance of OD.

In "Organization Development: Requiem or Reveille?" (Chapter Five), Tony Petrella, one of the foremost organization consultants, lays out what he thinks OD consultants should do if they truly want to develop organizational capability. His seven dimensions nicely frame the domain that must be considered and set a high bar, but one that consultants can find useful as a standard against which to measure themselves.

In Chapter Six, "OD: Wanted More Alive Than Dead!" Larry E. Greiner and Thomas G. Cummings, experts in the field of organizational change, trace the developmental history of OD and identify six orientations ("red flags") that detracted from the effectiveness of OD and laid the seeds for strong resistance in the last half of the twentieth century. They then discuss how OD has "morphed" in the last decades. Even though this may have allowed the field to gain more acceptance, they raise the question of whether OD has moved so far from its original roots that its identity has been lost. Also, they note that this change has led to a new set of red flags that may limit OD's potential.

In Chapter Seven, "On the Demise of Organization Development," Chris Argyris, one of the founders of the field, argues that in spite of the fact that OD promulgates the value of "learning organizations," it is more driven by humanistic values that prevent the type of double-loop learning that the field would need in order to continue to develop. In laying out his argument, he challenges us with several examples of closed-loop reasoning by OD practitioners that protects them from taking an objective look at themselves and their actions.

In the eighth chapter, "Organization Development: A Wedding of Anthropology and Organizational Therapy," Edgar H. Schein argues that contemporary OD is "a conglomerate of many theories, practices, and value systems." But in all of this he suggests there are two underlying perspectives that OD consultants should have. Since they deal with groups and organizations, they should be more like anthropologists; since they are helpers in producing change, they need the skills of a (family or group) therapist who would think in systems terms. Schein then traces the history of OD and points out how the field got off course by focusing on the individual, resulting in many OD consultants today being naïve about culture and complex systems change.

In "A Paradigm for Professional Vitality" (Chapter Nine), Peter P. Vaill stresses the impact that T-groups had on the formative years of OD and argues that the early vitality and promise of the field came from three forces: an emphasis on process, experiential learning that was powerful and unforgettable, and a strong integrative culture. He suggests that OD relinquished the forces that made it powerful through fragmentation and loss of direction. Furthermore, he argues that until OD returns to these three variables, it will never recover its vitality or be able to connect itself to the new bodies of ideas and methods that are continuously appearing.

In Chapter Ten, "Ideas in Currency and OD Practice: Has the Well Gone Dry?" Barbara Benedict Bunker, Billie T. Alban, and Roy J. Lewicki raise the question of why there has been a dearth of new core concepts that could keep the field fresh and contemporary. After noting that such transfer occurred more readily in the past, they identify the barriers that have grown to separate the research and practitioner subcultures. They argue that it is these barriers, rather than the lack of relevant conceptual material, that are the problem in each area learning from the other. To illustrate their argument, they identify more than a half a dozen areas in social psychology that contain powerful and relevant theory and research that are relevant to OD.

We conclude in Chapter Eleven, "The Future of OD?" not with a summary of the previous nine chapters (they are of such value that they should be read on their own) but instead with our own assessment of why OD has not reached its potential. We argue that OD has a vital role to play in today's organizations and that much would be lost if it were declared "dead" or prematurely integrated into the field of change management (especially as a field with an exclusively bottom-line financial perspective). But we warn against three powerful barriers that must be overcome if the field is to truly reinvent itself: (1) the lack of O in OD, (2) too exclusive an emphasis on human processes, and (3) the deleterious effects of humanistic values. We are concerned that these forces are so embedded in the field that there may not be the courage to confront them and make tough choices.

Consequently this book lays out ten "answers" to the initial question of why—just when it should be so relevant—OD is so marginalized. But these various answers amount to no definitive answer.

That is our objective. We want to raise possibilities and demand of you, dear reader, to furnish your own answers.

In so doing, reflect on the multiple roles that you play.

First, if you are a consultant, are you—and do you want to be— an OD consultant? This is a field with no barriers to entry, and many people claim the label but do not engage in the practice as described by the various authors. It may be that you use various *OD techniques*. This is well and good, but it does not make one an OD consultant. We are all in favor of people saying they want to do team building, third-party intervention, conflict resolution, appreciative inquiry, visioning, and the like. These are all valuable approaches and can have useful payoffs to individuals and teams. But it does not mean that you are *developing organizations*.

Second, as an OD consultant, you have not only a responsibility for how you represent yourself (and whether you have the competencies you need to deliver on expectations that you can develop *organizations*) but a responsibility to the field itself. You are likely to be mentoring others who are starting off; what are the minimal competencies they should have? What do you think educational programs that offer a degree in OD should cover? What should be the function of the professional organizations to which you belong?

Third, for those of you who run OD programs in academia, what is included in the curriculum? Have you fostered the belief that "it is only process" and that knowing various organization functions is not relevant? Many of the contributors to this volume stress the importance of linking OD with strategy, and with aiding the financial success of the organization (be it for-profit or nonprofit). Are you offering that knowledge? Perhaps as important, are you legitimizing it as a necessary concern of your graduates?

Fourth, for those involved in the professional societies, what are you doing to help the field look at itself? We want to acknowledge as a positive sign that the major OD organizations have commissioned a study to assess the present state of affairs (Wirtenberg, Abrams, and Ott, 2004). However, will findings be put into practice? It is our experience that too many OD consultants tend to be more self-congratulatory than willing to engage in tough self-examination. (This being reflected in the fact that too often professional meetings tend to collude in supporting this behavior.)

Fifth, if you are an executive, what are you demanding of the (internal and external) OD professionals that you employ? Are you settling for people who don't really understand the entire system and are not able to intervene at the systems level? Burke (2004) raises the question of where internal OD folks should report. Are you relegating them to a position far down in the organization, which guarantees they will be largely irrelevant to developing your organization?

We believe it is time to take a tough look at the field. OD still has much to offer. But to continue the practice of pretending that all is well guarantees that OD will continue to be peripheral. We hope this book will be an impetus to such self-examination and then to true revitalization. Otherwise, as Jerry Harvey suggests, it might be better to pull the plug.

References

Burke, W. W. "Internal Organization Development Practitioners: Where Do They Belong?" *Journal of Applied Behavioral Science,* 2004, *40*(4), 423-431.
Wirtenberg, J., Abrams, L., and Ott, C. "Assessing the Field of Organization Development." *Journal of Applied Behavioral Science,* 2004, *40*(4), 465-479.

1

The Crisis in OD

W. Warner Burke and David L. Bradford

This book is based on the *premise* that OD should be more relevant today than ever before and the *observation* that, by and large, executives ignore OD or relegate it to the bowels of the organization. This leads us to a crucial and paradoxical *question*: "If OD is so potentially relevant, why is it often ignored?"

The Potential Relevance of OD

Today change is constant and inevitable (as are death and taxes). In fact, one could argue that producing and managing change is *the* core task of leaders—and isn't OD synonymous with change?

With exponentially increasing movement toward knowledge industries, tapping into and fully using human expertise is more important than ever before. Offering approaches that "tap into" member knowledge is a particular strength of OD.

Increasingly, knowledge is dispersed throughout the organization. Those below may have special training and expertise not held at the top. Further, they are likely to be closer to the problem and certainly to the customers. Because of this, more than ever there is a clear need to reduce the power gap in organizations. Executives and managers would no doubt agree that participative management has positive payoffs, but they frequently don't practice it. Another form of the gap, as Chris Argyris would put it, is a difference between espoused theory and theory in action. Rosabeth Moss Kanter has commented that "participation is something the top orders the middle to do for the bottom" (1983, p. 244). The gap between rhetoric and practice remains wide. Yet OD people know that *involvement leads to commitment*. Involvement of people in decisions that directly affect them is both a strength and a value of OD.

With globalization continuing to expand at a rapid pace and with the United States in particular being more diverse as a society than ever before, there is a need for valuing and use of differences. Coupled with this is greater need for learning across geographic, ethnic, and value differences. This requires learning about human differences, about the consequences of stereotyping, about cross-cultural dynamics, and about conflict management and cooperative resolution. Many OD practitioners have expertise in helping people address and deal with diversity.

If present conditions would make OD potentially even more relevant than in the 1960s, then why are certain anomalies so prevalent?

• OD practitioners do not, as a rule, sit at the table of power. It is unusual for OD practitioners to work with executives to help plan and implement strategy for the organization, to be involved in developing a new business model and implementing it through the hierarchy. Why are OD consultants rarely brought in when there is to be a merger or acquisition, or in planning whenever a major reorganization is to take place? (They may be brought in only afterward to clean up problems.)

• OD practitioners do not necessarily need to be experts in business strategy, but they often do not sufficiently understand the language and how profit is made and costs contained according to various business models. Most important, OD practitioners do not seem to have adequate knowledge of large-scale strategic organization change—that is, how a particular business strategy fits with the overall mission of the company, how a change in business strategy affects the culture and vice versa, and how the structure of the organization has to be changed. In short, OD practitioners do not appear to be experts about strategy implementation.

- Even where there is an internal OD function (far from universal in organizations), why is it so frequently buried within HR? The lead OD person may not even report to the head of HR but to someone lower down the hierarchy such as the head of human resource development. Just as likely there is a perception on the part of high-level executives that HR is one of the weakest functions in the organization anyway. Under these circumstances it is difficult for OD practitioners to experience positive regard, much less have organizational influence. In the early days of OD, circumstances of this kind were not the norm. Internal OD practitioners such as Sheldon Davis, Sy Levy, Harry Kolb, and Paul Buchanan had considerable influence.

- Ask OD practitioners today if they are doing OD and most would respond, "Of course." Our argument is the opposite. OD practitioners for the most part are carrying out piecemeal activities using OD techniques and tools but are not involved in a systemwide change effort. OD practitioners are busy (1) serving as facilitators for off-site meetings; (2) conducting team-building and visioning exercises; (3) serving as coaches for supervisors and managers; (4) helping to resolve conflict between bosses and subordinates, among peers (especially in a matrix structure), and between work units that need to cooperate instead of compete; (5) providing leadership training and development for supervisors and managers; and (6) conducting focus groups to clarify problems and issues that need attention.

There is absolutely nothing wrong with these activities; in fact, they are generally helpful to managers and beneficial for the ongoing survival of the organization. But the point is that these activities are not typically part of an overall system change initiative; therefore this is not OD as we define it and as the field has been defined for a long time.

The Definition of OD

OD is one form of organization change. It is planned (rather than unplanned) change that focuses on all levels of an organization— individual, group, intergroup, total system, and interorganizational— rather than limiting the practice to one or two levels, as in, say, management and leadership development. OD relies primarily on application of the behavioral sciences rather than on, say, industrial engineering. OD practitioners may not be opposed to application of industrial engineering, but their consulting is simply based much more on psychology, sociology, and cultural anthropology.

The *content* of OD should be very much about organization mission and purpose, strategy, leadership, management behavior, and ultimately about culture change, typically change in the culture to support a change in mission, strategy, or leadership.

The *process* of OD concerns implementation of change in the content areas we have just noted and follows a plan of phases and steps. Even though the emphasis is on *planned change*, much of OD work is dealing with *reaction* to these planned steps. In other words, considerable effort on the part of OD practitioners goes to helping leaders of change in the organization deal with *unanticipated* consequences to the change process, to initiatives and interventions that are planned yet do not result in outcomes that were considered in advance and anticipated.

In addition to relying on the behavioral sciences, the underlying theory for OD practice is open system theory. Any organization is considered in terms of having *input* from its external environment, *throughput* (action based on the input, producing a product or service), and *output* (the ultimate performance of the organization). A feedback loop connecting output back with input completes the open system framework; what an organization produces (output) enters the external environment via customers and other stake-holders and in turn affects the input, thus completing the cycle.

Finally, as with all theoretical systems OD is values-based. Most OD practitioners believe that it is appropriate and right to:

1. Pursue congruence of individual and organizational goals, to search for what is good for the organization, which should be good for the individual employee, and vice versa

2. Promote openness and honesty in relationships

3. Create opportunities for all organizational members to learn and develop personally toward full realization of individual potential

4. Redress any imbalance between individual choice and free-dom and organizational constraints; sometimes too much choice can be harmful to the organization and therefore constraints are in order, and sometimes organizational constraints are too restrictive regarding individual freedom and therefore should be lessened

5. Pursue collaborative (as opposed to imposed) change; those affected by the change process should be involved in designing and implementing the change process

6. Minimize the power discrepancy between individuals and between levels in the organization

7. Surface conflict between and among individuals as well as between and among units of people in the organization, and deal with these conflicts directly rather than avoid, ignore, or collude with these differences

These seven values are representative, not the universe of values for the field of OD.

The point is that the practice of OD is based on both the find-ings and methodology of applied behavioral science *and* a set of beliefs about the congruence of human and organizational behav-ior that is humanistic in nature.

What, then, is OD? From this discussion, we can offer a defini-tion of OD:

Based on (1) a set of values, largely humanistic; (2) application
of the behavioral sciences; and (3) open system theory,
organization development is a systemwide process of planned
change aimed toward improving overall organization
effectiveness by way of enhanced congruence of such key
organizational dimensions as external environment, mission,
strategy, leadership, culture, structure, information and reward
systems, and work policies and procedures.

The Early Days of OD

Two independent movements and organizations on both sides of the
Atlantic Ocean in the late 1940s set the stage for the emergence of
OD. In the United States, it was the T-group (sensitivity training)
movement and the organization then known as the National Training Laboratories (NTL), based in Washington, D.C., and Bethel,
Maine. On the other side, in the U.K., it was the group relations
conference and the sociotechnical systems movements located at
the Tavistock Institute in London. The people shaping these movements soon learned about one another and quickly began to
exchange knowledge and experiences. Gradually what began as
experiments in small groups ("laboratories") became accepted as
useful and beneficial methods with which adults could learn and
grow. They could learn more about themselves as individuals
and became more interpersonally competent, particularly in such
domains as conflict management, authority related dynamics, and
building trust.

Gradually (we're in the late 1950s now) these group-based
methods of learning and change began to be used in organizations.
If these individual learning and group dynamic methods were
applied systematically in organizations, then eventually the organization itself would be changed; at least that was the belief and
intent (see, for example, Argyris, 1964). In the U.K., Eric Trist,
Fred Emery, and colleagues were applying their sociotechnical and

group-based methods of learning and change in coal mines and in the textile industry in India. In the United States, T-group methods were being applied by such people as Herbert Shepard, Paul Buchanan, and Robert R. Blake in oil refineries, and at about the same time (1958–59) Douglas MacGregor and Richard Beckhard were conducting similar activities for General Mills. Soon thereafter Jim Dunlap and Sheldon Davis, internal HR professionals at TRW Systems in Los Angeles, were conducting group-based activities with organization change as the goal. They also brought in academically based external consultants such as Bob Tannenbaum, Charles Ferguson, Warren Schmidt, and George Lehner.

Beckhard and MacGregor were using both group-based and sociotechnical system methods at General Mills and were emphasizing participative and bottom-up management. They did not want to label what they were doing as bottom-up, so they chose the term "organization development." Apparently independent of MacGregor and Beckhard, Blake and Shepard were also beginning to use the same term. Thus, OD emerged and evolved. These were heady days. Exciting changes were happening with these relatively new methods of learning and risk taking, within important industries in the United States. Subsequently, major OD efforts arose in the 1960s in organizations such as TRW, General Foods (the Topeka dog food plant experiment was especially noteworthy), Harwood-Weldon Manufacturing, Union Carbide, Esso (now Exxon Mobil), Pillsbury, Dow Chemical, Proctor & Gamble, the U.S. State Department, and the Episcopal Church.

It should be noted that although OD leadership came from internal professionals, notably Sheldon Davis at TRW, Harry Kolb at Esso, and Sy Levy at Pillsbury, the predominant lead came from academically based scholar-practitioners: Beckhard, MacGregor, Warren Bennis, and Edgar Schein at MIT; Argyris at Yale; Tannenbaum and Schmidt at UCLA; Paul Lawrence at Harvard; Blake and Jane Mouton at the University of Texas; and Shepard at Case Western University. Scholarly folks and practitioners worked together in forming the OD Network in the early and mid-1960s, as well as launching the first OD training program in 1967 at NTL, the Program for Specialists in Organization Training and Development. NTL served as the initial coordinator for both the PSOTD (later called PSOD) and the OD Network. Demand for the PSOD and the ODN grew rapidly. The 1960s and early 1970s represented the period of greatest growth for the field of OD. There was much excitement and tremendous promise.

But times, and OD, have changed. The promise and expectations from the 1960s and 1970s have not been realized. Thus we are back to our original question. If OD is potentially so much more relevant today than when it started, what happened? Where did it go off the tracks? Is it possible to regain the relevance it would appear to deserve?

We asked a dozen leaders in the field to answer this question. Several of them were founders in the field, and all have had extensive consulting experience. What follows are not scientific treatises but rather their personal statements from reflection and practice. We end with our answer to the question and then our prediction of the future. Can OD reach its potential, or is it doomed to be relegated to the sidelines?

References

Argyris, C. "T-groups for Organizational Effectiveness." *Harvard Business Review*, 1964, 42(2), 60–74.

Kanter, R. M. *The Change Masters*. New York: Simon & Schuster, 1983.

2

The Future of OD

Or, Why Don't They Take the Tubes out of Grandma?

Jerry B. Harvey

Recently I visited an old acquaintance who was hospitalized. Several friends told me he was quite ill. Sadly, I'd lost contact with him many years ago. We had known one another for a long time, but I can't honestly say that we were ever really close. I never found him easy to know, maybe because he went by a lot of aliases and although he was always a charmer I could never be sure who he really was. Nevertheless, since my informants told me that his death was imminent, I wanted to pay my last respects—but to be absolutely truthful, the longer he lived, the less respect I had for him. Ultimately, I don't know for sure why I felt constrained to see him. Perhaps I'm just sentimental, or maybe I went out of some convoluted sense of obligation.

My acquaintance was housed—or warehoused, depending on one's point of view—in the intensive care unit. From rumors I heard via the grapevine, that wasn't new. In fact, from what I understand, he had been in ICU for many years. Although being a layperson and therefore someone who is unqualified to make informed judgments regarding matters of impending life and death, I am convinced that he was barely breathing, if he was breathing at all. Personally, I have my doubts, even though he must have been breathing because he was attached to a respirator.

Someone, who I presume was a hospital attendant, or maybe a representative of hospice, was adjusting one of the many tubes that ran into various locations of his body.

"Who are you? Why are you here?" the attendant asked when I entered the room. He seemed surly to me. My inquisitor either wasn't friendly by nature or was just having one of those bad-hair days.

"I'm an old acquaintance of your patient," I replied. "I haven't seen him in a long time, though. We used to spend a lot of time together, but we sort of drifted apart."

"Well, you're lucky you came when you did," answered the attendant. "She's comatose. Look at that monitor over her bed. She's brain-dead, to be sure. Hasn't had a thought in years. She has a good heart, though. It's still beating strongly, but that's about all that's working like it should. If it weren't for all of these tubes and other gizmos, she would be a flat-liner for sure."

I was struck by the callousness of his statement.

"She?" I responded in total surprise. "Did you say 'she?' Are you sure about what you just said? Maybe I'm in the wrong room. When I knew her, she was a he," although I had to admit that, despite the ventilator providing oxygen, the array of tubes protruding from beneath the sheets, and the thick blankets virtually hiding my acquaintance from view, the person with whom I was visiting certainly had a lot of feminine features.

"You didn't know about her sex-change operation? Man, you've been away for a long time. Many of her relatives say she's never fully recovered from the complications that go along with that kind of surgery, particularly when they do it gradually, over a matter of years. Just between you and me, I've noticed that her relatives seldom discuss her surgery in public. In fact, many of them don't discuss it at all. The topic seems to be a no-no. I guess that all families have their secrets. You know what I mean: subjects that can't be discussed. I know my family does. We sure as hell don't talk about the fact that Uncle Henry is a drunk; at least we don't talk about it in public."

"How long has she been in this condition?" I asked.

"I can't really tell you for certain. Visitors tell me she's been in critical condition for ten years for sure, maybe up to twenty or longer. When they brought her in here, she was in such bad shape that she wasn't even able to tell the doctors what she did for a living. In fact, her original doctor, a Dr. Misciagna[1] if I remember correctly, said she spoke in gibberish—word salad. He says that while he was assigned to her case, she told him she did at least seventy-five different things for a living. He wrote them down for the purpose of keeping good records, but he said that he couldn't make any more sense of them than he could make sense of a table of random numbers.

"According to him, at various times she said she did empowering, massaging, deconflicting, leadershiping, coaching, gridding, sensitizing, feedbacking, spiritualizing, T-grouping, rolfing, quality managing, deep sensing, cheese chasing, change managing, appraising, diversifying, Myers-Brigging, renewing, life balancing, energizing, story telling, holistic knowing, mind mapping, group learning, team building, Enneagramming, reengineering, and a bunch of other stuff that I can't recall. The doctor's notes say that she was totally incoherent. He never figured out what was wrong with her, but if you ask me, I think she OD'd on something. I just don't know what."

"Did he attribute her incoherence to the sex-change operation?"

"Not that I know of—at least there's nothing in his notes about it if he did. All he said is that she appeared to be dangerously unbalanced."

"Well, what's going to become of her?" I asked.

"Mister, you've got me," the attendant replied. "If I had to guess, I'd say that her family is just going to let her slowly waste away until her heart stops beating and she dies. From their visits I can tell that they clearly love her a lot and seem like they desperately want to keep her alive.

"Most of them call her 'Grandma.' I'm not sure why. The name on her official records is Hope. She's been here for so long, the people down in the Records Department apparently have lost her full name."

Growing more and more frustrated in my search for information, I said, "Has anyone ever thought of taking all of those tubes out of Grandma and letting her die in dignity?"

"Maybe so," the attendant replied. "But no one has said anything to me about doing it. In fact, every few months a family member runs in here with some strange doctor in tow and starts yelling, 'I've found an elixir that's going to cure Granny. See if you can find a place to insert another tube.'"

"And you do it?"

"Of course I do. My job is not to reason why."

"Do any of the new cures ever work?"

"Obviously not. Occasionally one of them will perk her up for a little while and her family gets all excited, but whatever they bring inevitably loses its power. I've been around here long enough to know that's going to happen, and I'm sure that her family knows it, too."

"If you know that the cures aren't going to work, and the family also knows it, why do you keep putting new tubes into Grandma?"

"I told you. I do whatever the family and their doctors tell me to do, even if I believe what they're doing to her is absolutely crazy."

"That doesn't sound very rational to me," I said.

"Of course it's not rational," replied the attendant, who was obviously becoming irritated by our conversation. "But if it makes any difference to you, buster, I'm not about to be the one to take the tubes out of Grandma. I have to make a living doing something. And to make a living, I'm just like all the rest of her family. I need Grandma—I need Hope."

Note

1. Misciagna, M. "What Is Organization Development? A View from the Internet." Unpublished manuscript, George Washington University, Washington, D.C. The article is an excellent description, built from the Internet, of how OD adherents view their work. It also contains a thoughtful discussion regarding the role of what Wilfred Bion terms "pairing"—hopeful expectation devoid of reality—in the practice of OD.

3

Contemporary Challenges to the Philosophy and Practice of Organization Development

Robert J. Marshak

For more than a decade there have been consistent concerns and questions raised in the academic and practitioner communities about the state of organization development (OD). The main observation has been that OD is not playing a central role during a time of extensive organizational change worldwide. In his 1993 Distinguished Speaker Address to the Organization Development and Change Division of the Academy of Management, Robert E. Quinn lamented: "We are in an interesting situation. We live in a world where organizations are struggling as never before to make change. The demand is enormously high. Meanwhile we have a discipline supposedly centered on the issue of how to make change, and we seem to have little influence. Something is wrong" (Quinn, 1996, p. 4).

Those most concerned point out that in its early years OD was at the forefront of organizational change, inventing the foundational terminology, theories, and techniques still used today. In those years, OD practitioners worked closely with CEOs and heads of major divisions to bring change to highly bureaucratic organizations. Now, the story goes, all that has changed. Today most (but not all) OD practitioners find themselves left out of working at the highest levels on the major changes that have been transforming organizations and industries for the past ten to twenty years. Instead OD is viewed by a few as dead, and by many others as having become marginalized or even irrelevant to the central change issues facing CEOs of contemporary organizations. Concurrent with the perceived decline of organization development has been the rapid ascendance of another organizational change practice, called "change management," that has been spearheaded by the major global management consulting companies such as Accenture (formerly Andersen Consulting), BearingPoint (formerly KPMG), Cap Gemini Ernst and Young, and IBM Business Consulting Services (which acquired PriceWaterhouseCoopers Consulting). It is the practitioners of change management who now work closely with CEOs and heads of major divisions on transforming the world's corporations. The practitioners of organization development are left wishing to be involved but working mostly at lower organizational levels on less central issues, or with smaller organizations, associations, and nonprofits.

It is the intent of this discussion to look more closely at this situation, attempt to discern and describe some of the dynamics that may be involved, and conclude by offering a few suggestions about possible future directions for organization development. The presentation begins with an extended discussion of some of the major challenges and controversies confronting OD. These include issues related to the underlying humanistic philosophy or ideology of organization development, its relative inability to respond to a range of business trends since the 1980s, and some implications of the emergence and influence of postmodernism and the new sciences for OD theory and practice. Next, the shifting demographics of OD practitioners between 1986 and 2001 are reviewed along with some reflections on the possible consequences. Finally, initial ways to begin addressing the questions and issues raised in the presentation are discussed, including the need to begin differentiating at least three types of OD.

Challenges and Controversies

There are a number of interdependent considerations for trying to understand the present state of organization development. They form something more like a tapestry of interwoven challenges and controversies than a set of independent, causal variables. A central consideration throughout is the ongoing challenges and controversies since the 1980s to the underlying philosophy or ideology of OD. This is discussed in some detail here, followed by briefer discussion of other related controversies and challenges.

Humanistic or Business Orientation

One good way to help reveal the underlying philosophy or ideology of OD is to compare it to another related philosophy of organizational change, called change management. To begin the discussion we must first recognize that despite the generic qualities about the names *organization development* and *change management*, both are jargon or even marketing or brand names, used to describe a certain set of organizational change practices. It is also argued that they are terms representing ideological views on the processes and purposes of organizational change.

Briefly stated, the term *organization development* came into use in the late 1950s and early 1960s to describe a set of practices rooted in the behavioral sciences to create planned change in organizations (Burke, 1987; Cummings and Worley, 1997). Early practitioners of what became known as OD were heavily influenced by ideas and normative values based in social psychology and humanistic psychology—for example, the work of Lewin, Lippitt, Maslow, McGregor, Argyris, and the NTL Institute. The term *organization effectiveness* has also been used to describe basically the same practices.

In the 1980s, the major accounting and management consulting companies expanded their traditional practices to include "reengineering" or "business process reengineering" services. This ultimately led to the naming, or branding, of these new practice areas as *change management*. Thus, for a while at least reengineering and change management were virtually synonymous. As a practicing organizational change consultant at that time, I quickly learned from discussion with potential clients that I needed to carefully explore what they meant, and therefore what services they were seeking, when they used the term *change management*. In the early 1990s, in almost all cases, when I was asked if I did change management, what they really meant to ask was if I did reengineering. Additional background about, and a more detailed comparison of, organization development and change management is in Worren, Ruddle, and Moore (1999).

In change management, the assumption tends to be that specific changes can be identified and implemented using planning and project management techniques, while employing participative processes as a way to secure buy-in and support for the changes. Needed changes are identified, planned, and led by managers and executives using consultants as agents and resources to help direct or steer the change(s). These changes are almost always intended to advance the competitive and therefore economic and financial well-being of the organization and its shareholders. Other outcomes of the change may be important, but secondary to the economic objectives. From this interpretation, change management might also be considered ideologically to mean "engineering organizations for economic gain."

In organization development, in contrast, the assumption is that changes cannot be successfully identified, let alone implemented, without the true involvement of those responsible for doing the actual work. The purpose of involvement is to secure the best ideas and information to address the situation, with buy-in a side benefit. It is also usually assumed that there will be interdependencies and dynamics that cannot be fully anticipated or planned for, requiring an interactive process open to new developments and outcomes. Emphasis is therefore on identifying and facilitating effective change processes assuming that the proper process(es) will lead to the best outcome(s). Finally, OD envisions that change processes should lead to more humanistic organizations where greater emphasis on human development, freedom, creativity, and empowerment produces greater organizational efficiency, effectiveness, and economic return. For example, in the introduction to their seminal discussion of planning change, Bennis, Benne, Chin, and Corey (1961) assert, "The predicament we confront, then, concerns method; methods that maximize freedom and limit as little as possible the potentialities of growth; methods that will realize man's dignity as well as bring into fruition desirable social goals" (p. 2). From this interpretation, OD might also be considered ideologically to mean "facilitating human development for social and organizational gain." A short summary comparison of change management and organization development appears in Table 3.1.

Another way to quickly compare the underlying ideologies of OD and change management is to consider the everyday language and values associated with each. Despite the fact that both address how to create or manage organizational change, and in many cases they advocate similar principles and practices, the core emphasis is different. What is figure for one is ground for the other, and vice versa. The language and values, and therefore normative orientation, of OD are very much based in the language and values of humanism and social psychology. The language, values, and normative orientation of change management are very much based in the language and values of economics and business. See Table 3.2 for a quick summary to illustrate the point.

Ideologically, from an OD perspective change management is incomplete or misdirected because virtually by definition a directed, engineering approach to securing primarily economic ends does not fully achieve the real purposes of organizational change. If real organization change should include human as well as economic processes and purposes, then engineering change is inherently incomplete. One cannot engineer human development, dignity, freedom, creativity, artistry, and so on. Consequently, change implicitly or explicitly intended to create those purposes cannot exclusively use an engineering-for-economic-gain approach. In this sense, change management is an incomplete approach to organization change because it cannot create the normatively envisioned humanistic organization that should result from an OD effort.

Table 3.1. Comparison of Change Management and Organization Development

Change Approach	Emphasis on	Methods	Dominant Values	Management of Change as
Change management	Outcomes	Elite processes	Economic	Engineering and directing
Organization development	Processes	Participatory processes	Humanistic	Facilitation and coaching

Table 3.2. Language and Values of Social Psychology and Humanism vs. Economics and Business

Dimension	Social Psychology and Humanism	Economics and Business
Highest value	Human development	Financial return
Instrumental agent	Awareness	Money and resources
Image	Self-actualization	The bottom line
Location of values in action	Inner self	The marketplace
Icon	Enlightened and empowered self	Entrepreneur and business executive
Theme	The individual:	Business and markets:
	• Freedom	• Competitive strategy
	• Dignity	• Profit and loss
	• Empowerment	• Productivity
	• Emotions	• Return on investment
	• Spirit	• Efficient use of resources
	• Holistic integration	• Economic wealth

However, from a change management perspective OD is also incomplete, or at least somewhat contradictory or confusing, because OD seems to advocate *individual* development over *organizational* performance. The traditional OD response to this basic question of individual versus organizational needs and interests is to assert that in essence if you create a humanistic organization it will inherently be a high-performing organization.

Touchy-Feely and Bottom-Line Orientation

Given the language, values, and ideological orientation of OD, it should not be surprising that it has been labeled by its critics as "too touchy-feely" almost from the very beginning. For as long as I can remember, I have heard that approbation applied to OD along with requests to be more bottom-line oriented or less "airy-fairy" and deal more with the "nitty-gritty." Although these labels or epithets have been around for as long as OD, there is an important difference today. In the 1960s and 1970s the broader society was more liberal, more valuing of individual development and expression. Social values and business conditions were leading people to question the efficacy of the machine-like bureaucratic model of organization. OD was potentially both a value system and a way to free locked-up human and organizational potential. Forty years later, conditions have changed. Globally, most societies have become more conservative (or "moved more to the center"). Global competition and relentless cost cutting and job elimination have elevated the needs of the organization for competitive success over the needs of individuals. Ask not what your organization can do for you, ask what you can do for your organization . . . and be grateful you have a job. A more conservative orientation wherein organizational success allows the possibility of individual accomplishment is more the norm in most organizations I encounter today. As a consequence, the ideological orientation and emphasis of OD is more marginalized today than ever before. This is not just in terms of the values and orientations of today's managers and executives, but also of newer generations of would-be OD practitioners. As one Generation X-er commented in a plenary session at an OD conference held in the mid-1990s, "Do you have to be a hippie from the sixties to be an OD consultant?" An important issue facing OD therefore is the compatibility of the philosophical or ideological orientation developed in the 1960s with current conditions. Just as most liberal ideologies, whether they be liberal democratic, socialist, or communist, have had to adjust their philosophies in the past forty years, so too might OD need to adjust its underlying premises and values in some ways and to some degree.

Challenges from Downsizing, Reengineering, and Change Management

Serious challenges to the ideological orientation and practice of OD emerged in the late 1970s and early 1980s in the form of the downsizing and reengineering movements. The inability of OD to effectively respond to these business trends helped create a void that was ultimately filled by change management practitioners.

First, let us consider the OD response to downsizing. As an example, I will use my experiences in the late 1970s. At that time, President Jimmy Carter began efforts to reduce the size of the federal government, including the agency where I worked as a full-time internal consultant. At the time there was little written about downsizing, and nothing to provide guidance on how to do it. Over the ensuing three or four years, and continuing under President Ronald Reagan, I was involved in multiple efforts to downsize thousands of employees from my agency, eventually leading to elimination of my own job and staff. That's when and how I became an independent consultant! During that time period there never developed an OD position on downsizing, nor any methodologies, approaches, or interventions to address it. Many of the OD colleagues I interacted with at the time felt it should not and could not, as a matter of principle, become involved in eliminating jobs and careers. This reminded me of earlier debates at NTL-sponsored OD workshops in Bethel, Maine, toward the end of the Vietnam War, when the majority of participants generally felt it would be immoral to provide OD services to the military. Today, more than twenty-five years later, as downsizing efforts continue unabated, there is still no OD position on whether or not it is acceptable to be involved in downsizing, nor (if acceptable) are there any specific OD methodologies, approaches, or interventions to guide how to address it (Worley and Feyerherm, 2003). Also, there was and still is some question whether or not the principles and practices of organization development will work during the more conflictual, self-protective, and trust-destroying dynamics often associated with a downsizing effort. As a colleague remarked to me in 1979, "OD practices work when organizations are growing, not when they are in decline."

Next, consider what happened regarding reengineering and OD. In the late 1970s and 1980s I had many OD colleagues who were heavily involved in workplace redesign efforts, primarily using sociotechnical systems (STS) design principles and methods. At that time STS was an accepted, if not dominant, aspect of OD practices. By the 1990s OD practitioners working on work redesign efforts using STS principles had largely disappeared. What happened is a revealing story. First and foremost the market for workplace redesign efforts was successfully taken over by the major accounting and management consulting companies. Prior to their entry into the market, individual or small groups of OD-oriented practitioners provided craftlike redesign services, usually emphasizing the "socio" as much as or more than the "technical" dimensions of organization design. The major consulting companies entered the market in the mid-1980s offering standardized business process reengineering services, typically emphasizing technical over social dimensions, while still using many of the same STS principles and methodologies. They also offered their services in a more ideologically friendly package and on a scale (thousands of consultants) impossible for the mom-and-pop OD practitioners to match. At the same time, many (but not all) OD practitioners were openly skeptical or opposed to reengineering interventions, considering them to be or to have become nothing more than thinly disguised ways to justify and carry out further downsizing rather than enhancing the capabilities of an organization and its workforce. Concurrent with this trend, fewer and fewer new OD practitioners were being trained in work redesign or STS principles and practices. By the 1990s presentations related to work redesign had vanished from OD conferences, and STS theory was largely absent from the major OD degree and certificate programs that were training a record number of new practitioners (AU/NTL, Bowling Green, Case Western, Columbia, Fielding, Pepperdine, NTL, and so on).

Finally, in many ways change management was spawned in the mid-1980s by the major accounting and business consulting companies responding to the downsizing and reengineering movements. By the 1990s it could be argued that change management, not organization development, had become the dominant brand of organization change in most large corporations. In addition to the differing ideological orientation of change management, it also strongly incorporated and integrated business strategy and information technology along with the traditional business disciplines into its principles and practices. Many of the people-involvement change practices used in OD also became a part of change management, but to a lesser extent and with another ideological focus, as previously discussed. In the meantime, OD practitioners (with some exceptions) never really embraced or integrated strategic planning, information technology, or the business disciplines into their practices. Instead they opted to continue advancing and refining ideas and techniques related to the "softer side" of change: organizational culture, diversity, large group methods, organizational learning, mental models, and appreciative inquiry.

The net result of these and other factors, along with the fact that most corporations were now confronted with requirements to restrategize their businesses and incorporate information technology to increase productivity and cut costs (including people costs), was that by the 1990s change management had become the OD approach of choice in the executive suite of most major corporations. Certainly some OD practitioners were, and still are, involved in important change efforts at the highest level of major corporations, but they have become more the exception than the rule and never as comprehensively involved as the major change management consulting companies.

Challenges from Human Resources, Executive Coaching, and Extra Lean Organizations

In OD, the role of the consultant is to partner with responsible managers and involve those affected by any potential change(s) in processes that lead to improved results or relationships. The managers and employees are expected to assume ownership of the change by learning new skills and behaviors and by doing the change work themselves, while the OD consultant suggests and facilitates the process. In operationalizing this approach, early OD practitioners were advised to start at the top and cascade efforts down through the organization. Unfettered access to the top of an organization was considered to be critical, and early internal OD staffs positioned themselves to be independent of the Personnel Department and report directly to the CEO. When I worked as an internal consultant in the 1970s, my staff was called the Organization and Management Development Staff; we were a staff division separate from and equal to the Personnel Division. Today, there are many more internal OD staffs and capabilities than thirty years ago, but few if any report to the CEO. Most, in fact, are part of the Human Resource Division and usually exist in some combination with training, executive or leadership development, or succession planning, thus blurring and confusing the difference among OD, training, and HR planning. Despite what is asserted in theory, OD in practice in many organizations has become, and is thought of as, a human resources function, with all the limitations and expectations associated with that.

Another challenge to OD comes from the recent exponential increase in executive coaching. In OD, a consultant might coach an executive or manager incidental to his joint work on a change effort that could include multiple two- or three-day retreats and workshops. Now this same executive can meet alone for one or two hours in the privacy of his own office to discuss how to develop himself, work more effectively with others, and improve his area of responsibility. Though not the same as OD, executive coaching offers a viable service and consequently a substitute addressing human and psychological dimensions. It also can be consumed in smaller and less demanding time increments, in the comfort of one's own office, and where the manager has more control than would be possible in a facilitated group setting. In that sense, regardless of whatever else one may think of the recent explosion in executive coaching, it has taken market share away from organization development. In fact, partly because both heavily involve psychological and people dimensions, many OD practitioners today also market themselves as executive coaches as a way to take advantage of the market boom in coaching.

Finally, the trend since the 1980s toward very lean organizations may also have some consequences for OD. In most of the organizations where I consult, people are extremely busy, working long hours with little or no slack time or resources. What they want is someone under their direction to do the work for them, or to furnish a more or less turnkey operation. This extends to change efforts as well. Following the OD principle of getting the client fully involved and learning the skills to manage change themselves is sometimes experienced as simply too time-consuming and requiring too many scarce resources to be a realistic option for an overworked and understaffed executive. The classic interpretation, of course, is that this is a form of resistance. It might also just be a form of reality in today's high-pressured, twenty-four/seven, very lean organization.

From a harried executive's point of view it may sometimes be better to hire your own virtual organization change staff to manage the change, under your auspices. Thus an additional way to look at the ascendancy of change management consultancies is that they offer themselves as temporary, virtual change management staffs to busy executives managing very lean organizations.

Modern to Postmodern Controversies

Among the many streams contributing to the original formulation of OD was a strong positivist orientation rooted in mid-twentieth-century social science research methodologies. The whole premise of data-based change (for example, action research and survey research methods) presumes the existence and validity of an objective, discernible reality. By the 1980s, however, constructionist and postmodern approaches were beginning to heavily influence the social sciences with ideas about multiple realities and the inherent subjectivity of experience (Bergquist, 1993). Whether intended or not, these ideas seem to have influenced or been incorporated into OD thought and practice since the mid- to late 1980s. Whereas change management was integrating ideas predominantly from the objective business sciences, OD practitioners began incorporating more constructionist and postmodern ideas from the behavioral sciences, especially psychology, sociology, linguistics, and anthropology. The development of appreciative inquiry in the 1980s, based in part on social constructionist premises, is but one example of this trend. There has also been increased interest in multicultural realities and the influence of consciousness and mental models on organizational behavior. OD practitioners also seemed much more interested in the "new sciences" (Wheatley, 1992) than the traditional ideas from physics and biology that had helped shape the original formulations of OD theory. A partial listing of a new series of practitioner-oriented books published by Pfeiffer since 2001 is shown in Table 3.3 to help illustrate my point.

Table 3.3.   Some Early Titles from the Practicing Organization Development Series

Title	Focus
Appreciative Inquiry: Change at the Speed of Imagination	In a constructionist world, the power of a positive (rather than a deficit) consciousness
Beyond Change Management: Advanced Strategies for Today's Transformational Leader	Transformational change requires transforming the consciousness of leaders
Facilitating Organization Change: Lessons from Complexity Science	Application of the new sciences to organizational change
Guiding Change Journeys: A Synergistic Approach to Organization Transformation	A cross-cultural guide to psychological or archetypal transformation
The Conscious Consultant: Mastering Change from the Inside Out	Clarifying one's consciousness and choices to better influence change

Although certainly not monolithic, this shift in interest and emphasis places contemporary OD and its practitioners sometimes at odds with traditional OD and with most business executives who still adhere to the premises of an objective, quantifiable, and measurable world. The increased emphasis on transforming consciousness, operating from multicultural realities, and methods that tend to be more about creating common social perceptions and agreements than data-based analysis all contribute to distinguishing a significant range of contemporary OD from its traditional roots.

This shift potentially exacerbates (or perhaps helps define) the differentiation between early and recent adherents of OD. It also raises the legitimate question of whether or not contemporary OD is becoming philosophically as well as methodologically different from traditional OD. Since many of the postmodern ideas influencing contemporary OD come from scholars based outside of most business schools, the shift may also be contributing to the increasing distance between some academics and business executives on the one hand and many (but certainly not all) contemporary OD practitioners on the other. When this shift is combined with the advent of change management, both trends beginning in the mid-1980s, it is perhaps no wonder that by the end of the 1980s and early 1990s, business school OD academics were beginning to declare OD dead or ineffectual.

Shifting Demographics of OD Practitioners

So far this discussion has highlighted some of the shifts from traditional to contemporary OD and the advent of change management, all beginning in the early to mid-1980s. Concurrent with these changes there has also been a significant shift in the demographics of OD practitioners. Although precise data are not available, a recently published summary of the changing demographics of membership in the OD Network is a revealing proxy. Table 3.4 summarizes some of the key shifts between 1986 and 2001 in who identifies with being an OD practitioner.

Table 3.4. Shifts in OD Network Membership from 1986 to 2001

Category	1986	2001
Total membership	1, 938	3,960
Women	39%	55%
Men	61%	45%
Median age	44	50
Over fifty	25%	48%
Doctoral degree	28%	7%
Race	Predominantly white	Predominantly white
Roles	No data available	Internal 41%, external 41%, academic 3%

Sources: Minahan (2002) and Minahan, Hutton, and Kaplan (2002).

During this period there was an increase of more than 100 percent in the number of OD Network members, potentially reflecting the growing market for organizational change consultants. A majority of these practitioners are now women, whereas in 1986 more than 60 percent were men. Practitioners are also older, are equally likely to be internal as external, and have significantly fewer doctoral degrees, but are still predominantly white. Finally, only 3 percent of practitioners belonging to the OD Network in 2001 identified themselves as full-time academics. This dramatically reflects the ongoing differentiation between scholars and practitioners of OD, at least in this particular association. The original OD scholar-practitioner ideal, it seems, has differentiated into either mostly scholars or mostly practitioners of OD with fewer and fewer scholar-practitioners.

Considered separately or as a whole, these shifts raise a number of questions and invite speculation about their meaning and potential impact on the practice of organization development. The shift from OD practitioners being mostly men to mostly women is perhaps most notable. Has this happened because a greater percentage of women in recent years have been attracted to or been "allowed" to enter the field? Is it because men are now less attracted to OD or are seeking opportunities elsewhere?

These questions leave us with a sort of chicken-and-egg causal quandary. Is the increase of women in OD at least partially a reflection of men leaving or avoiding a perceived-to-be-declining field of practice, or is the perceived decline or marginalization of OD a reflection of the increasing number of women practitioners since the mid-1980s?

Regardless of the reasons, if the historic biases toward women in the workplace continue to any degree, then a field of practice dominated by women could be susceptible to the same biases and stereotypes. For example, women and OD are too emotional and touchy-feely, women and OD don't have what it takes to address the tough issues, women and OD contribute best in supportive roles dealing with relationships and feelings, and women and OD belong in housekeeping functions such as human resources. Of course, if any validity is given to these stereotypes, then the interpretation that OD is too soft and irrelevant to contemporary business issues precisely because it has become a field mostly of women gains credence. Not surprisingly, I have heard both views expressed. This alone suggests that the valuing and roles of women and OD in contemporary business organizations are not entirely independent phenomena. It also makes one wonder if the majority of change management consultants are men or women.

The decrease in doctoral-level practitioners from more than one in four to less than one in ten raises a similar chicken-and-egg quandary. Is the increase in academic concerns about the current state of OD a reflection of the decline in doctoral-level practitioners, or is the decrease in doctoral-level practitioners a reflection of the decline in OD? There is also the question of the potential impact resulting from having fewer doctoral-level practitioners. The early books and articles that helped create and give legitimacy to OD were written mostly (but not exclusively) by scholar-practitioners who implicitly called for consultants well versed in objectivist behavioral science theories and methodologies in order to facilitate action research interventions with client systems. The decline in OD practitioners trained in social science research and methodology, the hallmark of most traditional doctoral programs, could therefore be a contributing factor to the shift away from a more or less "pure" action research approach to a wider variety of facilitated programs, events, and interventions. This shift could also be manifesting itself in the developing body of OD publications, where the orientation is more about "how to do it" than "the theory of how to do it." All this could end up increasing the relative distance between OD practice and established social science research, theory, and methodology, thereby contributing to the ongoing differentiation between scholars and practitioners of OD.

The aging of OD practitioners (at least OD Network practition-ers), where almost one in two is over fifty, may have some values-based or generational implications. As previously noted, OD came of age in the 1960s and classically reflects the liberal values and mores of that period. Thus the values and orientations of traditional OD may be more attractive to the baby-boomers who came of age in that era than to following generations. The comment, "Do you have to be a hippie from the sixties to be an OD consultant?" succinctly conveys the intergenerational tension. Some of the differences between tra-ditional and contemporary OD may therefore reflect tension between older and younger practitioners over what should be the controlling values and orientations of organization development.

Finally, we must wonder about the combined impact of these shifts on the acceptance and practice of OD in today's business orga-nizations. In the 1960s the OD consultant knocking on an execu-tive's door was likely to be an externally based white male with perhaps a doctoral degree. Today the OD consultant is likely to be a white woman without a doctoral degree who is perhaps an inter-nal HR employee. Exactly how this shift in demographics, in a field notoriously known as being too touchy-feely, affects perception about and practice of OD is open to further inquiry and debate. However, in any consideration of what has happened to OD, the changing demographics of practitioners needs to be an integral part of the discussion.

Paths Forward for OD

Clearly there are many challenges and questions confronting con-temporary OD. What, if anything, should be done is also full of controversy and conjecture. From the discussion so far, however, there seem to be a few givens and two types of option.

First, something needs to be done about definitions and terminology. When practitioners, academics, or managers talk about OD, are they referring to traditional OD, contemporary OD, human resources OD, or something else? When people say OD is dead or irrelevant, which OD are they talking about? What is needed is some form of taxonomy to define, compare, and contrast the variations of OD that have developed over the years. On the basis of this discussion, three types of OD that might profitably be distinguished are summarized in Table 3.5:

1. *Classical OD*, based on the original humanistic values, principles, and premises developed in the 1950s, 1960s, and 1970s combined with objectivist, action research methodologies (for example, data-based interventions focused predominantly on behavioral processes such as data feedback team development)

2. *Neoclassical OD*, which maintains a primarily action research orientation but augments or amends the original humanistic values with more emphasis on business values as well as on contemporary business issues and processes (for example, system redesign or transformation efforts that might include "rightsizing" to help configure an organization for competitive success)

3. *Social Interaction OD, or New OD*, which presently ranges from humanistic to business values but has been heavily influenced by postmodern constructionist and new sciences orientations (for example, appreciative inquiry, which is based on a constructionist worldview)

Table 3.5. Three Types of OD

Orientations	Modern, Objectivist	Postmodern, Constructionist
Predominantly humanistic, with some business values	Classical OD	New OD
Humanistic, with more business values	Neoclassical OD	New OD

As an additional reference point, the values-based distinction suggested here between Classical and Neoclassical OD is similar to the difference Worley and Feyerherm make between the "traditionalist" and "pragmatist" camps of OD (2003). They do not, however, differentiate between modern- and postmodern-based OD.

One difficulty among many in creating such taxonomies is that establishing typologies is typically the work of academics, and it is unclear who might do such work given the distance between today's OD scholars and practitioners. Convening a group of academics and practitioners to jointly explore classification schemas concurrent with an academic or practitioner conference might be a first step. Some organizational change typologies already exist in the literature, but they do not focus on differentiating the various types of OD. Instead they classify OD as but one of many approaches to organizational change (Huy, 2001; Palmer and Dunford, 2002). Until and unless there is better and more established philosophical and conceptual clarity about what we are talking about, it will be difficult to do anything regarding the current state of organization development. Another benefit of such clarification, of course, comes in the marketplace. Right now there is enormous brand confusion about what ideologies and services are offered by people calling themselves OD consultants. Classical, Neoclassical, and New OD consultants all claim they are doing something called "organization development" yet may offer widely divergent services and types of expertise.

Another set of issues worth exploring requires further research. These issues include what exactly dead or marginalized means, and who is practicing what type(s) of OD and with what impact. With respect to what is dead or marginalized, there are several important dimensions worth clarifying. For example, are OD principles, or practices, or philosophy, dead or marginalized? From my observations a great many of the practices and even principles of Classical OD are now routinely incorporated in change management, even in the everyday lexicon and behavior of most managers (although not Classical OD ideology). If OD principles and practices, but not necessarily ideology, are incorporated in whole or part into everyday management, coaching, change management, knowledge management, training, and so on, should we consider Classical OD to have been an enormous success or a marginalized failure?

In terms of who is practicing what types of OD, it might be revealing to find out who was an advocate of, say, Classical, Neoclassical, and/or New OD. This might help clarify why there are such differing perspectives on whether or not "OD is in trouble," and it could help create a conceptual bridge to foster more effective dialogue among academics, executives, and consultants. Another set of questions worth closer study relates to the changing demographics of OD practitioners. Exactly who and what has been marginalized? Have the principles and practices of OD been marginalized, or just women practitioners of OD? Is an OD practitioner with an advanced degree perceived differently from another practicing OD? Do they use different approaches and methods or get disparate results? These and other related questions are all worth exploring to help determine what, if anything, needs to be addressed.

Given this armchair analysis, and absent the research I have described, I offer two intentionally contrasting "ideal type" options for the OD community to ponder. Pursuing both simultaneously without conscious intent, as seems to be happening now, is likely to obscure the issues and confuse the marketplace.

One option is *intentional creation and legitimization of a Neoclassical OD*. This would require updating and rebalancing classical organization development in ways that ultimately make it closer to, but not identical with, change management. First and foremost, this involves rebalancing the ideology of OD to be less exclusively and stridently humanistic while incorporating more economic and organizational values. The classic formula that a humanistic organization would inherently be a high-performing organization would need some rethinking and rebalancing of values and beliefs. At the same time, the core humanistic values of OD cannot be abandoned or subjugated. This is philosophical work of an order similar to Chester Barnard's famous declaration of faith at the end of *The Functions of the Executive:* "I believe that the expansion of cooperation (the organization) and the development of the individual are mutually dependent realities, and that a due proportion or balance between them is a necessary condition of human welfare" (1938, p. 296).

In addition to a rebalanced ideology, Neoclassical OD would maintain an action research orientation while incorporating and integrating into its principles and practices the latest developments in the business disciplines and information technology—not totally or exclusively, but to a much greater extent than is the current situation. This also means that the presumed competencies and education of Neoclassical OD practitioners would need to be modified to reflect these additional knowledge and skill areas. The amount of education and knowledge required to be a proficient Neoclassical OD practitioner would also increase, reflecting the new mix of principles and practices. Given that many of the practitioners of change management have an MBA or other advanced degree, it would be reasonable to assume that a master's degree with additional training in people or business disciplines would be minimally required. None of this, however, will be possible until someone or some process is able to cogently and persuasively present a renewed ideology for OD. This will not be easy, but it is essential.

The second option is to *more purposefully articulate and legitimate a "New OD."* The New OD would or could be ideologically similar to Classical OD but more self-consciously based in postmodern, constructionist approaches in the social sciences, as well as the latest developments in the "new sciences" such as chaos theory and complexity science. The New OD might have even greater emphasis on the psychology of consciousness or mind-sets, as well as how to use social interaction, in large and small groups, to create meaning and reality. Its core methodologies would be based more on constructionist social and symbolic interaction than on problem-solving, objectivist action research. Such emphasis would not necessarily negate other OD practices, but it would ultimately require them to be practiced consistently with the philosophical premises of the New OD. This too would require modification of the education and competencies of New OD practitioners and might also require the equivalent of a master's degree with some additional training.

A conscious choice to be a New OD practitioner would also most likely be a conscious choice to be at the margin for most major, for-profit organizations. This would not necessarily be a bad thing. Historically, OD practitioners and academics have operated at the margin where they could have an impact on but not be incorporated into the system. It is only recently, with the success of change management, that many OD practitioners have wanted to be incorporated into mainstream business. Focusing on New OD would also allow academics and practitioners the opportunity to discover and invent new social technologies, which in time could become mainstream practices, as was the case with Classical OD.

Is Classical OD dead or dying? Perhaps, although it is certainly still practiced and preached by some practitioners and most academics. Are Neoclassical OD or New OD the only choices? No; both could be pursued, but probably not by the same person. In fact, it could be argued that right now all three forms of OD are being practiced. Unfortunately, all three are using the same brand name, creating confusion in the marketplace and an inability within the OD community to make choices and create clear focus and alignment around change ideologies and methodologies. OD is not at a crossroads; that point was passed in the 1980s. It is currently on multiple, unnamed paths without a clear sense of direction for any of them and formidable competitors in the marketplace. The paths need to be named, the requirements spelled out, and clear choices made.

References

Barnard, C. I. *The Functions of the Executive*. Cambridge, Mass.: Harvard University Press, 1938.

Bennis, W. G., Benne, K. D., Chin, R., and Corey, K. E. (eds.). *The Planning of Change*. Austin, Tex.: Holt, Rinehart and Winston, 1961.

Bergquist, W. *The Postmodern Organization: Mastering the Art of Irreversible Change*. San Francisco: Jossey-Bass, 1993.

Burke, W. W. *Organization Development: A Normative View*. Reading, Mass.: Addison-Wesley, 1987.

Cummings, T. G., and Worley, C. G. *Organization Development and Change* (6th ed.). Cincinnati, Ohio: South-Western, 1997.

Huy, Q. N. "Time, Temporal Capability and Planned Change." *Academy of Management Review*, 2001, 26(4), 601–623.

Minahan, M. "OD Network: Our Evolution and Growth." *OD Practitioner*, 2002, 34(2), 50–54.

Minahan, M., Hutton, C., and Kaplan, M. "What OD Practitioners Want and Need for Success." *OD Practitioner*, 2002, 34(2), 55–60.

Palmer, I., and Dunford, R. "Who Says Change Can Be Managed?" *Strategic Change*, 2002, 11(5), 243–251.

Quinn, R. E. "The Legitimate Change Agent: A Vision for a New Profession." *Academy of Management ODC Newsletter*, Winter 1996, pp. 1–6.

Wheatley, M. J. *Leadership and the New Science*. San Francisco: Berrett-Koehler, 1992.

Worley, C. G., and Feyerherm, A. E. "Reflections on the Future of Organization Development." *Journal of Applied Behavioral Science*, 2003, 39(1), 97–115.

Worren, N.A.M., Ruddle, K., and Moore, K. "From Organization Development to Change Management." *Journal of Applied Behavioral Science*, 1999, 35(3), 273–286.

A Historic View of the Future of OD

An Interview with Jerry I. Porras

David L. Bradford and Jerry I. Porras

DAVID BRADFORD: Jerry, thanks for doing this. Let's start at the beginning. You have had a long involvement in OD. What led you into the field?

JERRY PORRAS: My involvement in OD started at Cornell when I entered the MBA program. As part of the core curriculum I was required to take an OB (organizational behavior) course. Up to that time I'd never really taken a course in human behavior. I was an undergraduate electrical engineering major and my coursework consisted almost solely of math, science, physics, and engineering. Clay Alderfer had just joined the Cornell faculty fresh out of Yale, where he had been mentored by Chris Argyris. He and Tom Lodahl, who had been at Cornell for a while, decided they were going to experiment with the OB course. So each week they offered a required lecture the first session and an experiential activity the second session. For the second session we had a choice of either a case discussion group or a T-group.

I knew what a case discussion was like but had never heard of a T-group. In one of my riskier moments I said, "Well, I don't know what this T-group thing is all about, but let's try it." So I took the T-group section and, much to my surprise, found that it opened up a whole new life to me. It exposed me to experiences that I had never had before or, for that matter, had never even understood existed.

I really enjoyed the T-group process and soon realized that I could work well and effectively in that type of setting. As a result, I took a lot of other courses in OB, and collectively they wound up changing my career path. I decided not to go back into the business world, which was my intention when I started the MBA program, and instead get a Ph.D. in OB. I asked Alderfer for his advice on which Ph.D. programs might fit me best. He said, "Well look, you're interested in groups. You're interested in human transformation processes. Probably the best place to go to is UCLA because they're really doing both better than anyone else." I was fortunate to get into UCLA and went with the initial intent that I wanted to learn how to use groups to transform people.

If you recall, in the early 1960s groups (T-groups, sensitivity training groups, encounter groups) were being used primarily to transform people without much concern for the setting the group participant came from. The idea was to make everyone more inter-personally competent so that they could interact more effectively with each other in whatever situation they found themselves. At UCLA, they were running groups mainly for all types of people with only a relatively minor emphasis on people specifically *in organiza-tions*. However, by 1968, when I arrived, the primary focus had changed to one of targeting managers for transformation using group dynamics. The theory, very simply, was, "Let's transform the ways managers think about themselves and the ways they relate to peo-ple and solve problems, and once we've done that we can send them back home to transform their own organizations."

So upon entering UCLA I was really into the power and potency of groups to help people transform themselves—period. I wasn't too focused on the idea that, once personally transformed, people could then transform the larger social systems of which they were a part. At UCLA I quickly began to focus more deeply and specifically on the use of groups to transform organizations. The UCLA faculty had begun developing approaches to using group dynamics to build the capabilities of an organizational team. So team building became the dominant intervention technique for transforming organizations at UCLA. This fit very well with my interests, and I was very excited about being a part of the program.

To give you a simple bottom-line answer to your question, I think that in the beginning the thing that made OD attractive to a lot of people, including me, was the excitement and the energy that come from being involved in transforming people. To see people who were very interpersonally incompetent evolve into ones who are, for example, more self-aware, less defensive, accept feedback, listen better, become more empathic, openly express and deal with their feelings, share their power, confront conflict, and help others develop and grow was an incredible experience. I believe a lot of people got into OD in those early years because of T-groups and the intoxication of being involved in personal growth.

As a little aside here, I think I need to clarify something so that you'll better understand why the field of OD was so central to me for so many years. As I got more and more into T-groups and the introspection they trigger, I grew increasingly aware of a fundamental question I had about myself: "What lasting contribution do I want to make with my personal energies and life's work?" I discovered that I really wanted to dedicate my efforts to creating a better, healthier society. I think my ethnic roots and encounters with racism in my earlier years came into play here. I had experienced an unhealthy society, and I wanted to do my small part in making it better.

The basic question triggered by this thinking was, "How do I help create a better society?" My answer was that I could do that by helping organizations of all types become healthier. This view has stuck with me to this day, and I believe that throughout my career all of my work has been dedicated to trying to accomplish this end. In the jargon of *Built to Last*, my personal purpose is to help create a healthier society by creating healthier organizations. This is where I have been coming from since the very beginning of my career. Now, the fit with OD is that, historically, it also has been all about helping organizations become healthier.

BRADFORD: Let's pick up on that theme. You were at UCLA from 1968 to 1972. That was the period in which there were grand hopes that OD could help organizations become healthier. Can you spell out exactly how OD was seen as a tool to produce these healthier organizations?

PORRAS: I think the basic belief at that time was that OD processes could really transform people, make them psychologically healthier, in the ways I described earlier. Then, through the use of these improved interpersonal skills, people in the organization would develop more powerful ways to solve problems together, increase their participation, share power and decision making, get things done more effectively and efficiently, and so on. All of these outcomes were linked to the notion that if you could help people get more psychologically healthy, they could do these things better, and they could then help their coworkers grow in these same ways. When all that happens you wind up having a more effective, more successful organization. That, I believe, was the OD model at that time.

BRADFORD: You are talking about different levels of analysis, and I wonder, What was the main emphasis? Your last comment, about personal growth releasing the potential within the individual, is at the individual level, as contrasted to a group—as contrasted to intergroup change. I'm afraid you are going to say "all of the above," but was there a primary focus?

PORRAS: I think the focus definitely was more at the personal level. Because if you just take the units you are talking about—the individual, interpersonal, group, intergroup, organization—the West Coast perspective was that every link in the chain ultimately is driven by individual personal growth. You cannot have better interpersonal relationships if you've got psychologically sick people, or less-than-emotionally-healthy people. If you don't improve interpersonal relationships, you can't have effective group behavior. And so on up the chain.

So, I definitely think the early West Coast OD perspective was that organizational improvement starts with individual growth— that you have to become a healthier individual in order to trigger all these other things or to make them possible. It doesn't necessarily mean improvement at all the other levels will occur, but it's more likely to be an outcome if you start out changing the smallest unit in these layers.

As I said before, when I first arrived at UCLA, the heavy emphasis was on personal growth, and the tool to create it was the encounter group or sensitivity training group. Team building was not yet the main focus, although it was beginning to grow. In this model, strangers came together and experienced themselves and each other in such a way that everyone grew in their ability to understand themselves and their own behavior and interact more effectively. Once the group experience ended, participants would then return to their back-home settings and help everyone they came in contact with to grow interpersonally also. This would happen because of the returning individual's increased openness, willingness to share feelings, reduced defensiveness, increased sensitivity to the needs of others, increased caring, improved ability to give and receive honest feedback, and on and on.

If the individual was returning to an organization, and especially if the individual was a manager, then behaving in these ways would develop the individual's subordinates and subsequently improve the performance of the entire work group. This dynamic would unfold through some sort of magical process with the individual now being a different person, influencing everyone around him or her to also become a different person. When this occurred, the work group would become more effective. If enough work groups were seeded with sensitivity training group alumni, then the whole organization would begin to change the way it functioned and achieve improved performance.

It was a naïve model.

As experience grew using this perspective, it became clear that the model didn't work, and the main reason it didn't work was that individuals returned to their home setting and couldn't overcome all of the existing organizational dynamics that had pushed them to behave in the pre-group experience ways. To compensate for that, the model evolved into one that said, "We need to teach these processes to work teams, not individuals." The emphasis then shifted to developing the team as a whole, and this is where team building began. It took the processes used in sensitivity training and merged them with the preexisting team processes needed to accomplish a specific organizational task.

The OD technology then grew to include intergroup team development and a whole host of other approaches, all based on the basic experiential learning processes used in the early sensitivity training groups.

BRADFORD: Thinking about where OD was at the time you finished your Ph.D. at UCLA and went to Stanford, what was your early research all about, and where did it lead you as your career developed?

PORRAS: I thought that maybe the way to make greater inroads into understanding the change process was by measuring the impact of OD interventions on key individual and organizational variables. My intention was to use these findings to develop a framework that described the change process. With this framework I could then more intelligently define and measure the impact of any OD intervention as well as begin to understand how the change process unfolds.

I did several long-term projects assessing the impact of various OD interventions measuring the variables targeted for change and the impact they have on various measures of organizational performance. I also did meta-analyses of the existing research in assessing the impact of OD to try to get an overall picture of the outcomes of numerous studies. All of this helped me to develop my perspective on the change process. The model that grew out of all this work attempts to describe why organizational change takes place as a result of an OD intervention.

One of the psychological theories that had intrigued me a lot beginning around 1986–87 was social cognitive theory, as put forth by Al Bandura. It really helped me begin to understand why OD works or doesn't work. Social cognitive theory, put very simply, focuses on the cognitive processes of people and on the environments they operate in. It also emphasizes the use of cognitive processes to make conscious decisions about behavior.

I started evolving to a perspective that, for organizations to change, everyone in the organization has to change their behavior. And if people don't change their behavior, you don't get organizational change. That's sort of a simple place to begin, and a lot of people criticized it saying, "Well that's old stuff. You're focusing on the individual again, and we know that that doesn't work." I said I'm not focusing on the individual; I'm focusing on the conditions that happen in the organization that cause individuals to change their behavior. If you don't get them to change their behavior, you don't have organizational change. And so social cognitive theory fits that way of thinking very well. Let me explain how.

I believe that the two desired outcomes of effective OD interventions are organizational performance improvements and individual personal growth. The organization wins, the individual wins; that's the optimal situation. Now, I also believe that these two outcomes are driven by individual behavior change. If that's true, we have to ask ourselves, What causes individuals to change their behavior in an organization? My answer derives from social cognitive theory.

People change their behavior as a result of changes in the environment in which they work. So you change the structures they work in, you change the design of their job, you change the cultures they are embedded in, you change the physical settings they have to work in, you change the technical processes that guide their work, you change the reward systems, etc. To the degree to which all of these changes are consistent with each other, the signals about behaviors that the person should engage in will be fairly consistent, and people will be bombarded by this same message everywhere they turn. If quality is desired, the boss is saying it, the reward system reinforces it, the machinery allows you to produce quality, the physical setting lets you talk to other people so you know whether you are producing quality, the systems give you quality information, etc. The result of all of this is that you are more likely to produce quality work.

BRADFORD: Let me break in; this is fascinating. Jerry, we started off talking about OD, and now organizational change. Would you say at this point you've stopped doing OD in your professional life? Or is OD still there for you?

PORRAS: Well. Define *OD* for me.

BRADFORD: That's just what I was going to ask you to do! Earlier on, you talked about some of the values around participation, releasing potential, involvement, valuing the individual, etc. These imply a highly collaborative approach. But one doesn't have to use collaboration to change many of the environmental factors you have been talking about. They could be imposed. That's why I'm wondering if you see yourself looking back at this point as having left OD. Or is OD part of what you are doing?

PORRAS: Well, I think what happened to me is that the term *OD* became irrelevant to me. But I think the values are important. My view is that you can redesign the environment that people work in using various collaborative models. You might not involve every single individual in every case, but frequently you can certainly involve individuals that represent the various constituencies affected by the change—which makes it a participative activity.

So many of the values that attracted me to OD in the beginning are still relevant to me—although, I must admit, they can be violated when you think the way I've been thinking the last few years.

BRADFORD: I want to come back to something you just said: "OD became irrelevant to me." Say more about that.

PORRAS: I think what has happened, and it's probably true today, is that OD is everything and as a result OD is nothing. In an attempt to stay organizationally relevant, people who had traditionally been doing team building, or personal growth work, began to gravitate to other approaches for driving change in organizations. And so OD became more than just human-process-driven interventions. It became whatever OD consultants were doing. In fact, OD as a term stopped being fashionable for lots of people and organizations. Many organizations stopped saying they did OD because the label (and maybe the entire field) had become a cliché. Furthermore, for many OD didn't have much value or respect because a lot of OD groups in organizations hadn't produced a hell of a lot of useful, lasting change that people could point to. So organizational effectiveness became the *in* term. It then evolved to organizational transformation, then organizational learning, and so on.

BRADFORD: Again, I'm going to take you off track because you made a wonderful comment when you said, "A lot of OD groups in organizations hadn't produced a hell of a lot." Why do you think that's true?

PORRAS: I think it's primarily true for two reasons. First, OD became too technique-driven. People in OD didn't have a conceptual framework to guide their work, to help them see the big picture from which they could decide what actions to take. Instead, OD practitioners began to see the reality they faced as an opportunity to apply whatever change techniques they had in their toolkit. Often, the technique didn't totally fit the requirements of the situation, so it didn't make things better. In the worst case, less-proficient OD practitioners were like the kid with a hammer who saw everything as a nail. The result was that whether you needed it or not you were sent to a T-group, or got team building, or process consultation, or role analysis, or third party consultation, or confrontation meetings, or whatever.

Second, from what I said at the beginning, it's naïve to think that if you just focus on changing people's awareness of their behavior and learning new behaviors and being able to exhibit them in a sort of isolated pristine space that you create in a group, then they will return to their back-home organization and continue behaving in the new ways. I think that that was a naïve view. The important factor missing was that you also have to change the context in which people operate, as well as changing people's sensibilities and awareness, in order to have any hope of getting sustainable new behaviors.

BRADFORD: Dick Beckhard frequently used the phrase "We have to put the organization, the O, back into OD." Is that part of what you are saying?

PORRAS: Yes. Part of the reason why OD hasn't been as successful as it could have been can be traced to the roots of the field. Back in the 1950s and 1960s the early founders were primarily psychologists, who at that time were trained to look at the internal drivers of individual behavior and individual development and much less at the environment that the individual operates in. For the most part their orientation was not to pay attention to organizational context factors such as, How do we change the reward system? How do we restructure the place? or How do we design jobs in a different way? Over time, approaches evolved taking the environment more into account. Probably the most prominent of these was the sociotechnical systems approach, which married issues of technical design with human behavior factors. I think there was great potential in these ideas but they just never took off, and I can't fully explain why.

BRADFORD: Given what you just said, one would think that the reengineering movement would have been ideal for people in OD. And yet OD rejected it. Do you have any sense of why?

PORRAS: Well, I think the reengineering movement was driven by a different group of people. They were not psychologists; they were basically more general management consultant types who came primarily with an analytical orientation—focus on the numbers, focus on the work processes—not on the human processes.

BRADFORD: But those trained in sociotechnical systems thinking were very quantitative and very exact.

PORRAS: They were. They had an engineering base.

BRADFORD: So it is interesting because this could have been an opportunity to marry the two ways of thinking you're talking about. And yet the OD field rejected it.

PORRAS: That it did. In thinking about it, there seems to me a series of reasons for the rejection. As I said, those pushing reengineering were trained in major consulting firms that had a strong analytical orientation. They tended to poo-poo all the soft human behavior stuff. This didn't create a very hospitable climate for OD folks to team up with them. Another reason relates to the value system driving reengineering, which was in sharp contrast to the value system behind OD. For example, the value system in reengineering keeps the power for the ultimate decision in the managers. Yes, people down the organization get involved and do problem solving and make recommendations or suggestions, but in the end there is no power sharing; the final decision is made by the manager. Finally, reengineering focused almost exclusively on the work processes and didn't seem to have any room for including the human processes people use to get work done.

BRADFORD: Let me try a fourth hypothesis. I wonder if the main argument for reengineering was the bottom line—that this will save us money, probably by getting rid of unnecessary work and workers. And I wonder if the humanistic tradition that you have talked about that underlay OD made those folks leery about touching anything that might lead to downsizing.

PORRAS: I think you're absolutely correct. And actually when you look carefully at most reengineering efforts—and there have been some studies that assessed the long-term effects of reengineering projects—they didn't work. Reengineering works for a while, when the organization gets the immediate cost savings of laying people off, but it doesn't build capacity. So I think the hypothesis you propose makes a lot of sense, and it also speaks to one of the potential benefits of OD. Rather than a process that results in people losing their jobs, OD seeks to create dynamics that lead to a more effective organization, which allows for expansion of the activities of people, for example, putting people in other types of jobs rather than laying them off.

BRADFORD: Can you give me an example of how this works?

PORRAS: Yes, let me give you an example from a Procter & Gamble plant that I knew about. The first-level manufacturing workers invented a device that would control a substantial portion of a highly automated process. This meant that fewer workers could now produce the same amount of output. I've forgotten the exact figures, but it was somewhere on the order of a production line that previously needed a team of ten people to run it, now you only needed seven. There were about ten lines in the entire operation.

Now, what is a plant manager going to do once he finds out about it? Well, first of all, apply it to all the lines. OK, so now what are you going to do with the extra thirty people? Classical reengineering would say, "Lay them off and capture the cost saving." But P&G had more of an OD orientation that said, "Let's find other things for them to do. We're going to expand the plant—let's put some of these folks on the redesign team. We've got people visiting us—let's put some of these folks leading plant tours. We've had some quality problems related to the functioning of our machinery—let's put some of these folks on analyzing that problem and coming up with some solutions."

Instead of firing people, they found other types of activities for them to be involved with. There are always problems in a plant. Apply the extra personnel time to their solution, and that way you keep everyone busy and deal with plantwide needs at the same time.

Over time, as people left on their own accord, they weren't replaced, and the workforce size dropped to take advantage of the technology. But it didn't drop to exactly the number of people required by the new technology. It was someplace between the original number and the technology-defined number (the theoretically most efficient number). The slack that was left over continued to be used to help the plant become more effective.

BRADFORD: That's a useful example. You talked before about your thinking of how organizations change that led to your stream analysis approach. What was then the progression to your seminal work, *Built to Last*, that you did with Jim Collins?

PORRAS: Jim Collins was teaching at Stanford, and we started to have conversations about how organizations change and develop. One of our questions was, What does the ideal organization look like? All of the talking that people have done about this question has been largely speculative and often in very vague terms. We talk about participation, commitment, and the like, but we really don't have any sort of tangible evidence that this is the best way to go. So one of the things driving the *Built to Last* research was to try to understand how an ideal organization is managed—"ideal" being organizations that have been highly successful for very long time periods. Not these flash-in-the-pans that are great for five or six years and then they disappear. So my interests evolved from trying to look at the process of how organizations can be changed to looking at what we want to change toward. What's that elephant look like? Let's describe that in its entirety, as best we can, and then go back and ask, Now what are the processes that get to that?

The process I described is not something that I consciously plotted out a priori. It evolved and I'm making more sense of it as I look back. But, in some ways I think my career has been kind of living OD from the point of view of just believing in my process and that my process will lead me to successful effective outcomes. And so I was following one process and evolved into another process without a lot of conscious strategizing and plotting and decision making about it.

BRADFORD: What does the research that led to *Built to Last* tell you about OD? Would you say to managers, executives, CEOs, "Use the processes of OD and you will end up with a company that is built to last"?

PORRAS: I think that there's a high potential for that. There's high congruency because some very significant findings in *Built to Last* fit with OD principles, for example, the role of values and purpose, and the passion for change. Concerns about values and purpose have been floating around the field of OD throughout its history. Values—who you are—and purpose—what contribution you are making—that's part of the personal growth model. The better you understand that, the better you are able to contribute to the environment in which you work.

BRADFORD: Is it that *values* are important, or the specific values that OD espouses?

PORRAS: More of the former than the latter. What was a very surprising finding in *Built to Last* was that *there wasn't one ideal set of core values* for all of the visionary companies. More specifically, there was no single core value held by all of the visionary companies. In contrast, OD says that there is an ideal set of values. Maybe one of the reasons that OD hasn't prospered and really grown over the years is because it has tried to tell people that "our values are the only right values." There are a lot of people in the world with a lot of different views in a lot of different circumstances, and maybe some of the OD values are right for them, but not all of them. And there's no, or little, accommodation for that in the OD perspective.

When I first got into OD, the values were very much humanistic values. In fact Bob Tannenbaum noted that the field had been espousing values but had never clearly enumerated them in one place. So he wrote an article spelling out those values. In that era it had a huge impact on the field, because it really did clarify OD values and emphasize that essentially they were humanistic values. But what we found in our research was that *having values* was what was important, not what the values were in particular. Now this makes for some kind of scary possibilities. You can say, "Wow, the Mafia might very well be a visionary organization."

Enduringly great organizations have values, and not all of the values are ones that everyone would like. And so it really speaks to a very heterogeneous view of the world in which all organizations don't have to be exactly alike in terms of what their values are. Where they do have to be alike is in the fact that they have strong, powerful values that guide them. You gravitate to one, and I gravitate to another. But hey, you and I are different, so why should we force all of our beliefs to be exactly the same? The notion of equifinality (you can get to the same end point through different paths) is one we preach in open systems theory, but not one that OD necessarily follows with respect to the issue of values.

BRADFORD: And I'm wondering if that doesn't limit the effectiveness of many OD consultants. That they are only going to be effective insofar as their values are congruent with the organization, but will be ineffective if there is any incongruity.

PORRAS: Exactly. And let's face it, there are relatively few organizations and organizational managers who have values totally congruent with OD's values. I think organizations with OD values sit out in the tail of the distribution of organizations. They are not in the middle.

BRADFORD: Let's now move to purpose. The other thing that *Built to Last* found was the power of purpose. And back to the point you were making before about OD having its roots in psychology. Purpose puts the organization central. Do OD's roots put the individual central? And what happens if the purpose is at all in conflict with the individual's needs?

PORRAS: Here's the way I think purpose plays a very powerful role for an organization. If an organization understands what its purpose is, clearly articulates and communicates that purpose, and lives that purpose—especially in who it hires—over time the organization will evolve into a state in which just about every employee's personal purpose is congruent with the organization's purpose. If it isn't congruent, the harsh reality is that those individuals should leave that organization because they never are going to fit. On the basis of the discrepancies in purpose, when critical decisions must be made the person wants to go one way while the organization, will push in another direction. So from a long-term perspective, it's more beneficial for both parties to part ways sooner rather than later.

Now, the problem is that most organizations don't have that clarity or consistency of purpose. They don't communicate it, they don't use it in their hiring, they don't use it in the way they evaluate people, and so all sorts of people with all sorts of different personal purposes are scattered throughout the organization, and some eventually gravitate toward the top. When that happens the misalignment reduces organizational effectiveness.

BRADFORD: Jerry, what's interesting is that your tone has changed. Ten minutes ago, when you were describing the P&G plan, you were talking about the value of holding on to people. Now you're sounding more hard-nosed about it: if they don't fit, they should leave.

PORRAS: Why is that incongruent? I don't understand the incongruency. Of course you should hold on to people. But you ought to hold on to people who want to be (and who should be) there. Hold on to those people who believe that through their contribution some higher-level purpose is being achieved. What is key is that they really believe it. And you don't want to hold on to people who don't feel that way, and they shouldn't want to be there either. So I don't see any incongruency in that.

BRADFORD: If I'm hearing you correctly, Jerry, it's not that you're saying we should hold on to people for whatever reason. You are saying that if people are terminated for immediate economic rewards, we ought to think very, very carefully about letting people go. But if there is a conflict around purpose, then it's in everybody's best interest that the individual leaves.

PORRAS: That is exactly right. If your first response is to lay people off just for the immediate cost saving, then you create an organization in which you don't have a lot of commitment. Instead, that produces a high degree of cynicism and all the traditional things we think are wrong with organizations. But if you fire people because they don't fit the purpose of the organization, or its values, that's a different issue. You need to get rid of them. If you do that, then you are behaving as a manager responsible to the other people left in the organization and to the organization as a whole.

BRADFORD: Let me push this a little bit further. Let's assume we have a big organization like GE when Jack Welch took over. And there is a sense of it being bloated. Are you saying in those cases one should just use attrition to cut it down by a third?

PORRAS: Well, it depends on how.

BRADFORD: If you had been an organizational consultant to Jack Welch when he became CEO, and he said, "We're a third over-staffed with people who are not necessary," given your values, what should you do?

PORRAS: That's a good question. I think if you've got the time, you let attrition take care of things. If you don't have the time, then I think you have to look at a set of variables. You have to look at the significance of the role the person is playing in the organization; how important is it? You have to look at how competent they are in the role; how much have they been contributing? Now those are usually the two things that are looked at when the decision is made to get rid of people. But there is a third factor that should be considered yet rarely is: how congruent are the personal values and the personal sense of purpose or beliefs of this individual with those of the organization? And I think you need to be willing to get rid of people who are very good on the first and very good on the second, but no good on the third.

In fact, Welch made the same argument. In his writings and his talks, he puts it this way:

> Think of a 2x2 matrix with one axis being the quality of the individual's contribution and the other the consonance between the individual's values and the values of the organization. Those who are *low in contribution* and *low in values congruence*, you kick them out, right? That's easy. If they're *high-high*, that's also easy. But what about the other two cells? Well, if they are *low in contribution* and *high in values*, you invest in them. You train them. You try to develop them. You try to keep them. You try to transform them from low performers to high performers. But if they're *high on performance* and *low on values*, eventually you have to bite the bullet and get rid of them.

And I believe this too.

BRADFORD: So you're saying it's easier to upgrade subperforming people than to change attitudes.

PORRAS: . . . than to change fundamental beliefs. I am not going to change your basic values. Your core values are fundamental to you. I cannot sell you a new set of core values. I can probably make you parrot what I want to hear about values. I can make you behave consistently with those values as long as I'm watching you, but I cannot make you really believe something differently. And when I'm not watching you, or when some really challenging difficult situation comes up, you'll revert to what you really believe and that will guide your behavior. So I don't think you can change those things. I think you can train and educate and increase the skills of people, but I don't think you can change their basic values.

BRADFORD: We tend to infer basic values from people's behavior over time, so wouldn't it be congruent with your values, Jerry, that if you see somebody act in ways that seem contradictory, you would first try to find out why they are acting that way to determine if they are secondary values or just erroneous beliefs?

PORRAS: Yes. We're talking about a process. I'm not advocating an arbitrary, "Well, Bradford, you acted the wrong way and now you're out." One looks for patterns of longer-term behaviors where that individual is consistently acting in ways that violate one of the organization's basic values. If you have a value of teamwork, and it's really seen as a core value of your organization, but there is this one individual who constantly does things that block the effectiveness of the team, that glorify himself or herself, and continues that behavior over time, then it's pretty clear that that person isn't compatible with the type of organization you want to run. And it's not to say your values are right and theirs are wrong; it's just a mismatch. And the best thing for both parties is for that person to find a new place where there is a better match. So I'm not advocating any sort of cruel, inhumane process for eliminating people who don't fit, but I am saying that in the end you really have to bite the bullet or you'll wind up paying the piper.

BRADFORD: Good. Let's go back to the third major finding from *Built to Last*, which was change, and link that with OD.

PORRAS: One of the key findings that we discovered in the *Built to Last* companies was that they had a very powerful orientation to change. It starts out with the organization having a passion for change, and that passion for change was often in the founders or the key transformational leaders in the early life of the organization. And central to OD is the notion of change, so that dimension is consistent with one of the basic principles of OD.

BRADFORD: Except change can be collaborative, participative, and bottom up, or change can be imposed. Did you find a difference in

Built to Last? Was change always participative and collaborative? Never imposed?

PORRAS: No, it varied—just as the companies varied in their value systems. But they all changed in ways that were consistent with their value systems. So if you have an organization that really values innovation and collaboration, like a 3M, then change occurs in a lot of bottom-up ways. HP used to be the same way. But in other places, change is much more imposed. I think at GE it was much more imposed from the top, with programs like Six Sigma and Workout. These were imposed programs. Some organizations have values that stress stretching and pushing themselves all the time, like Boeing. So they change by setting these audacious, difficult, and challenging goals. And they've continued to change themselves that way (until very recently for Boeing). On the other hand, there are organizations like Procter & Gamble where they evolve their products so they are continually improving themselves.

So built-to-last organizations change in ways that are consistent with their values, the sort of industry they are in, and the way they see themselves. And this is where we run up against OD again, in that OD says the only way you should change is through collaborative, participative models. OD practitioners could be more effective if they were to say that the way one should change should be consistent with the values that exist in the organization you are trying to change.

BRADFORD: Good. That's a great segue into pulling our discussion together. One of the articles in this book is a provocative piece by Jerry Harvey, who's saying OD is on life support and somebody should pull the plug. Early on, you were saying that OD became irrelevant for you as a concept. In this book, we are raising the question of whether OD could become a viable field. Do you think that's possible? Is it desirable? If it is possible, what would it take?

PORRAS: Let me first speak to whether it's desirable, before speaking to whether it's possible. I'm not sure it's desirable because I think OD has become an out-of-date fad in the minds of many managers. We might be better off just abandoning the term OD. What we're all interested in doing is helping organizations to change, to become more effective along a wide variety of dimensions. Let's focus on that.

By suggesting we abandon the term *OD*, I am not saying that we should throw out all that the field has stood for. Making organizations more effective will require making members personally more effective—not just in an instrumental way, but as human beings. That principle should not be abandoned. Organizations can only temporarily improve if there is no individual development. Long-lasting organizational effectiveness will only occur when there are long-lasting improvements in individual well-being and abilities. The individual has to gain in the long term for the organization to gain in the long term. That is a basic belief that OD has had from its origins, and it's still very relevant today. Some of these basic perspectives should be maintained, but in my mind the label doesn't buy us a lot.

And I'm not sure whether we need labels to identify ourselves and to sort out who is in or out. My fear is that any label would result in a new fad status for the field. After a few years the fad would wane and we would come up with a new one repeating the cycle. So I don't have an answer to that part, but I definitely think that many of the guiding principles should be maintained, such as that people should be treated humanely.

However, there are some OD principles and practices that should be abandoned, such as "we have the right values, and you have the wrong ones." Similarly, the belief that collaboration is the only legitimate way to operate and should be used in every situation should not be a universal value. Having more collaboration rather than less is attractive. But not "always collaborate" or "never collaborate." It depends on the situation.

Thus, we need to go through systematically and assess the key dimensions of the OD approach and look at each one and see what should be maintained and what abandoned. But I don't think the label *OD* is worth saving.

BRADFORD: What advice would you give to the local and national OD organizations and to the half-dozen or so OD master's programs that presently exist in various universities?

PORRAS: I think they ought to change their names.

BRADFORD: Just their names?

PORRAS: No, they should also systematically go through the analysis I'm talking about and update their efforts to map them into a broader reality. That will make their work more effective and hopefully produce practitioners who can help create healthier and more productive organizations. As I said at the beginning of our conversation, organizations are the linchpins of society, and making them healthier will result in healthier societies. That's what I'm interested in. The mechanisms we use for doing that can be varied, and there isn't only one way to do it. If people think there's only one way, they are not going to be successful or they'll be successful only with a subset of organizations. Instead, we need approaches that are sufficiently flexible so as to apply to a wide range of organizations. That will allow us to change more organizations more effectively than we've been able to do with traditional OD thinking.

BRADFORD: Thank you.

5

Organization Development

Requiem or Reveille?

Tony Petrella

For every complex question there is a simple answer.
And it's wrong.

         H. L. Mencken

A major premise of this volume concerns two questions: Has organization development delivered on its promise? Might OD be in decline? The editors tell me that most of the contributors believe the latter. I have a different view. My view grows out of my forty years of being a practitioner of OD on the ground, working with organizations from numerous industries and in many parts of the world. Over and over again I have witnessed my clients choosing to change to increase their own organization's effectiveness. What follows is a thumbnail sketch of the realms, forces, and factors that need to be addressed to be effective in this field of work. It also illustrates that the values and practice of organization development have made and continue to make a valuable contribution to the management and governance of large organizations.

  Experience suggests that one must first work within a comprehensive conceptual framework that applies in many situations. There are a few foundation blocks that always need to be in place. If ignored (and it seems they too frequently are), we risk failing. Though these principles might seem simplistic, they are profoundly important and serve to keep our work grounded and practical.

Further, although these principles are easy to articulate and understand, they are not always easy to employ. Learning how to work effectively to improve organizational functioning is not like learning algebra; the same formula doesn't work in every situation, and one must attune oneself, almost as an improvisational jazz musician attunes himself or herself, to the other players in the ensemble. The overarching conceptual framework is always a good touchstone, but the particular consulting mission often has to take a drastically new course of action depending on the demands of the particular situation. The requirement that this puts on the flexibility and creativity of the consultant is often quite taxing. It is not a good setting for someone who likes predictability and regularity. Nor is it good for the faint of heart, since the work often calls for the courage to stand apart and voice an unpopular point of view.

Richard Beckhard was fond of exhorting practitioners to "put the O in OD." He was saying that our work needs to place the functioning of the entire organization at the center of our practice if we expect to have an impact on improving organizational performance. He was concerned that practitioners too often were working in a fragmentary way on only one or two dimensions of organizational behavior. In this chapter the focus is on the *totality* of an organization's performance in relationship to its environment. That is a core belief of mine.

This chapter is an attempt to state first principles to improve the performance of the entire organization. If you want an inventory of methodologies and protocols that will fill up your intervention toolkit, this is not the place to find them. If you are interested in the basic conceptual building blocks required to lay the foundation for effective work on the goals of an entire organization, read on.

First Principles

1. The fundamental purpose an organization serves should be the primary touchstone for any effort to improve organizational performance. Purpose comes first.

2. An open-system framework serves best in understanding all sorts of connections, flows, and influences that an organization and its people are subject to when undertaking significant change. Many of these forces are generated outside of the boundaries of the organization.

3. People are the ultimate source in creating value, and that value is significantly increased through cooperation and collaboration.

4. Conflict is inevitable and requires the use of legitimate power.

5. An organization's culture is made up of the members' values, beliefs, and behaviors, which set the ground rules of appropriate organizational behavior.

6. Tension between continuity and change is healthy and eternal.

7. Vital leadership inside the organization is essential for all constructive change.

These principles can be looked at in three ways: (1) as the characteristics of an effective organization, (2) as the necessary ingredients of effective leadership, and (3) as the realms of organizational life that an OD consultant must be prepared to address. If any one is ignored or neglected, the organization will not be able to realize its full potential. If an OD practitioner is unable to constructively address any one of these issues, he or she is at considerable risk of failing.

Purpose Comes First

The primary societal function of a commercial corporation is creation of economic value, which determines the long-term sustainability of the enterprise. In a free market, a business organization must satisfy both customers and investors and do so in a way that is superior to the performance of competitors. Since failure in these realms prompts the leadership to seek change, it is wise for the consultant to be associated with change initiatives that enhance the business position of the corporation. The shorthand expression is to "make the business case" for the change initiative.

It is not up to the OD practitioner to make the business case personally, but he or she must work together with the appropriate leadership to make sure that the change initiative is shaped and articulated meaningfully. Too often among OD practitioners one finds a disregard or even hostility toward the profit motive in business organizations. Profit is to business organizations what oxygen is to humans; they need it to survive.

Any situation where an organization is challenged in the marketplace provides a great opportunity for both wholesale and wholesome change. But if the OD practitioners are not interested or involved in the core function of the corporation (the creation of value and the viability of the business), they are not likely to enjoy the chance to work with these remarkable opportunities. Profit is not our only goal. It is far too narrow a concept to use in defining our work and our mission, but we must include it in our work and be happy to pursue this as well as other goals.

Open Systems Framework

Any organization is a system in and of itself and must be understood in its entirety, as a total system. Russell L. Ackoff has applied systems thinking to the functioning of business organizations. Here is a simplified definition of a total system (for a complete definition, see Ackoff, 1994, chapter one).

1. A system is a whole that is defined by its function in a larger system (or systems). Stated more concretely, a business corporation is defined by its relationship to critical markets and to the environment in which it is embedded.

2. Every subset of parts can affect the behavior or properties of the whole, and none has an independent effect on the whole. More concretely, any critical function or department of an organization

can affect the performance of the entire organization, but this impact is determined by the *interaction* with other critical functions of the organization.

3. None of a system's parts has a defining function, behavior, or property of a system taken as a whole. It takes the whole organization to do a complete job, and no one part of the organization defines the organization's function or purpose.

4. The essential characteristics of a system depend on how its parts interact, not on how they act separately. The performance of an organization is not necessarily improved when the performance of any one part is improved; it takes integration of all the parts working together to use the improvement originating in one of the parts.

Far too many attempts to improve organizational performance narrowly focus on one part of the organization or one aspect of organizational work. Such efforts can produce some benefit, but it is folly to expect that the culmination of these efforts will affect total organizational performance in any significant way. That would require connecting all the related functions into a unified whole.

The head of any significant function can understand this reality, but the challenge is often gaining the cooperation of other related functions. The initiative can start in a single function, and even most of the work may need to be done in that function, but before real gains in performance can be ensured it will invariably require the assistance of other parts.

This conceptual framework allows one to determine the scope, depth, and magnitude of an organizational improvement effort. It also allows one to begin to see a change process as an interconnected series of steps that must be completed. It is not necessary to understand every moving piece to begin work. The pieces can be discovered—in fact will be discovered—only as one moves forward. But it is necessary to think in these terms to discover the critical interconnections adroitly and to understand their significance.

Let's look at a thumbnail sketch of an OD effort I was involved with that illustrates the utility of systems thinking. The work was with the mining division of a major producer of steel. The underground anthracite coal mines were no longer competitive with other sources of coal and were being closed. The corporation wanted to find ways to increase the mines' productivity. The particular mine in which our work started occupied one-half of a small mountain in Pennsylvania. Circumscribing the mountain, another mine owned by the same company occupied the other half of the mountain. To get there by car one would drive around the base of the mountain, a distance of approximately thirty miles. There were separate small mining towns on the two sides of the mountain, each being situated near the portal of a mine.

One major problem was the underground transportation system. The mine was old, and the mining was now being conducted deep, near the center of the mountain. The only track reaching that far into the mine had to be used for the three shift changes in a twenty-four-hour cycle of mining. Because the trip took so much time, and because it was only a single track, the incoming crew had to wait for the outbound crew to come out of the mine before they boarded and made the trip in. This meant that the mine was effectively shut down for approximately six hours out of twenty-four, causing a loss of productivity.

Running a parallel track was totally impractical, and for a few days the project team was stumped. But then one morning a mining engineer on the project team came in with a topographical map of the entire mountain that showed the underground passages of both of the mines. Eureka! The track in the other mine under the mountain was almost on a straight line with ours, and only about thirty yards of mountain separated them. Now the solution to the problem seemed simple. Cut through that wall, connect the tracks, and use the portal at one side of the mountain for the incoming crew while the outbound crew headed the other way, exiting the mine from the portal on the opposite side of the mountain. This was a technical solution to the problem. Almost.

As soon as this was proposed to the superintendent of the mine, he said it couldn't be done because of the ventilation problem it would create. Anthracite coal contains methane gas, which is quite volatile when released into the air. As the coal is cut from the seam, the gas escapes into the air and must be ventilated out of the mine. We consulted safety specialists who studied the situation for a few days and said that our solution would actually improve the ventilation. Problem solved. Almost.

After this opinion from the safety experts was obtained, the mining superintendent asked to meet with the whole project team. He entered apologizing and said that he had been up late the night before, full of shame for his reaction to our proposal. He had been so shocked and embarrassed by the simplicity of our solution that he just blurted out the first objection that came to mind, but the more he thought the stupider he felt that something so obvious hadn't occurred to him long ago. Then he said something highly insightful: "Probably the reason that neither I nor anyone else ever thought of this was that we have grown up thinking of these two mines as totally separate things instead of one big thing. We've always competed with that mine, we also competed on the football and baseball fields, and we have never thought of how linked we are. We will have a hell of a lot of objections to overcome (mostly from the managers of the other mine), but we will get this done and all of our jobs will be saved. I can't thank you enough."

This is a simple example of the kind of thinking that goes beyond analysis to synthesis. It almost always entails a shift in a way of thinking, and it is always a matter of putting separate pieces together creatively into a new and complete whole. The simplicity of the example comes from the ease with which one can visualize the physical reality of these mines. But don't be misled: the creativity inherent in synthesis always comes from seeing new forms of relationships in a larger whole.

People Create Value

Although it is crucial to keep permeable boundaries between an organization and external constituencies and developments, it must always attend to what may be the paramount constituents: the employees. One of the most encouraging developments in the mindset of managers over the past forty years is greater realization of the value that people can bring. This greater awareness is due to many factors, among them:

- Widespread emergence of "knowledge economies"

- Increasing rate of change

- Growing global competition

- Higher customer demands for quality in product and service

- Ease and rapidity of the flow of capital in global capital markets

- Complexity of the technologies employed

- Rising educational and skill levels of employees

- Changes in employee expectations, attitudes, and values

If one considers such industries as aeronautics, telecommunications, data processing, oil and chemicals, medical devices, financial services, pharmaceuticals, and a host of others, it is clear that none of them could exist, let alone succeed, without using the competencies that members bring.

Many managers understand that people are the ultimate source of value, but they often make the mistake of thinking this simply means one has to hire and retain good talent. Though necessary, that is not sufficient. Real value occurs when people work collaboratively and synergistically. Problems are too complex and knowledge is too dispersed for a few individuals to be the source of all answers.

From the point of view of the entire enterprise—the whole corporation—nothing is a more precious attribute or asset than a committed, cohesive, and cooperative workforce. To create a corporate culture that induces employees to cooperate is one of the most challenging tests of effective corporate leadership. Writing in 1963 on the subject of organization after retiring from years of successfully leading General Motors, Alfred P. Sloan came to the conclusion that cooperation is the essential principle of organization.

Coming from a totally different experience and with another set of interests, the psychoanalyst Alfred Adler made the bold assertion that "all the main problems in life are problems of human cooperation" (Ansbacher and Ansbacher, 1964, p. 1). In this statement he was recognizing the inherent and inseparable bond between an individual and the collective; no individual can develop fully without the cooperation of others. Recognizing this need for human association in a cooperative milieu and finding ways to enhance its realization is an absolute cornerstone of any effective consultation to organizations.

The field of organization development has made a significant contribution by stressing the value that people working collectively can bring. The past forty years have seen the emergence of numerous approaches that release the human potential in organizations. Work on conflict resolution, diversity, team building, interteam collaboration, and the like has dramatically increased the performance and human satisfaction that comes when people productively collaborate.

The downside is when these techniques are used not to release human potential but mainly to gain compliance. All too often, there has been much emphasis on "participation," "involving those affected by the change"—not out of the belief that their input would significantly increase the quality of the outcome but to overcome resistance to change. Such pseudoparticipation breeds cynicism and the charge that the consultants are a cover for management's exploitation of employees.

Conflict and Power

Although willing cooperation among individuals and groups is a goal for any effective collective effort, it is difficult to achieve in all instances. Individuals and groups have their own interests and needs, which often leads to the pursuit of conflicting goals. If this is compounded by the inevitable fact of limited resources and competition for promotion, authority, position, and status, frequently the best one can achieve in a large social system is a situation of mixed motives. Some degree of conflict always exists, and conflict requires constant managing.

Resolution of conflict and the decisions it requires is one basis for legitimate hierarchy, authority, and use of power. Dreams of resolving all of these issues through some sort of pure democracy, or through an all-knowing expert or technical rationality, are just that: dreams. Power implies the capacity to bring together both the resources and the necessary people in an initiative that accomplishes a particular purpose. No wonder people seek power; it can lead to accomplishment. More power suggests the potential for greater accomplishment.

Establishing formal and legitimate authority in hierarchical structures can help manage conflict constructively. The diversity of interests and the mixed motives of the membership of an organization create a dynamic tension that must be negotiated and resolved. The hierarchy constitutes a system of governance that is empowered to decide these issues; when it is done well it brings a degree of objectivity and rationality that can actually build cohesion, continuity, and stability in an organization.

There might be times when a system of absolute authority is needed to resolve these dynamic tensions, but a more viable approach often accepts pluralism and willingness on the part of those with authority to negotiate the differences between parties.

In this sense, an organization is a political system and a body politic. Currently *politics* is a dirty word. This is both unfortunate and unreal. Accepting the utility of political activity and the wholesome processes and outcomes that can result would be a much more mature and effective path to follow.

Even though hierarchy and power can be constructive forces in an organization, the misuse of power can lead to terrible consequences. Sensing this and knowing it from harsh experience leads to considerable anxiety, trepidation, and fear about the existence of power and its placement. This is why most organizations have a structure of checks and balances, in an attempt to produce fairness in decision making and appropriate use of authority and power. But no system is perfect, and inequities are a fact of life.

The ever-present question is, To what purpose are leadership and power exercised? For whose goals? whose wants and needs? These are questions of morality and must always be answered. How they are answered is as important as the questions themselves. Promulgating some doctrine and insisting that everyone follow it without independent thought and inquiry is not the suggested path. This is always a human struggle, almost in the form of a riddle, one that must be addressed again and again. For many reasons, including those deeply embedded in our psyche, this issue continues to confront mankind in crucial ways.

The anxiety and fear that people have about conflict and power often drive the issue underground. The issue is denied and kept hidden; it becomes almost a forbidden topic of conversation, a taboo. This only makes matters worse. Power that is not acknowledged or discussed raises a greater problem of hidden manipulation.

Nothing erodes cooperation and commitment more than a situation in which the purpose of the organization does not embrace and serve the wants and needs of all those affected. Too frequently, an organization has as its central purpose the exclusive benefit of some elite. This mostly has to do with distribution of rewards within the organization. It also arises whenever some members of the organization are exploited, in any of a variety of ways: (1) not receiving benefits others receive, (2) being excluded from privileges granted to others, (3) not being recognized or respected, or (4) working in settings that are dangerous or in any way inimical to health. Labor unions are one response to these problems. Some differentiation between people and roles is always appropriate given the difference in the value of the contributions made by particular individuals or groups. But conflict occurs when these differences become excessive. Today an argument can be made that executive compensation has become excessive relative to what ordinary employees receive.

OD consultants can play a crucial role in the legitimate use of power. They can surface issues that have been driven underground so that there is greater transparency and consciousness about how power and authority are being used (and misused). They can help an organization align the type and distribution of power with the core purpose of the institution.

But consultants can do this only if they are comfortable with power—their own power and the existence of power in the organization. There will always be asymmetrical balances of power between individuals, between groups, or among individuals and the groups they belong to. Wishing that it could be otherwise and acting as if this wish were true is to risk becoming dangerously disengaged from reality and perceived as naïve and thereby useless. Furthermore, as has been stated, there has to be acceptance and belief that organizations are political systems and that being such does not mean that they have to be manipulative or exploitative.

Power is more likely to be effectively used when it arises out of a set of values. One of the most basic values underlying the field of OD is the belief that leadership should be unifying and humanitarian. James MacGregor Burns, in his fine book *Leadership*, refers to this as moral leadership, where the leader "induces followers to act for certain goals that represent the values and motivations—the wants and needs of . . . both leaders and followers" (1975, p. 19). Rather than abhorring power, OD can work to help leaders along the path to effective moral leadership. Legitimate power, morally exercised, is a precious human capacity. As a Jesuit teacher of mine liked to say, "Power goes to those who bring hope." The exercise of power can enhance both an individual's and a collective's ability to make great contributions to society. But the moral caveat is always required: Whose needs are being served?

Values and Corporate Culture

A consulting project that I did with M&M Mars strongly highlighted the power of corporate culture. From the moment I walked through the door I was struck with their strong culture. Rather than a private office, I met my client, the head of manufacturing, at his desk in an open office. Like the bulk of the people who were employed at headquarters, he had a workstation in a very large office without partitions. In this setting it was easy to understand that this total collective of people was the client, not simply the executive sitting across the desk from me.

Our consulting work was a version of a sociotechnical approach, with equal emphasis on manufacturing efficiency and job satisfaction. The preexisting culture made proceeding along this path easy for us. The goal of our work was simply enhancement of what the organization was already intent on accomplishing. Out of multiple examples, what follows are two that illustrate the strength of the M&M Mars culture.

Mars was an absolute stickler about producing quality products. My first lesson in this came from two buyers of raw materials; one bought cocoa on the world commodity market, the other milk. Three policies governed their actions: (1) only the best ingredients were purchased, (2) reliability of supply was crucial, and (3) they were willing to pay a premium price for premium supplies and premium service.

A consequence of these policies and practices was that the costs of their supplies were considerably higher than if they had been willing to settle for a slightly lower-grade supply. With that in mind I asked them if the ultimate consumer would be able to discern a difference if they modified their buying policies to a slightly lower set of specifications. I couldn't tell if they were horrified or simply amused, but this was the answer patiently given: "It's obvious that you have never heard of incremental degradation." Asking what they meant led to this response:

> Let's suppose that you are right that the consumer wouldn't notice a difference. In fact there is some evidence that supports that contention. What would happen if we gave a bright young buyer a bonus for making that choice? And then suppose we continued this practice until one day a consumer actually notices the difference and is disappointed. What have we done? We've lost a customer, and that isn't good. But we have lost something else that is really very serious and hard to correct. As an organization we have lost the will, the knowledge, and the capacity to do things right, and this will not be easy to correct. That is incremental degradation.

I silently said to myself, *This is another indication of a strong organizational culture.*

One more event illustrates that this company had a strong corporate culture based on this principle of delivering value in the form of freshness and quality. This experience has to do with strict adherence to the recipes that were used, the expectation of personal responsibility in following the recipes, and added emphasis on the responsibility of people who held management positions. It is also about the use of sanctions to reinforce these expectations.

Most of the Snickers bars sold on the North American continent come from a large plant near Chicago. It was the time of the year when most of the production of the plants was geared toward producing candy that would be sold prior to Halloween. This is a critical time in the sale of this kind of candy because of the great volume purchased for this holiday. If there isn't enough candy produced to fill this demand, it is difficult to meet annual sales and profit goals.

The plant was having some difficulties on one of the production lines; the variance in the composition of the product was not what the recipe demanded. Noticing this, a worker on the line shut it down (this was routinely done when this kind of variance occurred). The plant manager was informed, and a team was hastily assembled to try to fix the problem. After some effort the line was restarted, but the variances were still too great and the people on the line shut it down again. The plant manager, who was quite concerned that this would lead to an undersupply for the holiday sale, ordered the workers to restart the line. They refused. He threatened to fire them if they did not. They started the line, and candy that didn't comply with specifications was produced.

That afternoon an employee on the production line called corporate headquarters and reported the event. Immediately the vice president of manufacturing was notified. The next morning he was on a flight to Chicago and went to the plant to learn what had happened. After a short time he verified the report of the production line associate. He had a brief conversation with the plant manager, who resigned that afternoon. It was all done with dignity and clarity. The rule of quality was paramount, and exceptions that were willful or negligent were not accepted. The news spread like wildfire. Once again, the collective will of this culture was affirmed.

I want to conclude this section on culture with a few essential thoughts:

- It is important to understand that a culture isn't built in the short run; it grows out of the experience of the members of an organization and takes time to evolve, stabilize, and become coherent. In the case presented here the culture was cultivated over two generations of family leadership.
- It is important to fashion a culture that is appropriate for the business of the enterprise and for the business strategy being employed. For example, in this case a pamphlet further spelled out the principle of quality: "It is the policy of Mars to design, produce,

and distribute products and services which are decisively superior in quality to the relevant competition." This is a statement of business strategy. It is also another statement of corporate identity.

• To build a strong culture there must be high congruence between what people say they value and how they actually behave. This is particularly true for the leadership, who must act in a congruent way in terms of what they say about their values, how they behave, the priorities they set, and what they choose to support and reward. People in subordinate positions are quite alert to all of these signals and believe what they witness and experience as being the "book" on the culture. Disembodied culture statements, rarely enacted, are not believed. To understand the real culture of an organization, look for what is done.

• Culture can and must be articulated; it is also pervasive, elusive, and a bit mysterious. It resides in the hearts and minds of the members of an organization. It is multifaceted and can be subtle and nuanced. It is historical and symbolic, enacted in many ways. It is a shared memory, a shared sense of reality, and a source of meaning and identity. It defines what it means to be a member and gives the whole corporation an identity.

• Culture is a response to the human need for order and stability. It also gives substance, significance, and meaning to the collective identity as well as the individual. It helps people answer the questions, Who are we? What do we stand for? How are we different?

For all these reasons the matter of organizational culture must not be taken lightly. It deserves considerable attention and work on the part of the leaders of the corporation. OD practitioners can be helpful in many ways. Leaders often understand their organization's culture tacitly but do not have it fully in their consciousness. Working to bring this material into the leader's awareness is a good place to start. The practitioner can also help a leader articulate and communicate the desired culture as well as keep the leader's attention focused on creating and sustaining organizational culture as one of his or her critical roles. The practitioner can point out and help verify where the leader's actions or policies conflict with the organizational values to be promoted. This extends all the way to the policies and practices used for rewards and recognition. Most of all, the consultant cannot collude with a client who wants a quick fix and is satisfied with slogans and posters. Hanging tough to make culture real and operative can be a challenging task for any consultant.

Change, Creation, and Tension with Continuity

The idea of change has always been central to the field of organization development; given contemporary conditions, change is the constant that all organizations face. Demands for change may come from the markets, which are the primary arbiters of the extent to which an organization is delivering on its core purpose. But change need not be just a response to failure or impending threat from a new competitor. It may simply be a response to a new opportunity that arises from new technologies, products, or services or the opportunity to enter a new market.

The change initiative can also incorporate other goals, such as the humanization of work. In fact, attaching other goals to key business initiatives is the best way to find the necessary support for important collateral purposes, particularly when it can be shown that they aid achievement of business goals. Far too many projects are undertaken in organizations without any attempt to make this connection.

Change is a process that is also about potential and therefore requires both inspiration and the will to generate. The metaphor that most expresses this view is that it is an act of creation. The history of civilization is full of the wonders of the creative and practical talents of people, sometimes out of the pure joy of the creative act in and of itself. So it is important to think about the overarching concept we use when we consider changes we are associated with, because our perspective always has an enormous impact on how we engage our clients and how we work.

Although change can be exciting and lead to a promising future, continuity is also highly valued. When change threatens to disrupt or dissolve what is central to an individual, group, or larger entity, stress and tension are the results. Individuals or larger entities always seek to preserve their core identities. Identity is crucial because it defines how parties make sense out of experience, how they choose to relate to the world, and how they create meaning in their lives.

At the organizational level, identity arises out of a particular history; the nature of the products and services provided; successes and failures; the larger business and social environments of which the organization is a part; and the nature of its leadership, past and present. An organization whose primary mission is research differs in these dimensions from a manufacturing organization, and they are both different from an organization that has distribution as its core function. These differences go on in countless ways. Furthermore, the organization's members, particularly the leadership, become identified with the organization and derive a good deal of their own personal identity in the process. Members who have a strong identification with the corporate ethos are rewarded and are usually highly committed to corporate goals, and those who are not highly identified or committed are not highly valued.

What is important in terms of considering change in an organization is the recognition that people will naturally cling to what they consider to be their own core values. If the organization has strongly represented these values in the past, people fear that this is about to change. Even though we might understand that an external world in flux is demanding that we change in some way, rather than being totally malleable in relationship to that demand we will strive to retain what is central to our individual and collective identities. Simply defining this phenomenon as *resistance to change*, a frequently used expression in this situation, is not helpful and can lead to an unproductive stalemate. Instead we need to discover what important parts of these identities can be carried forward while at the same time finding an appropriate response to the external demand for change. This allows us to create a new and different future while maintaining what is crucial from the past.

Effectively leading this kind of constructive and creative transition is a particularly important role for the leaders of an organization. Practitioners of OD must appreciate the sensitivity of people in such a situation and refrain from becoming radical proponents of change in a way that disowns important values from the past. Those who use appreciative inquiry in dealing with these changes are, in effect, being careful to value what was good about the past and demonstrating that these values can be brought forward into a new situation and continue to be relevant and useful.

Vital Leadership

Initiating and leading change can be daunting for the organization's leadership. To undertake significant organizational change, a leader must be self-confident, open-minded, courageous, persistent, and determined. Many managers who do a good job in times of reasonable stability are not suited for the task of leading change. Changing how an organization conducts its affairs takes strong leadership.

To be effective at leading organizational change, one does *not* have to be a transformational leader, as were Mao Tse-Tung, Mahatma Gandhi, and Martin Luther King Jr. They were visionary and revolutionary in their approach and able to mobilize masses of people to bring about great changes in the social structure of their society. They tapped into deep reservoirs of people's unfulfilled and unexpressed desires and were able to give them expression and form. Some of the same capabilities are required to lead organizational change effectively, though it is of a much more modest proportion.

The *vital leader* also needs to appeal to the hearts and minds of followers and must articulate and embody the desired future. This is true even though the change is less radical or revolutionary. Another difference between the vital leader and the transformational leader is that the change is likely to affect a smaller number of people. In spite of these differences, *vital leaders* must:

- Be able to visualize and communicate by word and deed a superordinate mission in such a way that the thoughts and feelings of members of the organization are mobilized into action

- Be able to act with authenticity and integrity, and garner truth and trust from others

- Be able to balance and integrate the needs of the group with the needs of individuals

- Be highly identified with the group and yet willing to stand apart in order to make judgments and decisions and employ power if required

- Be able to constructively manage conflict arising within the group as well as conflict between one group and another

- Be willing to rely on oneself and not succumb to the strictures and structures that have been put in place by others; this is especially important in creating major change

- Be willing to persist in the face of obstacles and go to great lengths to achieve important goals

- Be sufficiently aware of one's motivations, thoughts, and feelings so as to manage one's impulses and behave in a manner that is appropriate and constructive

Most people who would be vital leaders have tremendous ambition and a drive toward personal mastery. It seems that these leaders have deep personal needs to make a significant contribution to their organization, and often to society at large. Inquiries about their inner motivation and their understanding of the source of this energetic pursuit of higher ideals and aspirations are answered in various ways; however, a common quality is embodied in a Russian folktale: "[I do this] largely of my own free will and twice as much by compulsion." It is important for leaders to have this self-knowledge if they are to steer a steady course without losing their moral compass.

Leadership is crucial. Being social systems, organizations are basically about relationships among people. The relationship between leader and led is the *sine qua non* of cooperative collective effort. It's not good enough to have good people. Good people have to join together in cooperative and effective effort to ensure the continued success of a corporation. Achievement of organizational goals must include and incorporate the more personal goals of the working community, which is made up of all the employees. In this sense, we must understand vital leadership in the context of relationships that are created throughout the organization. Vital leadership must exist at all levels of the organization.

The need for vital leadership speaks to the crucial role that the organization consultant can play. The consultant needs both to support the leader in his or her efforts and challenge the leader to be more than she or he first envisioned. The consultant has to be personally committed and not take ownership for the change effort from the leader. The consultant must be aware of his or her own values and not impose them on the client.

In Conclusion

Has OD delivered on its promise? Might OD be in decline? Clearly the record has been spotty. Nevertheless there have also been some magnificent contributions to the understanding and conduct of effective collective effort. These outcomes have always been the result of using an appropriate conceptual framework and sensitive engagement with a particular kind of organizational leadership found in the client system. In this there is nothing new, and its truth has endured for forty years.

The OD consultant who can comfortably engage the leadership of an organization in addressing all the areas outlined by the first principles is a valuable asset for any organization. Those who cannot will always be only marginally relevant in any initiative of organization development.

References

Ackoff, R. L. *The Democratic Corporation*. New York: Oxford University Press, 1994.

Ansbacher, H. L., and Ansbacher, R. R. *The Individual Psychology of Alfred Adler*. New York: Perennial, 1964.

Burns, J. M. *Leadership*. New York: Harper Torch Books, 1975.

Sloan, A. P. *My Years with General Motors*. New York: Doubleday Currency, 1963 (reprinted 1990).

6

OD: Wanted More Alive Than Dead!

Larry E. Greiner and Thomas G. Cummings

The historical roots of organization development (OD) are traceable to the late 1940s and early 1950s, when it began to bloom but without the OD label attached at this point. OD's energy was fueled by an intellectual hothouse composed of various scholars from leading schools (Harvard, Michigan, Case, MIT, and UCLA at the forefront) who were concerned about developing a better and more positive understanding of the dynamics of change involving people and organizations.

In the early 1960s, the name OD became more commonly used as many of its proponents led it into a popular "movement" intended to "democratize" life in organizations. Not surprisingly, this movement gradually took on a faddish quality, especially after being given a lot of prominence, application, and success. However, the growing enthusiasm for OD was met by a backlash of critics and countertheories. As this criticism gained attention during the early 1970s, the OD movement began to wane and lose energy, never to return to its original form.

In this chapter, we will assess the evolution of OD and question if it still has value for the future. Today there are many troubling signs to suggest its possible demise. OD has virtually disappeared as the title of departments in many organizations. During the late 1970s and 1980s, OD became a bad word in many companies, and this remains so today. OD is rarely taught as a major field in universities, except by a small number of longtime adherents such as Benedictine, Brigham

Young, Case Western, Columbia Teachers College, and Pepperdine. Books and articles focusing exclusively on OD are now rare.

Nevertheless, signs of life still remain today. A few textbooks on OD continue to sell (Cummings and Worley, 2005; French, Zawacki, and Bell, 2005). Scholars in the Academy of Management still expound OD's virtues in sessions of the Organization Development and Change Division. The OD Network remains viable, with adherents coming together nationally and regionally for conferences and training programs. The American Society for Training and Development makes OD a key subject area for attention at its conferences. Among the practitioners, internal consultants continue to practice OD, but usually under a new title such as "organizational effectiveness" or "change management." The National Training Laboratories (NTL), where OD was nurtured for many years, still exists; however, a careful look at its website reveals hardly a mention of OD, except when cited as a single topic subsumed among many other programs. NTL once placed all of its activities under the OD label as its overarching concept and mission.

We believe that now is a good time to reevaluate OD. It has evolved through several definitions over the years. We begin with a short journey to observe what, in our opinion, has happened to OD. Our conclusion to this evolution and reevaluation is that OD is now currently in a weakened condition because of its gradual morphing into a variety of applications that may or may not represent OD in its original form. However, we believe that a newer, current version of OD can still play a vital role in the future if it reflects on its history, draws on its core philosophy, and focuses on key issues facing tomorrow's organizations.

Historical Perspective

Early Thinkers

Although many of us are already familiar with OD's history, we need to remind ourselves about the roots because they set in motion certain trends that took OD in a particular direction. This includes

OD's exciting startup, then development into a fad, and later diversion away from many of its original concepts by morphing into new forms that today might be unrecognizable to the field's forefathers. This is our historical account, but readers should match it with their own perspectives since historical analysis depends greatly on the particular observer's experience and opinions (see French and Bell, 1972, for an early historical account of OD).

The intellectual foundation for OD began in the 1940s with the research and writing of Kurt Lewin (1948) and his protégés. Their application of participative methods to small groups was found to lead to attitude change, higher performance, and greater commitment to individual action. Subsequently, various behavioral writers and researchers, largely from academe, picked up on this thinking to consider its broader relevance for creating change in organizations. Some of these scholars pursued a "micro" psychological approach to OD, while others went in a macro organizational direction. These various paths gradually came together in a complementary way in the late 1950s to form what was to be called OD.

The psychological side was represented by Abraham Maslow (1954), who argued for the inherent potential of individuals to pursue "self-actualization," which was more likely to be achieved under conditions of openness and personal recognition. Complementing Maslow was the work of Carl Rogers (1951), with his revolutionary notions of a new and less dogmatic approach to psychotherapy. His numerous and highly readable books advocated that people could change their behavior when engaged by others through methods of active listening and "unconditional positive regard."

The organizational side received its impetus from the writings of Chris Argyris (1957), who focused on what organizations could do to liberate individuals with higher-order needs. This view was supported shortly thereafter by Rensis Likert (1961) and his Michigan colleagues, who advocated organization-wide participation as a means to motivate individuals and thereby achieve greater performance.

Also feeding into these emerging psychological and organizational models were new theories of change and leadership. The change scholars, building on Lewin's simple but provocative theory of change phases in small groups—"unfreezing, changing, and refreezing"—began to extend these notions to entire organizations. This thinking was captured in a seminal book edited by Bennis, Benne, and Chin, *The Planning of Change* (1969), wherein most of the chapters, in one way or another, proposed the simple axiom that organizations could be changed through greater involvement of people in the change process. Their emphasis on helping organizations become more participative suggested a variety of benefits: reduced resistance to change, enhanced learning of new behavior, better solutions, and new cultural norms of openness.

The leadership side was represented in the thinking and writing of Douglas McGregor (1960), who proposed that different styles of leadership will result in different reactions from subordinates—more positive under "Theory Y," which was participative and democratic, and highly negative under "Theory X," which was oppressive and authoritarian.

All of this activity and theorizing about changing people and organizations was conducted by scholars under many university roofs, yet these same OD leaders often met with a lot of agreement at conferences where they shared ideas and eagerly awaited each other's next publication. Up to this point, OD was mostly an "intellectual crusade," with little thought given to making money from it.

OD Becomes a Movement

At this point, OD might be defined as a rough collection of scholarly ideas focusing on people and social processes in organizations and how to change and improve them. Somewhere along the way, the term *organization development* came into being as an overarching umbrella to include and embrace all of the previous thinking about the behavioral aspects of people involved in changing and developing organizations. We believe the term emerged informally at meetings of the academic founders and then became codified in their publications. OD rapidly gained credence and popularity among hundreds of practitioners in private and public organizations, especially within the personnel department.

A key organization promoting OD was National Training Laboratories, which began in 1947 as a division of the National Education Association, with training facilities in Bethel, Maine. The Bethel center provided training for people who paid to attend, although NTL was nonprofit. Much of this training was based on the use of T-groups, an educational technology resembling group therapy (although the T stood for "training" according to the advocates), to permit self-insight through open-ended discussion in small groups and feedback on member behavior (Argyris, 1964). The "trainers" for these T-groups were usually the early scholars and associates of NTL, who were paid a consulting fee for their assistance. The underlying premise of these groups was that causality for behavioral problems lay in an individual's perceptions, assumptions, and feelings concerning events and people around him or her. Therefore, the solution could be found in altering these elements with feedback in a sensitivity group led by a nondirective trainer.

Soon, many corporate practitioners, including corporate managers and staff who had received training at Bethel, began asking for consulting help to revitalize their organizations. They wanted to expose their managers to OD through the use of T-groups and other forms of sensitivity training as a means to change and renew their organization. In response, several consulting firms were founded to offer OD advice. One of them was Scientific Methods, started by Robert Blake and Jane Mouton, both early pioneers with NTL. Their contribution was the Managerial Grid (Blake and Mouton, 1964), a more structured approach for conducting interpersonal and leadership training than what was offered by T-groups. Blake and Mouton published several books on their approach to OD and were immensely successful in marketing their particular program to client organizations. Research on the success of their methods was mixed, however (Blake, Mouton, Barnes, and Greiner, 1964).

During this same period, there was a tremendous surge in OD activity as organizations asked for help in changing the styles of managers and improving their organization's performance. The emphasis here was on "reeducation" by exposing large groups of managers to intensive T-group-like exercises designed to provide interpersonal feedback and move these managers toward more open and trusting behavior. An additional goal was often to change the behavior and culture of an entire organization toward norms supporting greater openness; this required that a large number of managers be exposed to OD methods. The effects of these efforts were rarely studied, and when examined by systematic research the results were often mixed (Armenakis and Field, 1975; Boris, 1978; Morrison, 1981; Porras and Berg, 1978). The same ambivalence characterized research on changes in interpersonal relationships and personal behavior. Success often hinged on supportive factors in the organizational environment (Greiner, 1967).

Much about OD was recorded in a series of paperbacks from Addison-Wesley, written by well-known scholars and practitioners. In addition, publication of many other books and articles signaled that OD had indeed arrived. The OD Network, an association of adherents, was formed. OD practice became an integral part of the conference program of the American Society for Training and Development, which had thousands of members across the United States.

Like the growth of many management techniques, OD gradually took on characteristics of a fad. The more zealous proponents readily engaged organizations in OD, often performed with naïve idealism and without adequate diagnosis to determine if OD was appropriate to the situation. OD consultants were also earning substantial consulting fees. These proliferating OD programs relied on the application of earlier methods and theories to produce change in organizations; little attention was given to other issues facing organizations or to new theoretical development.

The definition of OD had now changed to an applied focus by practitioners on using sensitivity training and related methods to make organizations more responsive to people while also changing the members' styles to fit the changed organization.

Counterattack

During the 1970s, various critics began to rebel at the widespread use of OD, sometimes out of jealousy and other times out of skepticism about the promised results. OD was increasingly criticized for its cultlike activities, for forcing organizations to undergo an ideology of openness and use of T-groups, and for not achieving the desired outcomes. A provocative article called "Red Flags in Organization Development," by Larry Greiner (1972), summarized this criticism and warned about the possible future demise of OD. Here we briefly summarize the six danger signals, because the critics of OD began to take them seriously, and gradually much of OD moved off into new directions, although some early proponents kept going as they had been previously. The movement began to lose its early enthusiasm, energy, and adherents.

- *Flag one: putting the individual before the organization.* The obsession of OD with individual behavior change caused less focus on the formal organization—its strategy, structure, controls, and so on. As a result, OD neglected to address potential sources of environmental support and reinforcement for behavior change.
- *Flag two: informal before formal organization.* There was also an overemphasis on interpersonal values (openness, trust, and the like) in an attempt to change the informal culture of organizations, often at the expense of the design of the formal organization and its values of efficiency, hierarchy, and accountability. Again, an opportunity was missed to produce a wider impact.
- *Flag three: behavior before diagnosis.* OD was preoccupied with behavior change along the lines of OD's core values, not with diagnosing whether the existing behavior was compatible with the strategic thrust or culture of the organization. Thus, OD's goal of promoting more open and trusting relationships became the

normative model for change; it was taken for granted without questioning its applicability to particular situations.

- *Flag four: process before task.* With its emphasis on how one person should relate to others, OD became enamored with the human dynamics of working together, assuming that team building was the preferred alternative. In doing so, it neglected the realities of technology and the substantive problems in front of people. Contingency theory revealed that some jobs were inherently mechanistic and programmable; therefore they did not require much teamwork and openness for effective performance (Lawrence and Lorsch, 1969).

- *Flag five: experts before the manager.* OD programs were designed and conducted by expert consultants. NTL had become an elitist organization of trained experts. Their target of change was the manager in organizations. Unfortunately, managers were relatively uninvolved in the planning and conducting of consultant-led OD programs. They were simply supposed to be the recipients of change and to conform to the model being advocated by the consultants.

- *Flag six: package before the situation.* Potential clients for OD activities usually preferred packaged change programs: formal activities that were structured, tangible, and easy to explain to employees. Many OD consultants also welcomed this approach because structured programs were easier to sell and administer than open-ended and evolving efforts. The unfortunate result was that organizations were frequently shoehorned to fit the OD program's characteristics rather than customizing the program to fit the uniqueness of the client organization.

These six flags were among the more constructive criticisms. A satirical movie, *Bob & Carol & Ted & Alice*, was made to pan the superficiality of expecting people to readily engage in open and trusting relationships. Some academics argued that happy employees were not necessarily productive ones (Herzberg and Zautra, 1976). Journalists even questioned the sanity of executives engaging in such programs, some going so far as to accuse the consultants of being Communist-inspired.

In our view, the six flags portrayed a narrowing of OD's focus and an inability to embrace other aspects of reality facing organizations and their employees, such as strategic planning, work design, and global expansion. In addition, OD had for many proponents become an ideology—even a cult—with a proliferation of people acting as OD consultants in internal or external roles. Many of them were not well trained or qualified. OD's focus on democratizing organizations was frequently felt as threatening by the targeted managers, especially the power structure, because of its emphasis on change, democracy, and intimacy. Many critics questioned if OD's reliance on training programs as an educational intervention was sufficient by itself to produce lasting changes.

Changing Organizational Conditions

OD changed radically from 1970 to the present. It evolved and morphed into entirely new forms that seemed far afield from OD's traditional core. Of course, some of these changes were simply the natural evolution of any applied social science as new ideas and methods are invented and perfected. Other changes were unexpected and derived from OD's entrepreneurial spirit in responding to new demands placed on organizations by their environments.

As we describe shortly, organizations began to undergo (and continue to undergo today) an enormous transformation in how they are structured and managed. To some extent, OD played a role in helping to design and implement these changes. These efforts blurred the boundaries of the OD field and have made it more difficult to define what is and is not OD.

OD's evolution needs to be understood in the context of major trends shaping organizations over the last thirty years. As summarized in Table 6.1, these changes involved new demands from the economy, workforce, and technology, all of which greatly affected how organizations are managed. The economy has rapidly become more global, with diverse markets, political conditions, and cultures placing unique and often conflicting demands on how organizations accomplish work and transact business (Thurow, 1996). Laws, regulations, business customs, wage rates, and consumer tastes vary enormously across countries, requiring global competitors to make complex choices and trade-offs. These new and changing global conditions place a premium on how fast organizations can respond to them (Korten, 1995). In addition, U.S. society and government have given greater emphasis and scrutiny to promoting responsible corporate behavior.

In addition, the workforce has become much more diverse, educated, and contingent. This has resulted in new approaches to managing and developing human resources. Increased heterogeneity among employees has required new policies and practices that respect individual differences and cultivate cultural, ethnic, gender, and age diversity (Thomas, 1990). A more educated workforce has

Table 6.1.   Trends in Organizations and Their Contexts

	From	*Toward*
Economy	Domestic	Global
	Static, predictable	Dynamic, uncertain
Workforce	Homogeneous	Diverse
	Experienced	Educated
	Permanent	Contingent
Technology	Energy	Information
	Routine, mechanical	Complex, knowledge-based
	Mass production	Customization
Organizations	Bureaucratic	Organic
	Efficiency	Innovation
	Control	Learning
	Autocratic management	Strategic leadership

placed demands on organizations to improve compensation packages, to enhance opportunities for involvement in decision making, and to increase investment in knowledge and skills (Thompson, Koon, Woodwell, and Beauvais, 2002). A more contingent labor force can easily become less loyal and committed if employers fail to make significant improvements in the psychological and employment contracts that govern relationships with employees (Melchionno, 1999).

The technology that firms use to produce products and services has also been undergoing immense change. New information technologies have drastically redefined how work is performed, how transactions are conducted, and how knowledge is used (Drucker, 1999). Mechanical forms of work and routine tasks have been increasingly automated, leaving to human minds and ingenuity the more complex, knowledge-based work. The ability to furnish vast amounts of real-time information to anyone anyplace makes tasks more tightly connected and virtual. This enables workflows to become faster, cycle times to grow shorter, and production to be more flexible (Davenport, 1992). Products and services can then be more closely and quickly aligned to customer needs.

These economic, workforce, and technical forces have increasingly placed heavy demands on modern organizations to change themselves accordingly. New organizational forms have proliferated as firms seek to make themselves flatter, more flexible, and more responsive. Bureaucratic structures that promote efficiency and control have given way to more organic designs that favor innovation and employee commitment (Mohrman, Galbraith, and Lawler, 1998). Employees are increasingly being treated as a resource, not an expense. New human resource practices have evolved to attract, retain, and develop the best talent (Lawler and Mohrman, 2003). Because change, both internal and external, has become the order of the day, organizations are more oriented to learning than to control (McGill and Slocum, 1994; Senge, 1990). They seek to learn from their actions about how to change continuously and improve themselves. Competitive advantage derives from core competencies having to do with knowledge management, continuous improvement, and organization learning. All of these changes require strategic leadership to impart a compelling vision and motivate members to enact it.

The Morphing of OD

OD was not well equipped to deal with many of the demands and changes that we have described. It was geared more to a narrow range of topics, largely internal to organizations—team building, leadership style, interpersonal relations, and culture change—and confined mostly to sensitivity training and similar methods for making social processes more effective. As a consequence, OD's reaction to environmental change was varied as its adherents began to fragment and depart in numerous directions.

There were basically two sides to this departure, which we roughly divide between the "adapters" and the "holdouts." The adapters started to apply OD thinking to the new challenges facing organizations, while the holdouts stayed loyal to the old OD, practicing it where they could. In addition, a new wave of organizational scientists began to enter the market from schools with no formal OD training; these individuals offered their own solutions to organizational problems.

The OD adapters began to move in the directions outlined in Table 6.2. They heeded many of the early danger signals in Greiner's red flags. Moving ahead, the adapters developed new ideas and methods addressing not only processes of change but the surrounding organizational context, such as structure, rewards, and the design of work. Their values were still concerned with empowering people so organizations could become more effective. The Addison-Wesley OD series continued to report new ideas and applications well into the 1990s, covering topics from labor conflict to pay systems. At the same time, people trained in other disciplines, such as engineering, corporate strategy, and human resource management, significantly influenced these innovations.

Table 6.2. Trends in Organization Development

	From	Toward
Key targets of change	Individuals and groups	Strategy and structure
	Social processes	Work processes
		Human resource practices
Key stakeholders	Management	Management, employees, staff, customers, suppliers, etc.
Values	Humanistic	Humanistic and organization effectiveness
Change process	Problem-driven	Learning-driven
	Episodic change	Continuous change
	Expert-managed	Leader- or member-managed
Key change issue	Overcome resistance to change	Set positive vision for organization

The OD practitioners who adapted during this lengthy period typically chose to become more expert in the design of the formal aspects of organizations, especially with an emphasis on designs that gave more power to the workforce, such as decentralized profit centers. They let go of their attachment to sensitivity training methods but still contributed to the change process through internal consulting, managing offsite planning retreats, and arranging new forms of leadership training.

Many of OD's adaptive contributions were directed at the workforce. They rarely involved senior management or focused on issues external to the organization (interestingly, the same omissions occurred in the early days of OD). OD probably played its most significant role in helping to implement new work designs on the shop floor. Applying knowledge about sociotechnical systems, work psychology, and engineering, practitioners with OD training helped organizations design work that was more motivating, flexible, and responsive to change. These efforts were subsequently documented in research, showing how self-managed teams became more productive and satisfying than traditional jobs, especially in knowledge-work settings (Cohen and Ledford, 1994; Wall, Kemp, Jackson, and Clegg, 1986). Other OD practitioners helped to facilitate reengineering efforts that gave employees tools to continuously improve quality and work methods (Hammer and Champy, 2001).

OD also contributed to human resource management, frequently working with experts in personnel and industrial relations on traditional issues of employee and labor relations. OD professionals helped organizations select and train employees to fit the new structures and work designs described here (Kristoff, 1996). OD thinking also contributed to new types of reward systems aimed at making rewards more contingent on performance and skill learning in the workforce (Lawler, 2000). "Gain sharing," for example, tied rewards to measurable gains in performance of a team or business unit (Belcher, 1994). It encouraged members to work together to discover new ways to improve performance. Similarly, "skill-based pay" linked rewards to the number of skills or jobs that people could learn and perform (Lawler and Ledford, 1985). Workers learned new skills and broadened their expertise, thus creating a highly skilled, flexible workforce essential to better performance in a rapidly changing environment.

OD professionals, working mainly as internal consultants, have contributed to the change processes needed to introduce many of these innovations into organizations. Traditionally, OD viewed change as an episodic event directed by OD consultants who helped to identify problems, diagnose causes, and implement solutions. In contrast, these newer OD contributions were treated more as continuous learning in a lengthy transformation process managed by members from throughout the organization (Fisher and Tolbert, 1995; Mohrman and Cummings, 1989). This involved considerable innovation and learning-by-doing as members designed and tried out innovations, assessed the results, made necessary adjustments, and so on. Thus the capacity to change and improve was built into the organization so it could continuously adapt to changing conditions.

OD has also become involved with implementing new strategic plans in organizations, though rarely participating in the strategy formulation process. In dealing with strategy implementation, OD's contribution was mainly to design organizations so they supported and reinforced new strategies with lean and flexible structures that enabled the organization to respond more rapidly to changing conditions. In addition, OD thinking has stimulated a move toward "high-involvement organizations" that push decision making, information and knowledge, and rewards downward to the lowest levels of the firm (Lawler, 1986).

Occasionally, OD became involved in applied work on issues of organization learning and knowledge management (Argyris and Schön, 1996; Davenport and Prusak, 1998; Senge, 1990). In some cases, it helped organizations gain the capacity to learn continuously from their actions and make effective use of internally generated knowledge. This learning capability is essential if organizations are to constantly change and renew themselves, thus constituting a source of competitive advantage in a dynamic environment (Teece, 1998).

As the adaptive side of OD moved ahead, its values became more complex and diffuse. Traditional humanistic values of openness, collaboration, and trust frequently competed with values favoring organizational effectiveness, shareholder worth, speed-to-market, workforce diversity, and worker productivity. Consistent with this evolution, OD practitioners shifted their thinking about how to intervene in organizations. Traditionally in OD, resistance to change, both personal and organizational, was treated as the major obstacle to progress. OD once invested considerable effort in identifying sources of resistance and creating methods for overcoming it (Lawrence, 1969). Today, a more positive approach to change is emerging under such banners as "appreciative inquiry" (Cooperrider, Sorenson, Yaeger, and Whitney, 2001) and "positive organizational scholarship" (Cameron, Dutton, and Quinn, 2003). These approaches draw on people's vision, intrinsic motivation, and positive expectations for anticipating and implementing change on a continuous basis.

Today, OD has taken on an entirely new definition. Cummings (2005) synthesized several definitions after reflecting on what OD had become. He concluded that OD now encompasses diverse concepts and methods for changing organizations. Although several definitions of OD were previously presented (Beckhard, 1969; Beer, 1980; Bennis, 1969; Burke, 1987; French, 1969), the enormous growth of new approaches and techniques has blurred the boundaries of the field and made it increasingly difficult to describe. Cummings's definition seeks to clarify emerging aspects of OD while drawing on previous definitions of the field: "Organization development is a system-wide process of applying behavioral-science knowledge to the planned change and development of the strategies, design components, and processes that enable organizations to be effective" (2005, p. 5).

Deja Vu All Over Again—Or Is It?

As we saw in the last section, OD has clearly evolved over the years into many new forms, several of which may be quite unrecognizable to its forebears. In many ways, OD's contributions have been difficult to discern because rarely is the OD label used to describe these innovations.

Nevertheless, we believe that this evolution has been healthy, given the creeping faddism and limitations attached to early OD. At the same time, we now question whether this recent morphing of OD into so many forms may have strayed too far from OD's original roots, practices, and values. Have these recent innovations made traditional OD obsolete, or is reminding ourselves about OD's rich history of value for future innovations in the field?

The recent focus on strategy, structure, work design, human resource practices, and organization learning has achieved a lot. But in many ways, we believe, there has been an overcorrection to the red flags not only by OD but by the broader behavioral sciences and other disciplines involved. Though making progress, OD's traditional attention to social process and member participation has only occasionally been applied to solving the new problems facing organizations, and many times these values have been neglected or downplayed altogether, not just by OD but also by managers and other behavioral scientists. Values of business efficiency, expediency, and short-term gain have overridden the original OD values of involvement, trust, and openness (now called "transparency"). Frequently, the organization's decision makers have omitted OD—and, more important, people—from the solution.

In this new millennium, we believe that trust and the quality of human relationships are now more important than ever in predicting both career and organizational success. Human capital is now being described in terms of competitive advantage (Pfeffer, 1998). At the same time, the context for relationship building is decidedly different from what it was in the early years of OD, which focused on manufacturing (not services), domestic business (not global), face-to-face teams (not virtual organizations), and so forth.

Consequently, we believe that now is the time for a serious reevaluation of OD and its future—to remind ourselves of OD's original roots as we and others have described them, and then for all those concerned with social process, change, and enhanced human and organizational capabilities to move forward with innovative solutions for resolving a new set of problems facing organizations.

We see several new red flags facing OD today, but if they are confronted effectively, then OD can evolve again and make a major contribution. At its core, OD brings a concern for and set of methods to address issues of change, process, and relationships—all conducted within a value set of participation, openness, and trust. But in our opinion this is not enough to move ahead; OD cannot go all the way back home again to rely solely on group methods, personal feedback, reeducation, and a singular focus on process.

These early precepts have to be modified and better integrated with the realities of problems facing today's (and tomorrow's) organizations. The content of these issues must be joined with effective social processes for solving them, and OD must be positioned with sufficient credibility and power to do so.

New Red Flag One: Neglected Involvement in Top-Management Decision Making

There is considerable evidence that the human resource function in many organizations is not involved as a full partner in top-management decision making (Lawler and Mohrman, 2004). From this omission we surmise that OD, which is usually subsumed under HR, is also not involved in major decisions affecting the entire organization. This absence from power circles has frequently been the fault of OD because it avoided power dynamics in organizations and championed methods and values that favored less powerful organization members (Greiner and Schein, 1988). To be included at the decision-making table, OD will have to become more comfortable with power while gaining the necessary personal qualifications, acquisition of which likely includes prior successful performance in line operations, rising to the top of HR, and maybe even one's acquiring an MBA degree to signal that one understands and empathizes with the broader substantive issues facing organizations. At the same time, OD practitioners must demonstrate competence in helping to resolve important issues that senior management regards as within its scope of decision making.

New Red Flag Two: Neglected Involvement in Strategy Formulation

One of the major issues facing senior management is how to develop a coherent strategic plan that has the commitment of leaders and employees throughout the organization and also leads to competitive advantage. Unfortunately, this challenge is generally addressed by management consulting firms and planning departments—often to the exclusion of OD values and methods. However, most strategic planners and consultants are not trained in OD and thus may naïvely assume that the content is unrelated to the process for developing the plan. But behavioral processes and human input do indeed affect the content of strategic plans. Decisions about who to involve in planning and how to conduct the planning process will have a significant affect on the content and outcome (Greiner, Bhambri, and Cummings, 2003). A prime example of how OD can contribute to strategy formulation is described in the Mega case series, where OD-trained strategy consultants involved a senior management team in changing their company's strategic direction (Greiner, 2005). In this case series, the OD consultants use retreats and participation to facilitate a planning process that fully explores and develops the content necessary for a sound plan that also carries with it the commitment of those involved. This exercise is more than a simple visioning experience, an approach used in the past by some OD consultants. It involves concepts of economics, finance, operations, and marketing and places them within a special planning format necessary to bring out deeper issues.

New Red Flag Three: Neglected Involvement in Mergers and Acquisitions

We detect little current evidence that OD is involved in the difficult issues surrounding mergers and acquisitions. Too often merger deals and plans are drawn up only by financial experts and lawyers interested solely in completing the transaction. However, this goal has often caused the experts to overstate the potential synergies and downplay the difficulties of implementation. The result is that most mergers fail to live up to expectations (Buono, 2005). OD needs to become more involved in the earliest stages of the due diligence and negotiation process of a merger. This can help both parties bring out and assess objectively more complete information about each organization's needs and capabilities. Also, OD can help the acquiring firm address postmerger integration issues; on the other side, it can assist the acquired firm to communicate more completely its situation and needs to the acquirer. Because many conflicts and misunderstandings are likely to be experienced, OD practitioners will need to possess broad knowledge about the financial and legal aspects of mergers, as well as demonstrate strong negotiation skills.

New Red Flag Four: Neglected Involvement in Globalization

To date, OD involvement in the globalization process has been confined largely to cross-cultural training and international conferences. However, international companies face a range of behavioral and organizational issues that cut across country boundaries, such as developing global managers, choosing foreign partners, understanding cultural differences, assimilating foreign nationals, negotiating with foreign governments, and managing with a global mind-set. Although OD practitioners cannot be specialists in all these areas, they need to become more aware of them and how to facilitate their solution. They can also design training programs intended to produce global managers as well as team up with content specialists more knowledgeable on the business issues. OD needs to take a global perspective in all its work.

New Red Flag Five: Neglected Involvement in Alliances and Virtual Organizations

Today, many companies participate in alliances and business ventures over which they have little direct control. Moreover, firms have increasingly turned to outsourcing their noncore business functions so as to focus their strategy and perform better. Obviously, these external relationships cannot be managed entirely through contracts and hierarchy; instead, they require a good deal of trust and strong interpersonal relationships. Even though OD has developed effective methods for working on these issues within organizations, it needs to extend them to help people work more effectively across organizations where structure is limited and authority relations are ambivalent. In addition, employees need to gain insight into their own motivation and preferences because those with high need for structure and direction are unlikely to be successful when working across alliances and joint ventures. Aspiring managers need to learn how to lead teams composed of people from other organizations that are outside their control and how to resolve conflicts in these groups without escalating decisions to a higher level. Much of OD's traditional experience with team building in matrix organizations is relevant here (Davis and Lawrence, 1977), although the context is likely more complex than in the past.

New Red Flag Six: Neglected Involvement in Corporate Governance and Personal Integrity

Recently, we have seen many problems arise out of corporate and individual greed. The negative results have been widely felt, including the demise of companies, loss of jobs, and prison terms for corporate leaders. Society has also been hurt by a loss of credibility for its institutions and leadership. To its credit, OD has long addressed ethical issues related to its practice (DeVogel, Sullivan, McLean, and Rothwell, 1995). Unfortunately, this attention has had little impact on the broader issues of corporate governance and organizational ethics. They are closely related: bad governance leads to bad ethics and vice versa. Governance issues begin in the boardroom where new laws must be supported by a group process of confrontation, openness, independence, and teamwork. OD has much to offer at this level, but it will be unreachable unless the OD practitioner has sufficient credibility and representation in senior management (Nadler, 2005). There are only a few existing OD approaches for helping employees gain personal insight on ethics and integrity (Maister, 2005). The personal integrity issue can be addressed by OD through assisting organizations in preparing a "code of conduct" and offering additional training for employees, both experiential and knowledge-based. Employees need to gain suf-ficient personal insight so they can recognize ethical conflicts when they appear and then be prepared to resolve them responsibly. OD's original values of personal reflection, openness, trust, and human character should prove invaluable in these efforts.

The Next Era

Rather than acting as a polarizing force by choosing sides between, for example, process and content, or being a revolutionary tool for democratizing organizations, or ignoring the formal strategic needs of organizations, OD needs to reach out and create integrative solutions to the major issues facing tomorrow's organizations. We think it is OD's challenge to apply its core values and methods as a foundation for creatively helping organizations and individuals address these major issues. We have suggested a few approaches for resolving the new red flags, but many more must be designed and implemented by OD out of a newfound innovative and entrepreneurial spirit.

We believe the next era for OD signals a series of challenging applied issues involving the link between substantive content and social process. Here OD can contribute, but only if it gains access to key decision makers in organizations, and ventures into issues it may have avoided in the past, many of which are external to the organization. It must improve the organization's and the individ-ual's capability to embrace both content and process solutions. No longer can OD assume that substantive issues will be solved by offer-ing only a smoothly functioning set of behavioral processes. OD must become more substantively aware in searching for synthesis solutions with positive content and behavioral consequences. OD will move ahead only if it is taught more frequently to students and executives, if it acquires practical knowledge about the substantive issues facing organizations, and if it gains in power and reputation with decision makers for helping to solve important problems. Otherwise, OD will likely fade into irrelevance.

References

Argyris, C. *Personality and Organization: The Conflict Between System and the Individual*. New York: HarperCollins, 1957.

Argyris, C. "T-Groups for Organizational Effectiveness." *Harvard Business Review,* 1964, *42*(2), 60–74.

Argyris, C., and Schön, D. *Organizational Learning II: Theory, Method, and Practice*. Reading, Mass.: Addison-Wesley, 1996.

Armenakis, A., and Field, H. S. "Evaluation of Organizational Change Using Nonindependent Criterion Measures." *Personnel Psychology,* 1975, *28*(1), 39–44.

Beckhard, R. *Organization Development: Strategies and Models*. Reading, Mass.: Addison-Wesley, 1969.

Beer, M. *Organization Change and Development: A Systems View*. Santa Monica, Calif.: Goodyear, 1980.

Belcher, J. "Gainsharing and Variable Pay: The State of the Art." *Compensation and Benefits Review,* 1994, *26*(3), 50–60.

Bennis, W. *Organization Development: Its Nature, Origins, and Prospects*. Reading, Mass.: Addison-Wesley, 1969.

Bennis, W. G., Benne, K., and Chin, R. (eds.). *The Planning of Change*. New York: Holt, Rinehart and Winston, 1969.

Blake, R. R., and Mouton, J. *The Managerial Grid*. Houston, Tex.: Gulf, 1964.

Blake, R. R., Mouton, J., Barnes, L., and Greiner, L. "Breakthrough in Organization Development." *Harvard Business Review,* 1964, *42*(6), 133–155.

Boris, S. "OD Evaluation—A Different View." *Group & Organization Studies,* Dec. 1978, *4*(3), 396–398.

Buono, A. P. "Consulting to Integrate Mergers and Acquisitions." In L. E. Greiner and F. Poulfelt (eds.), *The Contemporary Consultant*. Cincinnati, Ohio: South-Western, 2005.

Burke, W. *Organization Development: A Normative View*. Reading, Mass.: Addison-Wesley, 1987.

Cameron, K., Dutton, J., and Quinn, R. (eds.). *Positive Organizational Scholarship: Foundations of a New Discipline*. San Francisco: Berrett-Koehler, 2003.

Cohen, S., and Ledford, G. "The Effectiveness of Self-Managing Teams: A Quasi-Experiment." *Human Relations,* 1994, *47,* 13–43.

Cooperrider, D., Sorenson, P., Yaeger, T., and Whitney, D. (eds.). *Appreciative Inquiry: An Emerging Direction for Organization Development*. Champaign, Ill.: Stipes, 2001.

Cummings, T. G. "Organization Development: Foundations and Applications." In J. Boonstra (ed.), *Dynamics of Organizational Change and Learning*. Chichester, U.K.: Wiley, 2005.

Cummings, T. G., and Worley, C. G. *Organization Development and Change*. (6th ed.) Cincinnati, Ohio: South-Western, 2005.

Davenport, T. *Process Innovation: Reengineering Work Through Information Technology*. Cambridge, Mass.: Harvard Business School Press, 1992.

Davenport, T., and Prusak, L. *Working Knowledge: How Organizations Manage What They Know*. Boston: Harvard Business School Press, 1998.

Davis, S., and Lawrence, P. A. *Matrix*. Reading, Mass.: Addison-Wesley, 1977.

DeVogel, S. H., Sullivan, R., McLean, G. N., and Rothwell, W. J. "Ethics in OD." In W. J. Rothwell, R. Sullivan, and G. N. McLean (eds.), *Practicing Organization Development: A Guide for Consultants*. San Francisco: Pfeiffer, 1995.

Drucker, P. "Beyond the Information Revolution." *Atlantic Monthly*, Oct. 1999, pp. 45–57.

Fisher, D., and Tolbert, W. *Personal and Organizational Transformations: The True Challenge of Continual Quality Improvement*. New York: McGraw-Hill, 1995.

French, W. "Organization Development: Objectives, Assumptions, and Strategies." *California Management Review*, 1969, *12*(2), 23–34.

French, W., and Bell, C. "A Brief History of Organization Development." *Journal of Contemporary Business*, 1972, *1*(3), 1–8.

French, W., Zawacki, R., and Bell, C. (eds.) *Organization Development and Transformation: Managing Effective Change*. (6th ed.) Burr Ridge, Ill.: McGraw-Hill/Irwin, 2005.

Greiner, L. E. "Antecedents of Planned Organization Change." *Journal of Applied Behavioral Science*, 1967, *3*(1), 51–86.

Greiner, L. E. "Red Flags in Organization Development." *Business Horizons*, June 1972.

Greiner, L. E. "Mega (A-D)." In L. E. Greiner, T. Olson, and F. Poulfelt (eds.), *Casebook for the Contemporary Consultant*. Cincinnati, Ohio: South-Western, 2005.

Greiner, L. E., Bhambri, A., and Cummings, T. "Searching for a Strategy to Teach Strategy." *Academy of Management Learning and Education*, 2003, *2*(4), 402–420.

Greiner, L. E., and Schein, V. E. *Power and Organization Development*. Reading, Mass.: Addison-Wesley, 1988.

Hammer, M., and Champy, J. *Reengineering the Corporation: A Manifesto for Business Revolution*. New York: HarperBusiness, 2001.

Herzberg, F., and Zautra, A. "Orthodox Job Enrichment: Measuring True Quality in Job Satisfaction." *Personnel*, 1976, *53*(5), 54–68.

Korten, D. *When Corporations Rule the World.* San Francisco: Berrett-Koehler, 1995.

Kristoff, A. "Person-Organization Fit: An Integrative Review of Its Conceptualizations, Measurement, and Implications." *Personnel Psychology,* Spring 1996, pp. 1–49.

Lawler, E. E. III. *High Involvement Management.* San Francisco: Jossey-Bass, 1986.

Lawler, E. *Rewarding Excellence: Pay Strategies for the New Economy.* San Francisco: Jossey-Bass, 2000.

Lawler, E., and Ledford, G. "Skill-Based Pay." *Personnel,* 1985, *62,* 30–37.

Lawler, E., and Mohrman, S. *Creating a Strategic Human Resources Organization: An Assessment of Trends and New Directions.* Palo Alto, Calif.: Stanford University Press, 2003.

Lawler, E., and Mohrman, S. "Human Resources Consulting." In L. E. Greiner and F. Poulfelt (eds.), *The Contemporary Consultant.* Cincinnati, Ohio: South-Western, 2004.

Lawrence, P. "How to Deal with Resistance to Change." *Harvard Business Review,* 1969, *47*(1), 4–12.

Lawrence, P. R., and Lorsch, J. *Organization and Environment.* Homewood, Ill.: Irwin Dorsey, 1969.

Lewin, K. *Resolving Social Conflicts.* New York: HarperCollins, 1948.

Likert, R. *New Patterns of Management.* New York: McGraw-Hill, 1961.

Maister, D. "Professionalism in Consulting." In L. E. Greiner and F. Poulfelt (eds.), *The Contemporary Consultant.* Cincinnati, Ohio: South-Western, 2005.

Maslow, A. *Motivation and Personality.* New York: HarperCollins, 1954.

McGill, M., and Slocum, J. *The Smarter Organization: How to Build a Business That Learns and Adapts to Marketplace Needs.* New York: Wiley, 1994.

McGregor, D. *The Human Side of Enterprise.* New York: McGraw-Hill, 1960.

Melchionno, R. "The Changing Temporary Workforce." *Occupational Outlook Quarterly,* Spring 1999, pp. 24–32.

Mohrman, S., and Cummings, T. "Self-Designing Organizations: Learning How to Create High Performance." Reading, Mass.: Addison-Wesley, 1989.

Mohrman, S., Galbraith, J., and Lawler, E. *Tomorrow's Organization: Crafting Winning Capabilities in a Dynamic World.* San Francisco: Jossey-Bass, 1998.

Morrison, P. "Evaluation in OD: A Review and an Assessment." *Group & Organization Studies,* 1981, *3*(1), 42–70.

Nadler, D. "Consulting to CEOs and Boards." In L. E. Greiner and F. Poulfelt (eds.), *The Contemporary Consultant.* Cincinnati, Ohio: South-Western, 2005.

Pfeffer, J. *Putting People First.* Boston: Harvard Business School Press, 1998.

Porras, J. I., and Berg, P. O. "Evaluation Methodology in Organization Development: An Analysis and Critique." *Journal of Applied Behavioral Science*, 1978, *14*(2), 151-173.

Rogers, C. *Client Centered Therapy*. Boston: Houghton Mifflin, 1951.

Senge, P. *The Fifth Discipline: The Art and Practice of the Learning Organization*. New York: Doubleday Books, 1990.

Teece, D. "Capturing Value from Knowledge Assets: The New Economy, Market for Know-How, and Intangible Assets." *California Management Review*, 1998, *40*, 55–79.

Thomas, R. "From Affirmative Action to Affirming Diversity." *Harvard Business Review*, Mar.–Apr. 1990, pp. 107–117.

Thompson, C., Koon, E., Woodwell, W., and Beauvais, J. *Training for the Next Economy: An ASTD State of the Industry Report on Trends in Employer-Provided Training in the U.S.* Alexandria, Va.: American Society of Training Directors, 2002.

Thurow, L. *The Future of Capitalism*. New York: William Morrow, 1996.

Wall, T., Kemp, N., Jackson, P., and Clegg, C. "Outcome of Autonomous Workgroups: A Long-Term Field Experiment." *Academy of Management Journal*, 1986, *29*, 280–304.

7

On the Demise of Organization Development

Chris Argyris

The editors argue, correctly I believe, that OD is experiencing a demise. They point out that:

- OD started with high expectations and with having significant influence at the organization level in major corporations.

- Contemporary conditions would suggest that there is an even greater need for OD approaches, given the pervasiveness of change.

- Yet OD has appeared to diminish in importance and is usually relegated to the bottom of the organization.

To understand what caused this demise, it is necessary to get at the designs for action that OD professionals use when they plan and implement their activities and programs. To understand the designs, it is necessary to make the distinction between the espoused designs and the "theories-in-use" that were actually used. The former do not explain demise. Indeed, if the espoused designs had actually been used, OD would not have experienced its diminution.

Instead the problem is the reasoning mind-sets that OD professionals commonly rely on.

Reasoning Mind-Sets

There are two reasoning mind-sets that dominate human action in organizations: *productive reasoning* and *defensive reasoning*. I suggest that during the early days, no matter what OD perspectives were developed, most of them were expected to meet the criteria of productive reasoning. However, I believe that it is fair to claim that OD consultants increasingly used defensive reasoning to define their practice, even though it was defensive reasoning that inhibited the kind of learning that OD stood for. Moreover, the defensive reasoning mind-set of OD blossomed during the very time in which the design and management of organizations became increasingly dominated by productive reasoning.

A productive reasoning mind-set is in the service of learning, informed choice, and personal responsibility for the effectiveness of one's action. Productive reasoning sanctions transparency. The test of the validity of claims is conducted by actions that can be independently verified. Productive reasoning admonishes actors to strive vigilantly to assure themselves that they do not realize they are kidding themselves and others.

The productive reasoning mind-set is the basis for development of managerial disciplines such as accounting, economics of the firm, information technology, finance, marketing, and strategy. In other words, responsible human beings managing organizations learn to value and trust productive reasoning (Jensen, 2000).

Defensive reasoning cannot be objectively verified. (That is the source of its attractiveness!) The purpose of defensive reasoning is to protect human beings and their systems from threat. A defensive reasoning mind-set seeks tests that are self-referential. That is, the logic used to *make* a claim is the same as the logic used to *test* the claim. This is the orientation of, "Trust me, I know what really goes on in the system." Such logic is self-referential in the sense that the individual states that the validity of his claim is that he knows it to be true. Defensive reasoning resists transparency and personal responsibility.

The consequences of defensive reasoning include escalating errors and self-fulfilling and self-sealing processes. This prevents testing not only the effectiveness of an outcome (single-loop learning) but also the assumptions behind the system (double-loop learning). Ultimately this leads to feelings of helplessness and acceptance of helplessness. The actors believe that they are victims. Helplessness is explained by more helplessness. Finally, actions produced by defensive reasoning are covered up by making them undiscussable. The undiscussability is also covered up.

Examples of defensive reasoning mind-set have been documented (Argyris, 1990b, 1993; Argyris, Putnam, and Smith, 1985; Argyris and Schön, 1996). Several recent well-known examples are Enron, Arthur Andersen, the Catholic Church, school systems rewarding children who cheat on tests so that the school's funding will not be cut, and the demise of alternative schools (Argyris, 1974). An analysis of the space shuttle *Columbia* accident suggests that the actions of the NASA bureaucracy, which early on led to its success, eventually may have aided and abetted the disaster (*New York Times*, 2003).

Organizational Inner Contradictions

Defensive reasoning and productive reasoning exist and grow side by side. Human beings are skillful at both. A dilemma arises because the coexistence of these two reasoning mind-sets produces inner contradiction. For example, whenever successful implementation of productive reasoning is threatened, human beings come to its defense by using defensive reasoning. As the transparent aboveground organizational world is strengthened, the underground world is also strengthened.

One important consequence of not dealing effectively with inner contradiction is that the underground world is strengthened in order to maintain the denial that it exists. However, if the underground bubble is pierced by a crisis that makes this world transparent, the user denies personal causal responsibility and places the responsibility on factors other than himself or herself. (Recall Enron and the other examples just cited.)

Some OD professionals are aware of these developments and espouse reducing them. The problem is that their theory-in-use is more consistent with defensive reasoning than with productive reasoning. But there are other OD professionals who are unaware of the inconsistency while they are producing it, and when they are forced to become aware they tend to place the blame on the system. They see themselves as somewhat helpless victims. All these reactions are consistent with a defensive reasoning mind-set (Argyris, 2000, 2004; Argyris and Schön, 1996).

The Problems of Humanistic Thinking

What has caused the change in thinking among so many OD professionals from productive reasoning to defensive reasoning? I think that much of the cause has to do with the rise of humanistic thinking, which grew in popularity in the 1960s. I did some work with a group of twenty-four OD consultants who described their orientation as *humanistic, interpretive, and existential* (Argyris, 1990a). They were asked to identify one or two illustrations of the core foundations of their professional practice. Once they listed them, they were asked how they would test the validity of these claims.

The response was that their perspective was humanistic. A humanistic perspective did not require independent testing of their claims. To do so would be to act inconsistently with their approach and take on a stance that was, in their view, too rational and scientific (that is, a productive reasoning approach). When asked to specify the criteria that they use to point to "too much" rationality, they responded that the question was inappropriate: "There you go asking us to be too rational and too scientific."

The problem is that those who hold the perspective defend it by claiming there is no need for some sort of a test that is independent of the reasoning they use to make their claims. This is a core feature of the defensive reasoning mind-set, namely that they serve the primary purpose of defending those making the claim and not the purpose of learning, especially double-loop learning. The problem is *not* with the substance of the position taken but with how it is crafted and defended.

The Case of John

I should like to illustrate my claim further by drawing on the distinction often made by OD professionals between emotional-subjective and rational-objective reasoning. I suggest that this distinction is self-protective, antilearning, and antieffective in helping others (such as clients) learn.

John is an active OD consultant who holds to the distinction between emotional-subjective and rational-objective. If my reasoning is correct, he should not be able to help clients learn to think and act more effectively.

John and I jointly designed an experiment to test the claim. I became the client. My position had two parts. One was that John's distinction inhibited learning. The second part was that I could be wrong and blind that I was wrong. I "hired" John to help me explore the degree to which I was wrong and blind. I did so because John claimed that my position was "too rational" and "too objective" (a claim similar to the one made by the professionals in related situations). We communicated with each other by e-mail over a period that exceeded six months.

John's argument throughout our dialogue was that it is valid to say there are two basic mind-sets in the domain of consulting. One is scientific, objective, and analytical; the other is subjective and humanistic. The former places feelings in the background; the latter gives feelings a prominent foreground position. He characterized my approach as objective and his as subjective.

The problem that I experienced with John was the reasoning processes he used to craft his claims and express them. For example, John often gave responses to illustrate his claims. I told him that I could not see how he went from his illustrations to his claim that his position was valid. I would describe the gaps and inconsistencies that I experienced in his responses and ask him to help me see where my reasoning was wrong and where I was blind.

John responded, in effect, that each of us held our own position. I was objective and scientific; he was subjective and humanistic. He would then add, "This in no way makes your position wrong."

If my position were not wrong, I would ask him how I could learn about my potential blindness. Isn't one of the key purposes of OD consultation to help human beings see where their position may lead to ineffective action? How would I, as a consultant, help my clients learn how to test the validity of their claims? Would not the clients understandably expect me to model such an approach? If I accepted his reasoning processes—in effect, that each of us is correct—how would I ever learn that I may be unwittingly kidding myself and others? How would he ever help to generate such learning for me?

Here are some illustrative comments taken from our e-mail correspondence.[1]

John's Statements

- It must be obvious by now, if the claims that I [John] am making are correct, your request [of how you test for the validity of your claim] is impossible to fulfill. There should not be a way to describe objectively a subjective mind-set.

- I believe that objectivity is likely to ruin the effect of emotional understanding. Making and sharing analytical observations will interfere with the conditions required to achieve the outcome that the client and the consultant want.

- My [John's] hypothesis is that people would trust you more, like you more, and feel better about their relationship with you when you adapt what I have been describing as an empathic/subjective mind-set as opposed to a distant/objective one.

- I am arguing that we cannot obtain objective answers regarding [emotional experiences] and that I cannot provide objective reasons why these objective answers are impossible.

- I have concluded from my experience that thinking about it too much tends to interfere with my ability to be an effective consultant.

- If I claim the truth about something is not the same for everyone, then I do not see how you can test other people's claims about that thing, whatever it is.

- Since I experience my own subjective feelings directly, a test [of their validity] is unnecessary.

- My reasoning is that if you feel something then for you, ipso facto, it is true.

As I read these claims, I expressed questions about how John might help me discover any potential blindness that I had.

My Reactions to John's Statements

- How can I learn from John about my errors if he tells me that objective understanding of his claims is not possible and that he cannot provide reasons that his "impossibility" claim is valid?

- If I were to accept John's position as correct, would it not require that I accept his reasoning processes that he uses to produce effective action? Would this not lead to my becoming dependent on him?

- If I were to accept John's advice that thinking about my position "too much" is counterproductive, what criteria would I use to judge when I am thinking "too much" or "too little" (if there is such a state as too little)?

This dialogue continued throughout the experiment. I finally concluded that I could not learn about my possible blindness and how to correct it. John responded in a way that surprised me. He said, in effect, that he did not understand our experiment to help me see and correct my blindness. I referred to our early e-mails where this was the reason that I hired him. He said there was a misunderstanding.

I do not think there was a misunderstanding at the outset. I interpret the claim of "misunderstanding" as a self-protective defense. I expressed feelings to John of betrayal. John responded to those feelings by repeating his claims that he never intended such an agreement with me.

From my perspective, John distanced himself from taking any responsibility to deal with my *feelings* by claiming there was an obvious misunderstanding. The irony is that his defense of misunderstanding was based on rational-objective reasoning. As his client, I felt that he reasoned in ways that made it possible for him to be blind to his part in the causal responsibility for the failure in our relationship.

In my experience, John's case illustrates one major reason OD is experiencing a demise. He appears to his client as incompetent, blind to his incompetence, and blind that he is blind. The basis of his skilled incompetence and skilled blindness is his defensive reasoning mind-set.

John's defensive reasoning mind-set is, in my experience, illustrative of much OD activity that I reviewed in my book on flawed advice (Argyris, 2000).

The Enfield Case

One of the major contributions of OD has been recognition that expertise can lie within the organization and not just at the top. The field has been quite creative in developing ways to reduce top management's unilateral control and increase participative opportunities for all involved.

This approach appears to have worked in the early days because the emphasis was on changing lower-level jobs and roles (that is, job enrichment and group control over immediate working conditions). There still might be many conditions where participation is appropriate today, but it has limitations when linked with defensive reasoning.

Take this example. Several years back, OD practitioners took a major role in designing and implementing a new organization, called Enfield, that was consistent with many OD values. The plant worked fine until it began to develop production and financial difficulties with the goals that the OD people helped to set. Rather than being able to test objectively whether worker involvement was the appropriate approach, the response was to increase worker participation. However, this became unmanageable given the goals that had been set. Consequently, the plant began to be managed in a much more traditional top-down way with tight measurements (of the nature that would make Frederick Taylor smile) being introduced (Argyris, 1990b).

The problem is twofold. First, without a productive reasoning mind-set, one tends to engage in the same repetitive behavior. A second problem is that this participative approach can be useful when the change deals with largely single-loop issues but is less productive when double-loop issues arise. (This is a point I return to at the end of the chapter.)

The Blind Leading the Blind: The Case of Tom

Another example of being caught in nonproductive reasoning involves the case of Tom, a senior OD consultant in a large corporation (Argyris, 2000). Tom was enthusiastic about a request by senior line management that the OD programs and the business problems be integrated. He and some line managers designed such a change program.

Subsequently, the enthusiasm and commitment of the line managers deteriorated. Tom became upset. He felt that the line managers were going back on their commitment, so he decided to confront them.

The line managers agreed that they were no longer enthusiastic because they felt that the integration of the "human" and "business" issues was not succeeding. They admitted they did not know how to accomplish the goal of integration. Moreover, they told him that they concluded he also did not know how to accomplish the objective. Tom admitted this was true. However, he expressed confidence that with genuine participation these problems could be overcome. The line managers disagreed. As one put it, such a participative process would be a case of the blind leading the blind.

OD Practitioners and the Tom Case

I would suggest that this trap of getting locked into defensive, repetitive reasoning isn't just a problem of this one individual (or a few); rather, it is an issue with many more practitioners in the field. During the past five years I have used the Tom case in workshops attended by OD and other HR professionals. The attendees are asked to read the case ahead of time. I then ask them to act as consultants to advise Tom as to how to prevent this problem from reoccurring. I begin the discussion with several excerpts from the tape transcriptions made by these consultants (Argyris, 2000):

- "I think the key [for Tom] is not to respond, but to be responsive."

- "Yes, I agree. Tom should try to develop, in some kind of a conversation, a real sense of what the survival issues are for the client."

- "Yes, and help the client to feel that all is not lost."

- "These are some ways that working to get this can really build some shared view of what it is that might be possible."

- "And try to frame that in terms that are pretty understandable for folks (which is difficult to do) to connect directly to business performance."

Let us reflect for a moment on their advice.

The advice is phrased in terms of end results: "be responsive," "develop . . . a real sense of the survival issue," encourage the client not to feel lost, and craft the conversation in understandable language.

The end results are not specified in ways that are operational. For example, what is the difference between *responding* versus *being responsive*? What is the nature of "some kind of a conversation" or building "some shared view" of what is possible? What is "understandable" language?

The contributions do not specify what Tom might say to produce these end results.

The causal theory in each bit of advice is not made explicit. This makes it difficult to test the validity of their advice. The speakers appear to believe that their advice is valid; they do not strive to test the validity of their advice.

When I asked the HR professionals to produce the conversations they would use with the "resisting" line managers, they were unable to produce the highly positive consequences they espoused in dealing with Tom. The conversations were consistent with an easing-in process. (Easing-in means asking the line managers questions that, if they answered correctly, would lead them to become aware of the ineffectiveness of their actions.)

There were two negative consequences of this easing-in strategy. First, the line managers did not believe their actions were ineffective. They believed that it was Tom who was ineffective, and this is why they refused to attend further sessions with him.

The second consequence was that the HR professionals sought data from the line managers that was largely on the affective level (again, our humanistic orientation) about their pain and disappointment on the job, which did not get at the task issues the line managers were concerned about. The line managers responded that their major pain was dealing with Tom. What follows are some examples of how these HR professionals would deal with the situation if they were in Tom's shoes. (I took the role of the line manager.)

HR PERSON ONE: First, I would start by asking the "resisting" line managers, "What is really on your mind at the moment? What keeps you awake?"

LINE MANAGER (LM): I'll tell you. I want to make sure that I get those darn business processes done because that is how I am being evaluated. I am a loyal manager—by that I mean a manager who produces the numbers, especially those I agree to.

HR PERSON TWO (BREAKING IN): I would not talk that way; I would ask what other things are on his mind.

LM: I am bewildered. You asked me what was on my mind. I told you. Did you hear me?

HR2: I think that I am trying to understand how come these ideas are on your mind. I want to understand why that thing is on your mind now.

LM: I am doubly bewildered. I thought I made it clear. I am striving to be a productive manager. So, I am going to produce according to the targets that I helped to set.

HR2: What kind of targets are we talking about?

LM: You know. Produce X and Y with Z quality and do so persistently.

HR2: What I am trying to understand is, given the targets, what is the disappointment at this point?

LM: The idea of disappointment is in your head, not mine. I am quite happy to do what I am doing. I am not feeling disappointed. In fact, if you would let me get on with my work, I would be quite happy.

I halted the role play and asked the group members to reflect. I said, "One of you began the session with the advice, 'Be responsive.' How responsive were you when you crafted this advice to Tom?"

HR PERSON THREE: Not very.

FACILITATOR: Would you please illustrate?

HR3: Maybe Tom was not totally listening to the line managers. I would be ready to roll up my sleeves and ask, "How can I really help these guys? How can we really enter some meaningful dialogue to address their problems?"

HR PERSON FOUR: And do so in a way to find out what's wrong. There has to be something wrong, or else there is not much leverage.

HR PERSON FIVE: I start with a different premise. I do not go to "sell" to anyone. I require that they come to me. It's not manipulative. It's just the way it is.

The discussion here again becomes abstract. What does it mean, concretely, to "roll up my sleeves" and "enter some meaningful dialogue"? The discussion also illustrates two assumptions often held by HR professionals: first, that to have progress the client must feel some pain, and second that HR experts should not "sell" but await initiatives from the line. In both cases, it is fair to ask why. The HR professionals seemed bewildered that I would question their two fundamental assumptions. They are unable to engage in double-loop exploration.

As the discussion continued, more of the participants began to make explicit their own sense of limitations:

HR PERSON SIX: I am sitting here thinking, "OK, let us admit that we do not know. Maybe we should say so and ask them to work with us to figure it out."

HR PERSON SEVEN: Yes, if we can admit that what we are doing isn't working, we would then all be aligned on that. We have no idea what the hell the right "what" is, but let's figure it out together.

When the HR professionals realized that they did not know as much as they should if they were to be helpful, they recommended shared dialogue and participation in order to figure out possible answers. But how can the blind responsibly hope to lead the blind? Imagine if other professionals—say, accountants—were to admit that they did not know how to produce a balance sheet and then asked their clients to participate jointly to prepare one.

To summarize, the HR professionals got caught in a closed loop by their defensive reasoning and were not able to break out of it in developing their interventions. Their advice was abstract, and it lacked explicit specification of how to produce the consequences that they advised; therefore it was difficult to produce an accurate test of the validity of their claims. Consequently, they gave themselves little opportunity to test where they might be unconsciously causing the very consequence that they advised against (making others defensive, acting inauthentically, bypassing their own defensive reasoning and actions, being skillfully unaware that they were producing these consequences while doing so).

Finally, the HR professionals had no theory that could be validated or implemented about how to integrate the technical features of organizations with the leadership, learning, change, and commitment that they espoused.

The argument being made is that OD professionals espouse productive reasoning and double-loop learning. However, their theory-in-use when engaging in difficult face-to-face interactions (in groups, intergroups, and organizational behavior systems) is consistent with a defensive reasoning mind-set. The same is true for many of the change programs that they implement in organizations.

The explanation for this is that most human beings hold theories-in-use whose fundamental reasoning processes, especially when it comes to double-loop issues, are dominated by a self-protective mind-set that ensures limited and short-range effectiveness of their interactions and programs (Argyris, 1952, 1990b, 1993, 2000; Argyris and Schön, 1996). Moreover, they are apparently unaware of inconsistencies and gaps while they are producing them.

This sets the stage for an additional cause of the demise of OD. The line executives are increasingly using managerial ideas that are founded on productive reasoning. Hence, if they see the limits of the OD perspective they may conclude that these limits should be accepted because OD is about the "soft stuff." This, in turn, leads line managers to distance themselves from the OD consultation by delegating it to the lowest hierarchical level and using fundamental OD approaches, such as team building and the like. Beyond the fundamentals, line management is likely to be cautious and skeptical about OD's long-term value, especially at the upper levels where double-loop issues require productive reasoning.

Difficulties with Double-Loop Learning

It is important to emphasize that all parties, at all levels, are programmed with theories-in-use. Learning how to improve performance in these existing theories (single-loop learning) is challenging enough because it requires examining one's existing level of competence. However, what OD has shown is that if you give human beings a genuine opportunity to create liberating alternatives, they will frequently take advantage of it to grow and improve. But this is mainly the case for single-loop learning.

It is a different situation with double-loop learning, which challenges one to examine the underlying assumptions behind one's theories-in-use and then entertain the possibility that such theories may be inappropriate. When this occurs, most resort to defensive reasoning. It is not unfair to suggest a generalization: give people a chance to create a genuinely liberating world and they will eventually fail and then blame others for their failure. This is consistent with the victim mentality of a defensive reasoning mind-set.

Ackoff (1999) has suggested some intriguing structural designs for organizations that he calls "democratic hierarchy." He reports, however, that executives have difficulty in implementing these ideas, even when they wish to do so. The problems arise when the requirements of the new structures require behavioral skills and a level of trust for double-loop learning that typically do not exist. Indeed, these consequences occur even when the CEO and chairman champion these ideas and when their immediate reports accept them (Goggin, 1974).

Conclusion

If human beings are to become more effective at double-loop learning, they have to become more skillful at using productive reasoning. If this is true, then it is even more important that OD professionals become skillful at productive reasoning and teaching others to become the same. They cannot hide behind such maneuvers as differentiating between the humanistic and subjective versus objective and scientific stance and hold this claim to be valid for OD consulting without defining a sufficient test of its validity.

I participated in many discussions during the early years regarding the differences between T-groups and several personal growth laboratories (Argyris, 1967, 1968, 1972). The differences were, in my opinion, papered over. This was consistent with the humanistic orientation I have described of "live and let live; everybody's right." In effect, all of us distanced ourselves from the difficult choices that we were facing. Why would the top management of any type of organization seek the help of OD practitioners with such a defensive reasoning mind-set?

References

Ackoff, R. L. *Re-Creating the Organization*. New York: Oxford University Press, 1999.

Argyris, C. "Diagnosing Defenses Against the Outsider." *Journal of Social Issues*, 1952, 8(3), 24–32.

Argyris, C. "On the Future of Laboratory Education." *Journal of Applied Behavioral Science*, 1967, 3, 153–183.

Argyris, C. "Conditions for Competence Acquisition and Therapy." *Journal of Applied Behavioral Science*, 1968, 4, 147–177.

Argyris, C. "Do Personal Growth Laboratories Represent an Alternative Culture?" *Journal of Applied Behavioral Science*, 1972, 8, 7–28.

Argyris, C. "Alternative Schools: A Behavioral Analysis." *Teachers College Record*, 1974, 75, 429–452.

Argyris, C. "Inappropriate Defenses Against the Monitoring of Organization Development Practice." *Journal of Applied Behavioral Science*, 1990a, 26, 299–312.

Argyris, C. *Overcoming Organizational Defenses*. Needham Heights, Mass.: Allyn & Bacon, 1990b.

Argyris, C. *Knowledge for Action*. San Francisco: Jossey-Bass, 1993.

Argyris, C. *Flawed Advice*. New York: Oxford University Press, 2000.

Argyris, C. *Defensive and Productive Reasoning*. New York: Oxford University Press, 2004.

Argyris, C., Putnam, R., and Smith, D. *Action Science*. San Francisco: Jossey-Bass, 1985.

Argyris, C., and Schön, D. *Organizational Learning II*. Reading, Mass.: Addison-Wesley, 1996.

Goggin, W. C. "How the Multi-Dimensional Structure Works at Dow Corning." *Harvard Business Review*, 1974, *52*(1), 54–65.

Jensen, M. A *Theory of the Firm: Governance, Residual Claims and Organizational Forms*. Cambridge, Mass.: Harvard University Press, 2000.

New York Times, Feb. 18, 2003, p. 1.

Note

1. All the comments on John's position have been read by him and approved as valid of his position.

8

Organization Development

A Wedding of Anthropology and Organizational Therapy

Edgar H. Schein

The field of organization development is today a conglomerate of many theories, practices, and value systems. In trying to make sense of this welter I have observed two consistent themes that are used yet seem to me close to the essence of OD. On the one hand, OD is about groups, organizations, and communities; hence OD practitioners must be well versed in anthropology; on the other hand, OD is about helping, and that requires the skills of a therapist, especially a group or family therapist familiar with the dynamics of complex systems.

For both of these roles, what is required is a kind of spirit of inquiry, humility, and self-awareness that allows phenomena normally out of awareness to surface. As my colleague Otto Scharmer put it recently, the OD consultant is a "midwife that helps reality to unfold," and this reality has cultural, political, social, and psychological elements in a complex interplay with each other.

To get a grasp of why this is so important in today's world, we need to look at some of the history of OD as well as some of the realities unfolding today.

History of OD

Looking first at its origins, one should note that the work of both the Tavistock Institute and Clinic in the U.K. and the National Training Labs at Bethel, Maine, in the 1950s was oriented toward communities, groups, and leadership development. Therapeutic communities had been developed in several European countries; the post–World War II reconstruction in England involved the Tavistock team of Trist and others with labor unions and management in the coal mines, while Rice and others developed new ways of organizing factories in the Indian woolen mills. Kurt Lewin was discovering in his work with Alfred Marrow how important worker involvement was when management tried to impose changes in work methods, and Muzafer Sherif was doing his classical studies of intergroup conflict in boys' camps (Schein, 1965; Sherif and others, 1961).

When the Bethel training groups started in the 1950s, a major portion of each day was devoted to role playing and to community-wide exercises to teach the participants how the community was a complex interactive system. The emphasis in the T-groups was on learning group dynamics and the relationship of members to authority and each other. It seems to me we have lost this historical perspective on groups and systems and have had to reinvent "large systems change" as if we knew nothing about it. How did that happen?

One set of forces derived from the success of the T-group as a personal learning tool. One could learn not only about group dynamics but about oneself, and the legitimizing of face-to-face feedback in "stranger" groups opened up a learning possibility that society more or less forbids. If your fellow participants were strangers with whom you would never have to work and whom you might never see again, it was possible to suspend the norms of face work and tell each other how we reacted to each other, even if this meant critical and negative feedback. Getting feedback, having "a turn in the barrel," became one of the preeminent learning goals that tended to override the learning that came from exercises, lectures, and community activities (Schein and Bennis, 1965).

It was probably inevitable that more individually oriented staff members would see in this methodology a powerful tool for helping individuals improve their own interpersonal competence, leading to the phrase "therapy for normals." This individualized focus and the various methodologies for getting people to look at themselves that resulted inevitably crept into OD, and we forgot for a time that OD was supposed to be work with groups and organizations, not individual work with leaders and managers.

Some of this bias was probably driven by the greater cost of organizational interventions in terms of both money and consultant time. Recall that Herb Shepard and Bob Blake working with Esso had evolved what Blake came to call the "managerial grid," which was a multistage intervention starting with individuals, moving to work units, and ending with total systems approaches (Blake and Mouton, 1969). Many organizations launched these programs but often found that they ran out of energy or money before all the stages were completed. It was simply easier for individual consultants to work with individual managers or small groups. Individuals working with other individuals also reflected the individualistic competitive U.S. culture, in contrast to the Tavistock work, which was usually carried out by research *teams*. The U.S. culture values teamwork if it is pragmatically necessary to getting the job done or "winning" but does not value group work intrinsically. The quip that "a camel is a horse put together by a committee" is a uniquely U.S. joke, and it is no accident in my view that the remedial OD books that sell the most are books on team building.

American pragmatism drove practitioners into tool development. The grid was a classic example of turning concepts and theories into tools that were even completely self-administering. In principle an organization could develop itself without a consultant by just following the steps that the grid program prescribed. If facilitators were needed, they could be developed inside the organization.

University Associates, later to become Pfeiffer, became a highly successful publisher of various kinds of exercises, scales, theory articles, and aids to trainers, all of which signaled that OD was becoming a mature industry, but one built more on tools than real understanding of cultural or even organizational dynamics. As OD became more popular, a great many of its practitioners entered from such other fields as HR, training, or education, and those practitioners were hungry for tools but did not have the sociotechnical background that the OD founders had.

With the writings of Abe Maslow, Douglas McGregor, and others, the OD field linked strongly with humanistic psychology, which was evolving on the West Coast around Tannenbaum, Bugental, and others and thus developed a strong value-based culture of its own. The mission of OD for many of its practitioners became "to make organizations more humane," a place where employees could achieve personal goals and even self-actualization through matching their personal goals with organizational goals rather than maintaining a primary emphasis on helping organizations to be more effective.

Out of the Tavistock work came another theme, the idea that organizations were sociotechnical systems. However, the idea that organizations were systems and the understanding of them as systems hinged on the ability to see both the technology on which the system's work was based and the social system doing the work. This idea was brought into the OD field and was immediately embraced by some practitioners, but for some reason it did not really catch on with the bulk of U.S. consultants.

Also largely ignored was the work of family therapists, especially the Italian group that built its entire therapeutic framework on the premise that the family was a tightly interlocked system and that working with this system required a sophisticated understanding of the systemic dynamics. For example, one huge insight was that one did not have to work directly with the problem person. If one worked with other family members and changed their behavior, the dynamics of the system would change sufficiently that the problem person would be positively affected (Campbell, Coldicott, and Kinsella, 1994; Palazzoli, Boscolo, Cecchin, and Prata, 1970).

The combined effects of these trends were loss of ability to design large-scale systemic interventions, lack of skill in working with complex systems, and (most important) lack of understanding of culture and its impact on individuals and groups. In fact, one could say that OD in the 1980s and 1990s was culturally naïve. The introduction of 360 degree feedback as a new and powerful tool and the current fad of "coaching" illustrates what I mean by cultural naïveté.

Cultural Issues Today

The logic of 360 degree feedback was to improve individual development by giving the person being developed better data about himself or herself. Inasmuch as the perceptions of subordinates, peers, and superiors are all relevant, the process encourages all the members of the role set to offer information to the person being developed. Suitable methods of confidentiality are employed to protect subordinates from being punished for submitting negative data to the boss, but little consideration is usually given to the existing culture and its norms around feedback, confidentiality, and what one does or does not share with the boss, and—even worse—to the impact of the entire process on the organization.

First of all, the method requires the members of the role set to make a decision about whether or not to give feedback to the incumbent, which involves them in a thought process that they did not necessarily agree to and that was awkward to refuse. Second, the method got them thinking along dimensions of relationships that they might never have thought about, so their cognition is being influenced in unknown ways. Third, sharing the process may encourage the members of the role set to share information about what they did or did not say about the incumbent, and in this sharing new attitudes and feelings are being built that are in no way anticipatable. If the existing culture is highly coercive and political, it might lead subordinates to discover that they each said some negative things about their boss and to build a coalition against the boss that was not previously there. Finally, if a person refuses to enter into the process, this information is often passed on to the boss, which changes the relationship between them in unknown ways. All of these consequences are above and beyond the issue of giving the incumbent some feedback from his or her role set. If the intervener is culturally aware of these impacts, the 360 degree methodology can be sold to the entire role set as an *organizational* intervention, in which case the client system can choose whether and why they would want to do this. Where the naïveté comes in is when the 360 is done for the sake of an *individual* with no consideration of the consequences to the role set and the *organization*.

The current craze for coaching presents a similar cultural naïveté. Very little attention is given to the issue of who pays for the coaching. This is crucial because it raises the question of whether the coaching is really socialization or indoctrination of the coachee into the organization ("coach him to overcome some of his problems in order to get ahead in the company") or whether the coaching is really a self-development tool for the individual that might even have the consequence of leading the coachee to realize that she is in the wrong organization and should leave (Schein, 2000). Organizational cultures differ greatly in the degree to which they coercively socialize new members, as opposed to creating a genuine developmental environment that encourages leaving if a mismatch is discovered.

Perhaps the greatest example of cultural naïveté is the highly touted consulting models in which "data gathering" and "diagnosis" are separated from the category "intervention." What every anthropologist and systems theorist knows is that measuring a human system, indeed any system, changes it to some unknown degree. In other words, data gathering is already an intervention, and how one gathers data should be decided by intervention criteria, not by the traditional physical science model criteria of reliability or validity. As I have argued in proposing "clinical inquiry" as the method of choice, it turns out that one can gather "better" (that is, deeper and more valid) data when one is in a helping clinical role than when one is a detached researcher or consultant (Schein,

2001). The reason is that most of the relevant organizational data are contextually buried in the culture, and if one is not helping the organization the members have neither the motive nor the ability to make explicit the deeper levels of their culture. In a helping relationship, however, it is possible to help insiders surface cultural assumptions that then aid observing and interpreting what is really going on. In this sense all helper activities and all forms of inquiry are simultaneously interventions and diagnoses in that what we do reveals data and those data in turn determine what we do next. It is an entirely intertwined process.

In summary, OD has drifted toward individual intervention, toward concern with tools and techniques, and toward a kind of humanism on behalf of employees. On the issue of techniques, the most telling data are the surveys that come around fairly frequently asking me which of thirty or more techniques listed on the sheet I use. The glib underlying but unstated assumption is that each item stands alone and represents a specific kind of intervention from which OD specialists can choose and ignore totally that the appropriateness of any one approach depends on a host of other factors present in the organization and its culture. Finally, the myth continues to be propagated that one gathers data before one intervenes, instead of recognizing that every contact with a client system is an intervention and that the intervention and data gathering are one and the same process. So where do we go from here?

Learn to Think More Like an Anthropologist

To think like an anthropologist one must first accept the reality of culture. Too many definitions that I find floating around are either wrong or superficial. Culture is for the group or organization what personality and character are for the individual: the sum total of what has been learned in coping with the external environment and in developing an internal identity and sense of integrity. Such learning starts out being a conscious coping with whatever problems the group faces. If successful, those ways of behaving become routinized. The beliefs and values that lie behind the behavior drop out of awareness and gradually become taken for granted as unconscious assumptions that cover all of the group's functioning (Schein, 1985).

If we understand culture in this way, we have to recognize that it is deep, extensive, and extremely stable. Culture gives the group meaning, predictability, and stability. Culture is the group's legacy of past successes. If we understand this, how can we go around advocating or bragging about culture change programs that we have been involved with? How can we offer culture surveys that tell a group what its culture is from just answering twenty-five survey questions? How can we ignore the fact that every group values and cherishes its particular culture even while complaining about it? How can we buy into simplistic typologies of culture when it is obvious that the essence of a group's culture is the unique pattern of assumptions based on its unique history? So the first rule of thinking like an anthropologist is to take culture very seriously and give deep respect to each organization's culture.

Of course our clients also misunderstand culture, so they often come to OD consultants with a request to do culture assessment and launch a culture change program. But it is our task to resist and help the client appreciate the complexities of the culture. If we are more aware of culture dynamics, we will recognize that our clients do develop ways of operating that are maladaptive; we must have models to help them solve problems and improve their functioning. But if we think like anthropologists, we will not start with the notion of changing the culture. Instead, we will ask what precisely the business problem is and what kind of new behavior is needed to fix the problem. Instead of dealing with high-level abstractions such as culture, we have to help our clients be entirely concrete about what is going wrong and help them figure out what they should be doing differently. Once they have figured it out, we can then contemplate with them the question of how their culture aids or hinders making the changes they have identified as necessary.

Analyzing the role of the culture must be done by the client with the help of the consultant, preferably in a series of group meetings that work their way through the levels of artifacts, espoused values, and underlying shared assumptions (Schein, 1999b). Culture is far too complex a pattern for us to assume that the consultant is able to assess it, but the consultant is definitely needed to help the client system surface what it has come to take for granted. In the process, it will be discovered that mostly the culture is a positive force for change, and only if some specific elements of the culture are a barrier to the change should one begin to think about how to change those particular elements. Then we will further discover that the best way to change some elements of the culture is to use other elements to make the change.

For example, when Alpha Power (a disguised name for a client I have worked with) had to make its employees more environmentally conscious and responsible, three aspects of the culture worked together to produce this change. The paternalistic and autocratic culture enabled it within a few years to train the entire workforce on how to diagnose and remediate environmental hazards. The high-tech engineering culture enabled inventing a whole series of instruments and tools to prevent hazards in the first place and locate hazards more efficiently. The bureaucratic culture enabled changing reward and discipline systems rapidly and efficiently to ensure that the new behavior required of employees was adequately rewarded and controlled. The culture did change insofar as the self-image of the employee was altered fairly radically, but it was the bulk of the culture that made this specific change possible.

In summary, I think OD practitioners have to be quite sophisticated about culture and develop the skills of helping clients deal with their culture issues. OD consultants should not go around advocating culture change, because this immediately identifies them as being culturally naïve. OD consultants should also become aware that they are in a culture themselves, one that is based on their own group's shared experience. The beliefs, values, and assumptions of a given set of OD practitioners are not necessarily appropriate for a given client system. If OD practitioners are selling certain values, they are no longer being OD practitioners but ideological salespeople, a role that reflects absence of cultural humility and once again cultural naïveté.

Develop the Skills of an Organizational Therapist

To be an organizational therapist, the OD practitioner has to recover lost models and skills of thinking about and designing large systems interventions. Too many OD practitioners assume that what works with their individual clients scales up to groups and that what works in groups scales up to the intergroup and interorganizational levels. The most obvious fallacy of this line of thinking is illustrated by what happens with growth and aging. The process is fundamentally different if we are talking about individuals and organizations. The individual evolves new behaviors and new systems but retains one ego and one physical body that is acting out whatever complexity has come with age. But the organization as it ages develops subgroups, subsystems, and subcultures that are physically separate entities and have the capacity to act independently. Corporate governance bears little similarity to the ego's governance of the personality because the parts of the corporation are physically independent and responsive to many egos.

For example, in analyzing the history of Digital Equipment Corporation (DEC) it is striking how critical decisions made early in its history by articulate, assertive, innovative electrical engineers through a process of open debate became gradually subverted by the fact that success, growth, and age led these same people to become heads of large functional and project groups who still debated out their decisions, but they were now acting as representatives of their units, not as individual thinkers. One could observe how rational, logical thinking became skewed by the need to protect one's turf and one's employees, and—most surprising of all—how little awareness there was in these same executives that they were now biased in their thinking (Schein, 2003).

Working with large systems composed of many subsystems raises vividly the issue of power and politics that many OD people are ill equipped to deal with because their own subculture is built on a value system that devalues power and politics. Working with systems raises the whole issue of centralization and decentralization. Working with systems raises the issue of how a system can differentiate itself sufficiently to meet the multiple goals and functions it has. A biological analogy of organs with single functions coordinating together breaks down when the organs are semi-independent divisions in geographically different areas coping with multiple agendas in their local communities.

As Rashford and Coghlan (1994) point out so clearly, the issues or problems addressed at various levels require fundamentally different kinds of interventions. At the individual level the main issue is bonding with the group and developing an appropriate psychological contract with the organization. At the group level the issue is managing the interpersonal issues deriving from identity, influence, and intimacy norms to build an effective team. At the intergroup level the issue is how to maintain coordination when power politics and distortion of communication arise owing to competitive intergroup dynamics. At the organizational level the issue is mission and strategy.

For each of these levels, OD practitioners have their own value systems, their own concept of a "healthy" state of affairs to be achieved, and therapeutic biases of how best to work with the client. From a systemic point of view the concept of client itself becomes ambiguous in that one is often working with "contact clients" on a project that is funded elsewhere by a "primary client" on behalf of a vague entity, the organization, as the "ultimate client" (Schein, 1997, 1999b). As social responsibility and environmental sustainability surface on a more global level, the concept of ultimate client shifts to community, society, or even the globe.

Implications

The world is becoming more interconnected, which means the ability to work across and within cultural units is becoming more and more important. For the OD practitioner to think more like an anthropologist is no longer an option; it becomes a necessity. Not only do OD practitioners have to develop the skills of working across cultures; they have to come to terms with their own culture and examine whether the thrust of their interventions is guided by what the client culture needs or what the OD culture wants. Since the OD field is today a mix of many subcultures, it becomes ever more important from a client's point of view to sort out just what the implicit goals of the OD consultant are and what model of health is driving his or her interventions.

As the world grows more interconnected and as we recognize that within organizations we have complex and interconnected systems, the skills of the therapist are relevant so long as the client is defined as the whole system. What the therapist brings to the party is relationship-building skills (Schein, 1999b). In any work with a human system and at any level within the system, the basic interventions will always be face-to-face conversation about something or other. What the OD practitioner must be able to do is build a good enough relationship to elicit valid data from the client so that they can work together on the right issues. The thought processes of the anthropologist are the key to identifying the right issues to talk about and focus on. Therefore the cultural and the therapeutic need to be wedded. Only then can OD begin to realize its potential.

References

Blake, R. R., and Mouton, J. S. *Building a Dynamic Organization Through Grid Organization Development.* Reading, Mass.: Addison-Wesley, 1969.

Campbell, D., Coldicott, T., and Kinsella, K. *Systemic Work with Organizations.* London: Karnac Books, 1994.

Palazzoli, M. S., Boscolo, L., Cecchin, G., and Prata, G. *Paradox and Counterparadox.* New York: Jason Aronson, 1970.

Rashford, N. S., and Coghlan, D. *The Dynamics of Organizational Levels*. Reading, Mass.: Addison-Wesley, 1994.

Schein, E. H. *Organizational Psychology*. Upper Saddle River, N.J.: Prentice Hall (2nd ed., 1970; 3rd ed., 1980).

Schein, E. H. *Organizational Culture and Leadership*. San Francisco: Jossey-Bass (1985, 2nd ed. 1992).

Schein, E. H. "The Concept of 'Client' from a Process Consultation Perspective: A Guide for Change Agents." *Journal of Organizational Change Management*, 1997, *10*(3), 202–216.

Schein, E. H. *The Corporate Culture Survival Guide*. San Francisco: Jossey-Bass, 1999a.

Schein, E. H. *Process Consultation Revisited: Building the Helping Relationship*. Reading, Mass.: Addison-Wesley-Longman, 1999b.

Schein, E. H. "Coaching and Consultation: Are They the Same?" In M. Goldsmith, L. Lyons, and A. Freas (eds.), *Coaching for Leadership*. San Francisco: Pfeiffer, 2000.

Schein, E. H. "Clinical Inquiry/Research." In P. Reason and H. Bradbury (eds.), *Handbook of Action Research*. Thousand Oaks, Calif.: Sage, 2001.

Schein, E. H. *DEC Is Dead; Long Live DEC*. San Francisco: Berrett-Koehler, 2003.

Schein, E. H., and Bennis, W. G. *Personal and Organizational Change Through Group Methods: The Laboratory Approach*. New York: Wiley, 1965.

Sherif, M., Harvey, O. J., White, B. J., Hood, W. R., and Sherif, C. *Intergroup Conflict and Cooperation: The Robber's Cave Experiment*. Norman, Okla.: University Book Exchange, 1961.

9

A Paradigm for Professional Vitality

Peter P. Vaill

In a small hotel conference room in Montreal in 1966, about fifteen men and women met as what was then called the Industrial Network. Among the attendees were representatives from TRW, Dow Chemical, American Airlines, Alcan, Pillsbury, Esso, General Foods, and other well-known corporations as well as representatives from Harvard, MIT, Case Western Reserve, and UCLA. One main piece of business was to formalize themselves as a division of NTL Institute for Applied Behavioral Science and transfer coordinator responsibilities from Jerry Harvey of NTL to Warner Burke, also of NTL. Five years later, Burke announced at the New York meeting of the newly named and newly independent "OD Network" that the association had grown to nearly three thousand members—quite a remarkable rate of expansion.

Unfortunately, the field of OD, which started with such promise, has not achieved it. Although the number of OD consultants has continued to grow, relatively few organizations use these consultants to play a significant role in their operations. What has caused this situation and the feeling of malaise that seems to go with it?

This chapter is concerned with what it will take to refocus and revitalize the field of OD. But before I address this issue directly, I think it is worth reflecting on the explosive growth the OD field experienced in the late 1960s and all through the 1970s. The field doesn't have to follow the same formula today, certainly, but we need some vision of what restoring the field would look like, and one place to look is in its own history.

No doubt the rapid growth of OD was due to a conjunction of many forces. An important one, which I shall not deal with further, was "demand," and I mean it just exactly in the economist's sense. The 1960s took many organizations into territory they did not understand, and they were entirely ready to listen to anyone who seemed to understand their problems and could offer solutions. OD was one such set of voices.

It is also important to say that the beginning of the new century hardly finds the OD field moribund or an empty husk. If it is a fad, it is certainly much longer-lived than most of the "flavors of the month" so characteristic of the management and planned change fields. Many thousands of individuals continue to call themselves OD consultants and have active practices. Degree programs in OD continue to enroll all the students they need. Publishers continue to commit themselves to OD books, as witnessed by the series recently initiated by Pfeiffer. Nonetheless, there is something wrong with the field that various task forces and study committees are hard at work trying to identify. This book is testament to that concern. The field doesn't have the focus and vitality that old-timers know it used to have. There is not the sense of mission that sparked so much work in the 1960s and 1970s. Perhaps of most significance, new theories and practices keep coming along that often don't identify themselves as part of OD; in fact, some take pains to differentiate themselves from OD, as if there were some kind of stigma associated with being part of OD. So it is still worth asking the question: What will it take to restore the vitality and sense of mission that was so characteristic of OD in its early years?

The Impact of the T-Group

One cannot discuss the growth of OD without discussing the role of the T-group. It may seem to be old hat now in the twenty-first century to undertake an analysis of the impact of the T-group. But since we are trying to understand how the OD field may be refocused and revitalized, we need to reflect on how we got to where we are, and it is not possible to do this without looking once again at the T-group. In the next few paragraphs I derive some meanings from the nature of the T-group that I think do point in some new directions for contemporary OD practice and for the OD field as a quasi-profession. I hope the discussion has a freshness and is not a rehash of what everyone already knows.

From the pervasiveness of the T-group in OD education and practice, I think three factors can be derived that need to be examined at greater length. First, T-groups and related group methods that emphasized direct human encounter gave OD an understanding of the *processes* by which human social problems could be worked through to their putative solutions. Second, T-groups brought learning about human psychology and relationships *to consciousness*; learning could be *felt* directly and unequivocally. Third, OD developed a *confident professional culture* that gave it visibility, drive, and powerful meaning to its members. These three factors gave OD the promise that this book seeks to help restore. I will now expand briefly on each of the three in preparation for assessing their meaning for present-day OD.

Sensitivity to Process

The "solution" that OD had was a sensitivity to interpersonal and group processes. "Process" in all its forms was seen as the strategic variable in understanding group events. By *process* I mean how a group of people work together, regardless of the subject they are discussing or the problem they are trying to solve. Moreover, this sensitivity to social processes extended from two-person relationships on up through small-group to intergroup relations. By and large, this sensitivity to process did not extend to whole organizations in the early years. There were many definitions of OD springing up in the late 1960s and early 1970s, but I think they had in common this process focus, this concern for how people worked together. In an earlier paper, I actually defined OD as a process *for* working on organizational processes (Sikes, Drexler, and Gant, 1989). As noted elsewhere in the present book, there is more content to OD than just this process focus, but I believed then and believe now that its process focus is one of the most distinctive things about OD.

OD people became very sensitive to communication processes, particularly those in which some members of a group were being marginalized. They also were quick to note top-down forms of communication and forms that obscured or denied underlying motivations and feelings. OD people were alert to hidden agendas and power trips. They were good at forecasting the results of a group process where communication dysfunction of this kind was present. They were adept at spotting events in human groups that they knew could lead to problems, such as failing to clarify the objectives of the discussion, failing to introduce new members, configuring the room in such a way as to make discussion difficult, or abruptly cutting off discussion of a sensitive topic. Indeed, the list of ways in which the group process can be mishandled is a long one; of course, human groups are still rife with such issues thirty years later. Behind group process, OD people learned about the processes by which feelings get expressed, including the processes by which they are distorted or suppressed. Of great importance was to learn processes for helping emotions to be more fully and authentically expressed.

It is also important to remember what is suggested by this word *process*. It means movement through time, especially change through time. Movement through time is in sharp contrast to a point of view that talks about how a group or other human system "is"—an essentially static view. Furthermore, this static way of talking about human systems implies that the group has always been this way and always will be, whereas a sensitive observer knows that how the group is now may not necessarily be how it was in the past or how it will be in the future.

The point is that sensitivity to group process has been an OD specialty from the beginning. The place, of course, where OD people learned these lessons in the 1960s and 1970s was the T-group. There are no statistics available that I know of, but it is a fair guess that in 1971, when Warner Burke announced there were three thousand OD Network members, virtually 100 percent of those doing OD knew what a T-group was; and probably at least 75 percent had been through one or more of these groups. A significant percentage were making some use of the T-group format in their own OD work, usually under the rubric of "team development."[1]

"Group process" became a standard phrase in the T-group lexicon. As will be discussed in a moment, however, group process was equated with what went on in a T-group, a misperception that was to have quite serious consequences in later years.

Conscious Learning and Laboratory Education

Process among human beings is an extremely elusive and even ethereal concept. Human beings live on many levels at once, both in their inner world and in what they communicate to each other. Verbal and nonverbal modes are common, as are multiple messages in one utterance. The timing of messages exchanged among persons is also extremely important in what people are able to make of each other. *The T-group produced conscious learning about group process.* The learning was not merely experience, and it was not osmosis. The learning was grounded in some simple theories and was directly felt by virtue of participation in the group. Most T-groups moved, in one way or another, from a state of rather superficial and inauthentic communication to much deeper and more authentic communication. The life of the group *was* this process of movement. Participants could live it minute to minute, both the excruciating pain and the extraordinary pleasure, as well as stretches when nothing seemed to be happening. The T-group brought learning about the processes of human relationships to consciousness. Many participants had never dreamed so much could be learned about their own behavior and others' as occurred in these groups. Perhaps more important, many participants had transcendent learning where they experienced the most profound feelings in themselves and others and could directly experience what difference this made in their relationships and in their own feelings.

So the T-group methodology showed participants both what is wrong with so much human communication and also what such communication is like when it is going right. Participants lived through this process and had the opportunity to participate by their own actions in facilitating the movement. The T-group therefore supplied OD with a framework for thinking about what is wrong with much organizational behavior and what is needed if it is to be improved. Group process was the right set of variables for understanding group behavior from the inside as well as the outside.

Because participants lived through the process of change in the group, they could see what kind of intervention facilitated movement and development and what kind didn't. The T-group experience taught OD people that simply declaring something was wrong with the way the group is working accomplishes little. Attempting to use power—and worse yet, manipulation—to effect the change doesn't work; indeed, the T-group showed that it makes things worse. The T-group powerfully taught the lesson of participation: for a group to become more effective, all of the members need to have a voice in group decisions and group process. "People support what they have a hand in creating" became virtually a mantra of the OD world of the 1960s, and this lesson was learned in the T-group. Again, participation could be seen as a delicate process that was central to the kind of movement a group might be trying to achieve.

The T-group taught OD what group processes are all about; what it takes to move from a less effective to a more effective state; how everyone needs to be involved in this movement; and that skillful interventions in the group process from time to time can help it move[2]; perhaps most of all, because the T-group experience was so intense and so personal, it brought learning about all these things to consciousness. The more generic name for the T-group methodology was "laboratory education." Clearly, participants in T-groups had unlimited opportunity to experiment with group process and the impact on it of their personal behavior, for the essence of a laboratory is conscious and intentional experimentation.

The T-group experience probably taught sensitivity to process more effectively than any other method. One can read books about process, of course. One can see it displayed in well-written case studies. One can observe it directly as a field researcher. But as a member of a T-group one is working with the process even as one is part of it under conditions of some frustration and even pain about the way things are going. Rather consistently, T-groups did work through their process problems, so each member was able to see what extraordinary things could be achieved among people, and what positive feelings emerged, once the process problems were resolved.

In a very real sense, therefore, the early OD *was* an understanding of group process; it possessed a methodology—the T-group and its various permutations—whereby organization members could learn process sensitivity too and presumably apply it to their own organizations.

A Confident, Dynamic Culture

The third factor in OD's explosive growth in the decade following the 1966 meeting in Montreal was that OD people were having all of these experiences together, and each person knew that all the others were having the same kind of experience. The OD world was a place of enormous synergy in the 1960s and 1970s. Everyone was on a steep learning curve about group process, elusive and ethereal as it was. Moreover, people were having these learnings together. The feeling was one of being involved in something terribly important. OD people realized that they had come into possession of genuinely esoteric knowledge—process consciousness—and that this knowledge was the key to a wide range of human problems. We may look back now somewhat wistfully, or perhaps a little cynically, at all the group experiences that were created in those years, but there was little if any cynicism at the time. Perhaps there was some skepticism about T-groups from their critics around the question of whether they had truly long-term effects, but

for those who immersed themselves in this culture there was excitement and a sense of unlimited possibility.

There were two primary places where people could participate
with each other in these learnings. One was at the Bethel, Maine,
training facilities of the NTL Institute (as well as a few other
locales run by NTL), and the other was the semiannual meeting
(until 1980, when the meetings became annual) of the OD Network. Both of these venues were extraordinarily powerful experiences of learning and renewal for those interested in OD.
Attending a T-group in Bethel, as is well known, became virtually
a rite of passage for OD people. The meetings of the OD Network
powerfully reinforced the evolving norms of inclusion, participation, and formation of deep friendships. The process philosophy
people were learning what was applied *to the OD meetings themselves*.
Though filled with substance about OD, an OD Network meeting
was not a stuffy academic affair. It was highly personal, supportive
of participants, and great fun. These factors should not be under-
estimated in what they contributed to the evolving OD culture. It
has been widely remarked that the T-group was crucial to the formation of OD, but I think the ambience of OD Network meetings
was also of great importance in helping the OD culture crystallize
and evolve.

It is not an exaggeration to say that the early promise of OD,
with which this book is concerned, was largely fed by these three
factors I have described: the T-group's continuous focus on group
process and its many related variables; the unforgettable learning
experiences that T-groups also brought into awareness about group
process and about what it takes to move from less healthy to healthier interpersonal relationships; and the stimulating culture that grew
up among OD people at NTL programs and OD Network meetings.
These were the experiences that led us to believe that in OD we
had hold of something truly special, something that promised true
"organization development" to all the thousands of organizations of
all kinds that were laboring in a frozen state with processes that

almost guaranteed mediocre results, chronic conflict, and little or no individual development.

A Paradigm of Vitality and Mission

There is a powerful lesson contained in the three factors and the interactions just discussed. More by accident than design, these three factors were what gave OD its enormous vitality and promise in the decade of approximately 1965 to 1975. By 1969, all the foundational books had been written. The NTL programs were fully under way and in many ways at their apogee. Corporate America was beginning to become aware of this new approach to organizational change called "organization development." The formative meetings of what was to become the OD Network were being held. Up to this point in our discussion, a great deal of emphasis has been placed on the T-group and its role in all of this, and deservedly so. But notice that the T-group per se is not essential! What seems to be essential are the three factors I have described. For a new field of human relations to achieve vitality and impact, it needs to (1) take a process view of its phenomena rather than one of static principles; (2) conduct itself in such a way that members, especially new members, can have intensive, conscious learning experiences about process; and (3) conduct itself in such a way that a culture of confidence, mutual support, and enjoyment evolves. This is what the T-group teaches us: it is a vivid case of *a paradigm of learning and change in human relationships that leads to spirit, vitality, and a sense of mission.* Since the remainder of this chapter makes use of this paradigm in various ways, let us give it a name: a "paradigm for professional vitality," or its acronym, PPV. It is important to note, however, that the OD field tended not to understand itself this way. The field thought it was the T-group itself, rather than its own fulfillment of the underlying paradigm of which the T-group was such a dramatic case. In later years, this misperception was to become of great importance.

Fragmentation and Loss of Direction

At the same time OD was evolving, other things of great significance were happening in the organizational world. Change was becoming a way of life as new technologies, new markets, new competitors, new governmental regulations, new societal tastes and values, and new employee expectations, to name a few, began to intersect in the board rooms of North American organizations of all kinds. This led to what might be called a series of crises of mission and purpose, with the attendant need fundamentally to rethink what the organization was trying to be.

All the various kinds of change that were going on quite naturally created many new organizational processes that management needed help in dealing with. In the same work already cited (Sikes, Drexler, and Gant, 1989), I observed that organizations were on what can be called a "process frontier," trying to develop ways of doing things they had never done before. I wondered whether OD would be able to respond to all the challenging new organizational processes that, on their surface at least, did not look very much like the interpersonal and group relations that OD understood so well.

For example, as the computer penetrated deeply into organizations, there arose a need for facilitating communication between highly trained experts in hardware and software and laypersons who needed the systems but had no idea how they worked (this problem still exists). But to be an effective facilitator of the communication between experts and laypersons, the OD person needed an understanding of the nature of the problem, and most OD people did not seem even to be aware that the problem existed. Suddenly, OD had to be interested in technology—something the field had actually been suspicious of and averse to. Moreover, the miscommunication between experts and laypersons was not a problem that could be alleviated by respecting feelings and each side's point of view. What the parties needed to understand, and invent methods for addressing, was the "expertise gap" itself.

Similarly, the encounter of U.S. organizations with competitors and potential allies from other cultures created another new set of processes that were not merely a matter of interpersonal sensitivity. The much deeper forces of culture were involved, and as with technology this required knowledge and skill with new subject matter for OD people. Working with the Japanese was probably the most dramatic example of this challenge in the 1970s, but in fact the problem appeared in as many forms as there were cultures around the world. Suddenly, Americans—especially OD people—needed to learn how to spell "ethnocentricity," and it wasn't easy.

The organizational world was filling with problems and challenges for which the T-group methodology was not the solution. OD people responded by inventing new approaches to these problems. But the approaches tended to be tacked on to OD, as it was then known.

All of the new content types contained their own process variables, which an OD consultant would need to understand and be comfortable with to make the kind of intervention that facilitates change. In each of the examples that follow, I have added in parentheses the type of process problem the example embodied:

- So-called mission and vision workshops, within the broader field of strategic management that contains the mission and vision issues (processes within senior management)

- Cross-cultural communication workshops and interventions, including what has come to be known as diversity work (processes heavily influenced by cultural forces)

- Large group interventions (processes beyond face-to-face communication)

- Structural interventions to make so-called matrix organizations and other kinds of new structures work better

(processes where top-down authority is reduced or missing entirely)

- Interventions intended to bring about "organizational transformation" (processes of fundamentally reinventing an organization)

- Applications of the principles of "organizational excellence" as popularized by Tom Peters (processes associated with achieving very high performance)

- A variety of projects that came under the heading of human resource development yet were remarkably similar to OD in values and objectives (managing human resources with increased process consciousness)

- Assistance in the design of sophisticated education centers for management and leadership development (educational processes beyond the traditional classroom)

- Facilitation of interorganizational relations (for example, merger and acquisition processes)

- Beginning in the late 1970s and ending in the early 1990s, the U.S. Army mounted an ambitious system-wide change program under the name of Organizational Effectiveness (OD processes integrated with military processes)

- Many OD people became interested in what was known as sociotechnical systems theory and practice (integrating the processes of technology with social processes)

- More recently, we have seen a great surge of interest in "total quality management" rise, flourish, and wane without much relation to OD at all, even though it has quite similar objectives to OD (integrating technology processes with organization design processes, and human resource processes at the level of the total system).

These are just a few examples of projects OD people got involved in from approximately the mid-1970s until the present. The proliferation of interventions continues, to which the recent upsurge of interest in executive coaching by OD people is testimony (teaching processes with executives). Many OD people have also recently become interested in what is called "change management" (integration of change processes with organizational strategic processes). It is related to OD but not the same thing at all, its adherents insist. The same might be said of the currently popular "emotional intelligence movement" (a new view of psychological processes).

The preceding paragraph is rather labored. In structuring the discussion this way, it can be seen how process variables are everywhere in the challenges today's management is facing. OD people have been right in the middle of these events. But they are not sure they are doing OD, especially younger professionals who never experienced the culture of vitality and a sense of mission that was so strong twenty-five years ago, because they think OD works only with interpersonal processes. It seems that OD is split in all directions. *It is the variety of all these interventions*, detached from (1) process consciousness, (2) experiential learning, and (3) a robust culture—the absence of PPV—*that has led to the confusion*. It is not hard, at any OD Network meeting, to find groups of people standing around puzzling over what OD really, *really* is. These are usually younger practitioners who did not experience the excitement of the decade from the mid-1960s to the mid-1970s. I have met students graduating with a master's degree from an OD program who confess that, though having read all the definitions, they really can't say what OD is.

Most of the new approaches mentioned here have come and gone in popularity, giving rise to the accusation of faddishness that is so often made about the organizational change field. Even though many of these new approaches are interesting on their own terms, they are only loosely related to traditional OD. I believe the paradigm of professional vitality (PPV) derived earlier explains why. If OD doesn't understand itself in terms of this underlying paradigm—and I don't think it does—it will not see what needs to happen in order for the new theory or method to have a truly synergic relation to the existing OD field. The PPV says, "Make sure you look at any new activity in terms of the process variables you will be working with. Be sure you pay attention to the way practitioners are going to learn how to work with these variables, rather than simply taking them in at a purely cognitive level. Make sure that these variables and these learning processes are integrated into the culture of vision and mission that has always characterized the OD field. If these three functions are not performed, the new content will be disconnected from the field, and as more and more content resides in this disconnected status, the field will feel increasingly fragmented and without direction."

PPV, in other words, blows the whistle on much of the shopping and sampling that is so widespread in the OD field today. The paradigm both explains the problem and provides a strategy for recovering a sense of mission and direction. The OD field is sophisticated enough to evaluate the variables that a given new approach contains. It knows more than enough about effective learning processes to design learning experiences that help students and practitioners develop a true sense of ownership of the new approach. As noted earlier, the OD field knows how to create conferences and workshops that foster a culture of confidence, vitality, and direction. It remains for the leaders of the OD field only to be mindful about these matters. In other words, *it is time to begin to guide the OD field, rather than let it evolve in whatever way it will—and the PPV provides the basic terms of guidance the field needs as it encounters new material.*

It is an interesting exercise to reflect on some of the bodies of ideas that have swept through the management and OD field and raise some questions about them in terms of the PPV idea. Organizational excellence, for example, as developed and popularized by Tom Peters, enjoyed great popularity in the 1980s and into the 1990s, but it has never been integrated into OD, and its popularity seems to have waned. Certainly through his research Peters got hold of a key set of process variables involved in excellence. But he tended to use a pure lecture method of presenting these ideas to potential practitioners; interesting as the lectures were, they did not produce learning that really stuck. Peters made some early efforts to build a culture among his users through his "skunk camps," but they also did not contain intensely involving learning experiences and as a result did not build the culture he was seeking.

The pure lecture method was also the principal means by which W. Edwards Deming attempted to popularize total quality management, and again the kind of learning that is needed for others to carry his work forward might not have occurred. Many TQM applications, moreover, were implemented in a top-down fashion, which is not the best way to develop a culture of committed users. The same kind of analysis can be performed on any of the fads that have come and gone; I think it will show that one or more of the three factors of PPV received little or no attention, leading the fad to lose its viability fairly quickly.

Some Positive Examples

Interestingly enough, there are four new bodies of ideas, not yet mentioned here, that have been doing just this mindful evolution of themselves. The four are the "organizational learning" movement as originally articulated by Chris Argyris (Argyris and Schön, 1978), and more recently by Peter Senge (Senge and others, 1999); Marvin Weisbord and his colleagues' "future search conferences" (Weisbord and others, 1992); the "appreciative inquiry" school as created at Case Western Reserve by Srivastva, Cooperrider, and their associates (Cooperrider, Whitney, and Stavros, 2003; Srivastva and Cooperrider, 1999); and finally the "open space conferences" invented by Harrison Owen and his colleagues (Owen, 1997). In all four cases, real care has been exercised in accurately stating the pertinent process variables. In all four cases too, the importance of the process of learning the new theories and techniques has held center stage. And in all four cases, it has been realized from the beginning that a new culture is being created, not just a new body of ideas. Each of the four has one or two founding fathers or mothers, but they have all gotten beyond that stage to create communities of professionals. Furthermore, in all four cases a great deal of publishing for practitioners has occurred with the intent of making the new approaches more accessible.

At the moment, none of these four bodies of work is part of mainstream OD, even though some of those involved have a long history with OD. The initiative probably lies with the OD field to build the bridges that are needed so that OD people can get involved in these newer fields without feeling they have to say goodbye to OD. It is important to remember that the three elements of PPV are pertinent to the evolution of these four fields; it is possible that these four fields, as well as others, would do well to pay attention to the three factors of the paradigm. It is possible for any one of these four fields to get so caught up in its own content that it fails to give sufficient emphasis to one or more of the three factors of PPV. Thus OD has a crucial role to play in having lived through the operation of the paradigm once already itself, in the form of the T-group, and is perhaps better prepared to contribute to the evolution of these four newer fields.

Summary and Conclusion

This chapter has reexamined the role of the T-group in the history of OD in order to understand how OD's extraordinary vitality and promise first evolved. In the course of reflecting on the role of the T-group, three major functions it played were identified: (1) the strategic importance of sensitivity to process variables; (2) the consciousness of learning and development that the T-group permitted; and (3) the use of T-group values and methods to create a culture of confidence, vitality, and mission. It was seen that these three functions actually constitute a paradigm, a paradigm for professional vitality, for any field to thrive; the T-group experience was merely one instance of it. The OD field was seen to have undergone considerable fragmentation and loss of direction in recent years, principally because one or more of the paradigmatic functions was not fulfilled. It was argued in conclusion that if OD wants to recover its vitality and connect itself to the new bodies of ideas and methods that are continuously appearing, it must take care that the three functions of PPV are fulfilled in each case. This is how OD will remain adaptive to the present and future as well as true to its past.

References

Argyris, C., and Schön, D. *Organizational Learning: A Theory of Action Perspective*. Reading, Mass.: Addison-Wesley, 1978.

Cooperrider, D. L., Whitney, D., and Stavros, J. M. *Appreciative Inquiry Handbook*. Bedford Heights, Ohio: Lakeshore, 2003.

Owen, H. H. *Expanding Our Now: The Story of Open Space Technology*. San Francisco: Berrett-Koehler, 1997.

Senge, P., and others. *The Dance of Change: Challenges to Sustaining Momentum in Learning Organizations*. New York: Doubleday/Currency, 1999.

Sikes, W., Drexler, A., and Gant, J. *The Emerging Practice of Organization Development*. Alexandria, Va.: NTL Institute for Applied Behavioral Science, 1989.

Srivastva, S., and Cooperrider, D. L. *Appreciative Management and Leadership*. (rev. ed.) Euclid, Ohio: Williams, 1999.

Weisbord, M. R., and others. *Discovering Common Ground*. San Francisco: Berrett-Koehler, 1992.

Notes

1. As early as 1967 I heard the phrase *team development* being routinely used at TRW Systems, Redondo Beach, California, to describe the primary focus of the OD work going on there.

2. See Roethlisberger, F. J. "Introduction." In A. Zaleznik, *Worker Satisfaction and Development*. Boston: Harvard Business School Division of Research, 1958, for the idea of a "frozen" group that has no capacity to change itself.

10

Ideas in Currency and OD Practice
Has the Well Gone Dry?

Barbara Benedict Bunker, Billie T. Alban,
and Roy J. Lewicki

How does the practice of organization development (OD) renew itself? People are saying the field is in crisis. In its early days, OD was the method of choice in planned change. Now, there are numerous methods available and an explosion of consultants dealing with change. Rather than having to sell people on the idea that change must be addressed and managed, organizations just want to know how to control its pace and cope with it. At the same time, organization development practice is accused of being faddist. Practitioners go to conferences looking only for something new to add to their wares. Clients are eager for the new and different, for any magic that will make change easier.

Where do new ideas for practice come from? Why are there not more new ideas that lead to innovations in practice emerging in the field today? We believe that the gap between theory-based research and practice, which has widened over the years, is one key source of difficulty. In this chapter, we explore two main sources of innovation: the translation of theory-based research into useful knowledge in work settings, and the invention by practitioners of new methods and concepts that are used as organizational interventions.

Note: The authors express appreciation to Robin Athey, Jean Bartunek, Peter Coleman, Don Ferrin, Jim Meindl, Dean Pruitt, and Ruth Wageman for helpful conversations about the subject matter of this chapter.

What Caused the Gap Between Theory and Practice?

The separation between theory and practice did not exist in the early days of OD. Kurt Lewin's pioneering research, studying groups in order to understand their dynamics and what constituted good leadership, emerged out of World War II. After the war, his students studied group process. They showed empirically how leadership affects productivity and satisfaction, how people's attitudes and behaviors are influenced by others. Sociologists and social psychologists began an intensive study of groups that generated findings that were useful to practitioners. The T-group movement translated some of the research findings into activities that demonstrated the predictable nature of some group processes. Also, people participated in these unstructured groups (sensitivity training or T-groups) in order to learn to recognize these dynamics in real groups. Lay people in all types of organization, from the Episcopal Church to the U.S. Army, were trained to use these ideas to improve their own groups and meetings.

As OD developed, it became the action arm of basic social and organizational research. There was continuous communication between researchers and practitioners, in many cases because they were the same person. As Lewin said, "Nothing is so practical as a good theory." From the 1950s through the 1970s, research and practice were relatively closely connected, and each encouraged the other's enterprises.

Then the changes began:

1980s

- Social psychology research attention shifts from interpersonal processes and group dynamics to cognitive processes, with decreasing interest in interpersonal and group-level phenomena.

- Practitioners are no longer on a faculty or regular readers of relevant research.

- The academic practice of organizational psychology moves its primary location from departments of psychology to business schools.

1990s

- Psychology becomes more focused on neuropsychology.

- Practitioners enter the field of OD with a wide variety and disparity of backgrounds. No common knowledge core is assumed or required. Knowing that someone is an "OD practitioner" does not tell you much about the person's training, preparation, background, or expertise and skill base.

Signs of Hope for Bridging the Gap

There is some new work that *is* bringing practitioners and researchers together, and it should be mentioned here. Some university researchers are exploring the conditions for collaborative research *with* practitioners (Amabile and others, 2001; Mohrman, Gibson, and Mohrman, 2001). In these interesting field studies, the subject of study was the process of organizational change as it was occurring. A university research group and a practitioner group collaborated on research to understand and test hypotheses in one case about organizational learning and in the other about team events and motivation. The collective focus of attention is the cross-professional collaborative processes that took place. The research describes the academics and practitioners as operating in two separate worlds, each having its own unique values and accepted styles of decision making. The studies make it clear that the gap is more than a lack of knowledge of each other's knowledge base or approach to problems. Two very different cultures exist. If this research spawns further collaborations, that work also needs to develop and specify methods for bringing these two communities together.

Other signs of hope indicate that the widening gap between research and practice has not been unnoticed:

- The *Academy of Management Journal* devoted a Special Research Forum section to this topic in its April 2001 issue.

- In the *Academy of Management Executive*, every issue has a section called Brief Reports, which abstracts and summarizes current research of interest to managers and executives.

- The Academy of Management—an organization of over thirteen thousand academics and practitioners— adopted this topic as its primary theme for its 2004 annual professional meeting.

- Occasionally, there is research that documents how removed actual organizational decision making is from what is known from research findings. One recent study describes seven commonly held beliefs in human resources practice that have been shown in research to be false.

In *The Handbook of Psychology*, authors James Austin and Jean Bartunek (2003) wrote a groundbreaking review chapter titled "Theories and Practices of Organization Development." Rather than just assess the new organizational research literature contributed by academics, as would be typical of similar review chapters, these authors also chose to review practitioner contributions to new thinking. They point out that academic researchers have been more interested in *change process theory* (Porras and Robertson, 1987), which describes the underlying dynamics or organizational "motors" that create change. In contrast, practitioners are interested in *implementation theory*, or the methods, techniques, and actions that practitioners use to effect change. The authors also examine the limited impact that each group has had on the other's thinking, writing. and research orientation. That no previous authors of similar review articles and chapters have considered discussing the contributions of practice and trying to integrate those practices with more academic research speaks for itself about the gap that needs to be overcome.

Research Areas and Their Distance from Practical Application

In this chapter, we have identified six promising research areas that could be translated into practice. As we will point out, they hold real promise but have not been fully explored. Some of this research appears to be farther away from practical application than others. We have decided to aggregate these research areas into one of three categories of closeness to application (see Figure 10.1). Research areas in the outer circle are most "ready" for or "friendly" toward quick application and are in fact being applied. In the middle circle are those research areas where there has been some effort at application, but these efforts are not widely known. They have not been adopted into currency by practitioners. Finally, the inner circle consists of more abstract ideas that hold promise but where some extensive collaborative implementation experiments would be required to develop the practical applications. We turn now to a consideration of these six promising research areas that, in their current state, hold different degrees of applicability to OD practice. Our selection is a sample and is not intended to be exhaustive.

The Outer Circle

Virtual Teams

The recent work on virtual teams is an example of an area where research results, and what practitioners are doing, are coming together to create useful new knowledge. The global economy necessitates virtual teams: teams that have a clear task, require team

Figure 10.1.   Three Degrees of Applicability

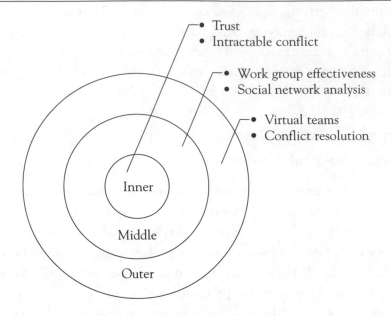

- Trust
- Intractable conflict

- Work group effectiveness
- Social network analysis

- Virtual teams
- Conflict resolution

Inner

Middle

Outer

members to work interdependently to accomplish the task, are geo-graphically dispersed, and communicate through technology rather than face-to-face (Gibson and Cohen, 2003). As a growing new phenomenon, they have attracted research interest. Today, consultants are using this research to prescribe and consult with virtual teams. Books on virtual teams vary in the degree of integration of these two streams, but most represent both sources of knowledge. From our review of the best-known resources, the most interesting are the books that do an excellent job of reporting theory and research in a form that can guide practice. Gibson and Cohen's *Virtual Teams That Work: Creating Conditions for Virtual Team Effectiveness* (2003) is an exemplar. These authors draw on actual studies of virtual team functioning, as well as ideas about effective team creation. As they outline the different issues that virtual teams must address, they use theory and research from several disciplines:

- Cross-cultural psychology (approaches to managing differences)

- Impact of technology (the advantages and drawbacks of different types in group dynamics)

- Reward systems (how we compensate people so as to increase their motivation and productivity)

- Social networks and knowledge management (how effective networks can increase information and problem solving within an organization)

We have seen "virtual team tip sheets" in one Fortune 500 company that seem to draw directly from this literature, evidence that this knowledge has entered the general domain.

Another resource written by practitioners is Duarte and Snyder's *Mastering Virtual Teams: Strategies, Tools, and Techniques That Succeed* (1999). This is more of a how-to book, but not without a theory base. Again, after orienting the readers to the unique characteristics of virtual teams, they describe the critical factors for any team, success factors, technical boundaries, and cultural boundaries. There is specific advice about how to start a team, how to define roles and competencies, and how to build trust. This book is full of charts, checklists, and activities to build virtual teams. It was written by two experienced practitioners using their own and other's experience as well as the research literature.

Conflict Resolution

Prior to 1980, work on conflict and its resolution was conducted by scholars working in separate scholarly domains: social psychology, labor relations, international relations, and community development. Little or no contact was maintained with practitioners. However, since 1980 the field of conflict resolution has been sustaining an active dialogue between researchers and practitioners. This dialogue was enhanced by several factors.

First, significant funding initiatives from the Hewlett Foundation and the National Institute for Dispute Resolution, beginning in the early 1980s, underwrote research and practice centers at approximately twenty American universities. These centers were designed to encourage collaboration among conflict scholars from departments across the campus, underwrite the development of extensive teaching materials, and support better outreach initiatives and collaboration with practitioners. Many centers have become self-sustaining by disseminating teaching materials or conducting applied projects and workshops that bridge theory and practice.

At about the same time, law schools across the country began to actively explore and advocate alternatives to litigation—specifically, mediation and alternative dispute resolution—as vehicles for resolving disputes.

Finally, several professional organizations, such as the International Association of Conflict Management, the Society for Professionals in Dispute Resolution, the Association for Conflict Resolution, and the Legal Educators Section of the American Bar Association, have explicitly designed their regular meetings and publications to bridge theory and practice. Many lawyers, particularly those practicing mediation and arbitration, have been consumers of some of this work, although the movement toward implementation has not been as extensive as many would hope. Although some critics have charged that conflict resolution practitioners still do not use 10 percent of the theory or research generated by scholars (Honeyman, 2001), the field of conflict resolution practice is much more sophisticated today as a result of this accumulated work.

Why is it that so few OD practitioners have immersed themselves in the rich research on conflict and its resolution, much less developed applied practical skills such as sophisticated conflict analysis or effective third partyship for the myriad interpersonal and interunit disputes in organizations? It would seem that this is a fruitful area for the expansion of practice and the development of new OD practitioner skills.

Negotiation. A parallel trend has occurred in the conflict subfield of negotiation. The ubiquitous role of negotiation in the lives of public and private sector managers helped fuel a strong demand for negotiation courses in business and public administration schools, as well as in executive seminars. Since faculty who teach these courses often have strong research interests in the discipline, these faculty have actively built research careers by studying negotiations in controlled laboratory contexts and prescriptively applying the findings in their teaching. Textbooks such as Lewicki, Barry, Saunders, and Minton (2003) and Thompson (2001) regularly incorporate these research findings into prescriptive advice for the negotiator. Specific areas of translating theory and research into practice include:

- The impact of using specific negotiating tactics on negotiator outcomes (Pruitt, 1983; Pruitt and Carnevale, 1993)

- How cognitive biases can distort a negotiator's judgment about negotiation processes and outcomes (Bazerman and Neale, 1992)

- How negotiation dynamics change when parties negotiate through agents (Mnookin and Susskind, 1999)

- What factors affect a negotiator's judgment of what is ethical or unethical conduct in negotiation (Robinson, Lewicki, and Donahue, 2000)

Again, although it is difficult to determine exactly how much research is actually being brought into practice, the prevalence and popularity of management courses that combine theory and practice in negotiation has served to significantly enhance practitioner knowledge and skill. Negotiation can be viewed as one set of influencing skills that OD consultants need for themselves and that may be used to educate clients. Yet again there seems to be little exchange among these areas of training and practice. We know of no OD practitioner who has become an expert in directly improving negotiation practice, nor do OD practitioners appear to offer advisory or consultative services to managers in contexts such as labor relations, the resolution of interunit disputes, the formation or management of strategic alliances and joint ventures, or the development and management of effective customer-supplier partnerships. Given the popularity of executive coaching among consultants, it is amazing that this rich area is untapped.

Mediation. Mediation is another big area in conflict resolution that, though widely practiced in the community, courts, and schools, has not greatly influenced OD practice. Social psychologist Dean Pruitt began to study mediation as it was developing in community centers around New York State. Mediation strategies were developed by practitioners and modified by them through extensive reflective practice. Pruitt (1983, 1995) did research to illuminate practitioner debates. For example, is it helpful or not to separate the parties? If mediation and arbitration is offered rather than mediation alone, does that affect settlements? Research helped mediators understand and develop best practices. Mediation as a tool in dispute resolution has become so popular that it has spawned specialized groups of full-time practitioners in community, the law (divorce mediation), and the schools.

Third-party skills are trainable and well researched. There are times when OD consultants need to use these skills or coach clients in their effective use. Imaginative programs are needed to explore the use of these skills in consulting practice.

Middle Circle

Work Group Effectiveness

For the last twenty-five years, social psychologist Richard Hackman and colleagues have been involved in a systematic program of research on groups. His theory of effective group functioning (Hackman, 1987) identifies input variables that are critical in designing a team that can be successful, describes group process as something that can augment or undercut team functioning (process gains and losses), and establishes three clear criteria for effective team functioning. Briefly, the product must satisfy the customer, the group must emerge as a better team, and individuals should have learned something. After the model was published, Hackman and his colleagues went into the field to do case studies of real teams to see if their theoretical ideas could be documented in different types of groups. In the concluding chapter, the practical implications of these case studies are captured as "tripwires in designing and leading work groups" (Hackman, 1990, p. 493). It is remarkable how many of these tripwires are created by the way a team is created, sponsored, and supported from its inception, rather than by improving processes during its working life (and it is this latter focus that has preoccupied organization development practitioners). Hackman believes the best way to increase the probability of effective functioning is doing the team setup right. This can be seen even more clearly in his latest book, *Leading Teams* (Hackman, 2002); more than half of that book is devoted to understanding the factors that are critical in the setup of an effective team.

In sharp contrast, OD practice working with teams has focused attention on *process consultation* or *team building*, which usually concentrates its efforts on the team after it is formed. Team building focuses on interventions into group process where the team learns from its experience about norms and roles, collaboration, conflict, or interpersonal interactions. Hackman proposes starting earlier, with the conditions that create the work team. He advises consultants and managers to put major resources into getting the launch of a team right: "These basic conditions provide the foundation for superb team performance, and no amount of coaching can compensate if they are badly flawed" (Hackman, 2002, p. 169). One wonders how OD practice would be affected if practitioners adopted this model of practice. It would certainly suggest that they should have a more active role in team design, rather than simply team management interventions. Furthermore, Hackman's research makes clear that if there is to be coaching, timing is important, as providing it at certain strategic moments increases its value. The critical moments are as the team starts its life, at the midpoint in its history, and after it has succeeded or failed at its task (Hackman and Wageman, forthcoming; Wageman, 1995).

OD practitioners also tend to use *process consultation* when working with teams. They often rely heavily on theories of group development (Tuckman, 1965), which, though intuitively appealing, are poorly supported by research and lacking in specific intervention direction. One wonders why the substantial body of research generated by Hackman and colleagues over the past fifteen years, published in reader-friendly language, providing clear guidelines for intervention, and illustrated with many case examples, has not been more widely discussed and incorporated into current OD practice. The Hackman work on teams fits our definition of the middle circle. It is interesting and well-researched work that is waiting to be discovered by practitioners.

Social Network Analysis (SNA)

Network analysis, the mapping of informal invisible contacts among employees, has a long history in academic research departments of sociology and communications. In the early 1990s, there was a surge of interest in networks among organizational behavior researchers, but this literature was quite abstract and technical and remained largely in academic journals, as is typical of ideas in the inner circle of Figure 10.1. More recently, the power of networking ideas has moved from the inner circle to the middle. Some researchers and people interested in knowledge transfer in organizations have taken these ideas and made them useful as diagnostic tools for organizational intervention. Selective application is occurring, but the techniques are not widely known or used by practitioners.

The key idea from network theory is that networks of informal social relations, which do not necessarily map on the existing organization chart, are nevertheless crucial to business effectiveness (Cross, Borgatti, and Parker, 2002). These networks often exist across the boundaries created by formal structures, work processes, geography, and culture, as they effectively map communication patterns, information exchanges, informal influence processes, and trust, especially among high-end knowledge workers. Often, executives do not know how important these informal and invisible networks are to the company's success (Cross, Nohria, and Parker, 2002; Krackhardt and Hanson, 1993). The goal of network analysis is to identify these networks, analyze a variety of transactions within them, and intervene both to strengthen them and to ensure that they lead to productive organizational dynamics. Thus a tool managers could use to strengthen collaboration and knowledge sharing was developed. In an analysis of forty informal networks, researchers found:

- Nonintegrated networks where two or more subgroups existed

- A network where a low power person was the most central person and a possible bottleneck to organizational effectiveness

- Networks where isolated members were not being well used as resources

- Specific individual roles in a network, such as central hub, knowledge broker, and boundary spanner, which needed to be strengthened or used more effectively

With the analytic tools provided by sophisticated network analysis, researchers were able to work with practitioners to intervene to strengthen the network.

Knowledge-intensive work in organizations such as consulting companies, pharmaceutical firms, and the World Bank require effective collaboration and innovation across internal organizational boundaries if they are to apply their knowledge resources to solve complex problems. There may be a variety of technical solutions available to improve knowledge sharing, but there is evidence that "engineers and scientists were roughly five times more likely to turn to a person for information than to an impersonal source such as a database" (Cross, Parker, Prusak, and Borgatti, 2001, p. 100). So these researchers initiated a program to help employees map and improve their ability to create and share knowledge in social networks. First they located the people managers turned to and mapped their networks. Then they developed five relational characteristics that further define the nature and function of these networks. Different questions were asked to identify types of network.

Five types of network were identified:

1. Knowledge network: Do network members know who has, or who does not have, specific information?

2. Access network: If network members know, can they gain access to the key people to use them as resources?

3. Source receptive network: If they can gain access, will those who make an inquiry be treated collaboratively? Will the resource really engage with the problem?

4. Source relationship safety network: If inquirers and knowledge holders do engage, how confident are the inquirers that exposing their vulnerability (asking for information) will not have negative consequences?

5. Energy network: Finally, how does interacting with this source affect the inquirer's energy level?

Research on energy networks found that:

- Energizers and deenergizers are easily identifiable.

- The higher your position in the energy network, the better your performance (better even than expertise) in several types of organization.

- People who are well connected to energizers tend to perform better.

- Interactions with a positive goal and in which people can contribute, are fully engaged, and have a sense of progress and hope produce higher energy levels (Cross, Baker, and Parker, 2003).

Depending on what the organizational situation requires, it is possible to diagnose a network on any or all of these aspects, and then structure an intervention to specifically focus on what is lacking and what is needed. When a good in-depth diagnosis is obtained, it may not be too difficult to figure out what action steps are required! Network researchers have developed the theory and then tested it practically in a number of interesting organizational situations with Fortune 500 companies and governmental agencies. We are aware that some consulting companies are developing social network analysis models for their own use, but SNA models, mapping techniques, and intervention expertise are not prominent in the offerings of many OD practitioners.

Of special interest to OD practitioners, social network analysis was used to study a structural change and reor-ganization in a school (Stevenson, Bartunek, and Borgatti, 2001). The goal was to achieve more integration across units of the school. The structural change that occurred was to propose a new role, an academic director, with more power to coordinate curriculum matters. During the year, administrators whose power was threatened by this change challenged the authority of the new role incumbent, which left this person feeling defeated in efforts to bring about better coordination. The school faculty and staff were very much aware of these dynamics, so the change effort appeared to have failed. However, a later analysis of the network dynamics showed substantial overall progress across the whole school in reducing structural autonomy and increasing cross-departmental awareness. The researchers suggest that with more time, and with the change objective not so heavily focused and concentrated in a single organizational role, this change effort might have appeared to school personnel to be more successful. They also suggest that change can be moving in more than one direction at the same time. Periodic snapshots of the social network can help practitioners identify what is happening and inform their intervention strategies.

The Inner Circle

Trust

Given how central trust is to effective group and organizational functioning, trust had been a remarkably understudied phenomenon. However, in the mid-1990s research efforts picked up significantly in the organizational and social sciences. There has been a wealth of research on trust, trust development, and trust repair in the past decade. A number of factors have driven this work: a recognition of the importance of trust in building a strong organization (Bruhn, 2001); the essential nature of trust as it contributes to the success of new organizational forms, such as alliances and ventures (Lane and Bachmann, 1998); and abuses and betrayals of trust by the leaders of many prominent corporations through broken promises, scandals, and corruption (McLean and Elkind, 2003; Toeffler, 2003). This research has tended to focus in several key areas.

Defining trust. Remarkably, there is little convergence on exactly how to define and measure trust. Researchers have defined trust as a belief in the other's ability, benevolence, and integrity (Mayer, Davis, and Schoorman, 1985) or as "an individual's belief in, and willingness to act on the basis of, the words, actions and decisions of another" (McAllister, 1995, p. 25). Researchers have attempted to specify types of trust (Lewicki and Bunker, 1995, 1996) and to suggest that trust and distrust are fundamentally different (Lewicki, McAllister, and Bies, 1998). Work in this area can be summarized as whether definitions focus on what trust is, who is trusted, what the types of trust are, and trust at what level (at the individual, group, or organization level; Dirks, 2003).

Although researchers have preoccupied themselves with issues of variable definition, few of the findings have been translated into practically useful knowledge. There are many reasons for this. First, trust formation and trust repair are indeed more complex than initially suspected. Second, researchers are in general loathe to translate their *descriptive* findings into *prescriptive* statements for practitioners, and the complexity of the trust-building and trust-repair process has enhanced this reticence. We believe, nevertheless, that there are now beginning to be interesting findings (discussed earlier) that could be the basis for collaboration. Unfortunately, at the same time that researchers know more about trust, a spate of prescriptive trade books on trust (Reynolds, 1997; Tracy and Morin, 2001), with certain limitations (Galford and Drapeau, 2002), fail to employ *any* research findings while engaging in extensive discussions of the "trust problem" in organizations and broad generalizations about ways to ensure and endorse trust.

Understanding how trust is built. At a recent professional meeting, Donald Ferrin (2003) reported sampling more than fifty recent articles on trust and suggested that more than seventy-five variables had been studied as factors that predict interpersonal trust. In attempting to make sense of this widely dispersed and divergent literature, Ferrin suggested that the questions of how trust is built could be grouped into two major areas: what causes trust; and when, how, and why trust develops over time. In the first area, he cited data from a number of studies about the impact of specific leader behaviors on follower trust. Specifically, leaders who are perceived as fair, have a vision of the future, and keep their promises are more trusted. Work by Simons (2002), on "behavioral integrity," is consistent with this line of thinking. This work has as-yet-unrealized implications for leadership development and executive coaching.

Repairing trust. There has also been an emergence of interest in trust repair. Is the old adage that "trust, once broken, cannot be repaired" really true? Lewicki (2003) reviewed this work and indicated that although several studies had demonstrated how trust could be repaired on the basis of the nature of the past relationship between the parties, the nature of the violation, and the types of repair action such as apologies and reparations for lost outcomes, much work remained to be done in clarifying trust repair dynamics. Kim, Ferrin, Cooper, and Dirks (forthcoming) studied the effectiveness of two responses to trust violations—apology or denial—after there had been a violation of competence-based or integrity-based trust. In terms of restoring trust, the most effective response depended on the type of violation. As this line of research develops, it is promising for all kinds of interpersonal and group-level situations where trust has been violated.

Although there are many more studies of interpersonal trust, there are some that deal with trust at an organizational level. For example, trust in managerial behavior, as expressed in human resource policies, has been studied. Not surprisingly, the stronger the perception that policies are fair, the more trust there is in management (Korsgaard, Brodt, and Whitener, 2002; Mayer and Davis, 1999; Whitener, 2001).

The work on trust building and trust repair is a ripe area for better collaboration between OD practitioners and researchers. Trust, or lack of trust, is a major problem in many organizations; at the interpersonal level a breakdown in trust contributes to ineffective leadership and dysfunctional teams, while at the organizational level it contributes to poor coordination and integration across functional units. Clearly, the practice field has moved beyond "blind trust walks" and "trust falls" as trust-building initiatives, and many OD practitioners have extensive experience in improving relations within and between organizational units and improving trust. There are many practical books on trust. For example, three recent books (Galford and Drapeau, 2002; Hastings and Potter, 2003; Kouzes and Posner, 2003) explicitly address ways that leaders can develop trust. There is some convergence in the ideas across these three books, but they contain little more than long laundry lists of factors that might affect trust in a leader and often dig deeply into character and personality rather than focus on behaviors that leaders can readily improve. Since the research field is currently mired in tedious discussions of the definitions of variables, variable measurement, and causal modeling, this is one area where practitioners could help researchers focus their thinking and test the relevance of selected practical ideas about trust building and trust repair. Enhanced dialogue between researchers and practitioners, as well as more clinical, ethnographic descriptions of trust-building and trust-repair initiatives in organizations, could significantly enhance the work of both groups.

Intractable Conflict

The management of intractable or protracted conflict—another potentially very important topic for organization consultants that falls in the inner ring of Figure 10.1—has not yet reached application but is an area where active research is occurring. Many long-standing disputes—within communities, across cultures, and between nations or religious groups—are viewed as intractable. Lederach (1997) suggests that globally approximately 25 percent of the wars being waged in the first years of the twenty-first century have persisted for more than two decades. Coleman (2003) describes intractable conflicts as recalcitrant, intense, deadlocked, and extremely difficult to resolve. Intractable disputes are characterized by factors such as a long time span, high conflict intensity, pervasive threat, strong motivation to harm others, and feelings of hopelessness of the parties about resolving the dispute. Coleman is engaged in developing a metaframework that seeks to understand and integrate the various intervention approaches to managing these difficult protracted conflicts. His goal is to use these approaches in a complementary fashion to deal with this type of conflict. This work holds promise for being helpful to practitioners in thinking about and intervening in high-intensity disputes.

Lewicki, Gray, and Elliott (2003) compiled and analyzed eight major case studies of intractable environmental dispute. They were particularly interested in the way that disputants framed four critical conflict elements: their own identity or sense of self in the dispute, the other party's identity, the specific environmental issues at stake in the dispute, and the parties' preference for particular avenues of dispute resolution. The researchers' argument is that differences in these frames and the compatibility of the frames affect the tractability of these disputes. They found that disputes became more intractable when parties had strongly positive frames of their own identity, strongly negative characterizations of the other parties, differing definitions of the key issues under dispute, or different preferences for how the disputes should be resolved. These researchers not only offered many insights to practitioners on how framing dynamics can exacerbate conflict but opened up significantly new avenues of research on the role of perception, language, and cognition in the ways parties frame disputing dynamics, and alternative reframing strategies for disputants and conflict resolution practitioners alike. Working with the concepts and skills for framing conflicts, if developed, should be of great interest to consultants working in organizations. Although organizations are not warring states, interdepartmental battles that never end and interpersonal acrimony that goes on for years can be very dysfunctional in organizational life. Gray and others on this project have been experimenting with training procedures designed to help parties reframe their views of self, others, and the issues in a dispute in order to improve dispute resolution (Lewicki, Gray, and Elliott, 2003).

Another interesting idea in protracted conflict is the current discussion of the timing of interventions using the concept of "ripeness" (Druckman, 1986). The idea is that intervention when a conflict is "ripe" is much more likely to be effective than at other times. Both parties have to reach a level of being fed up enough that they are willing to engage. Recently, researchers have begun to look at how disputes evolve over time, with an increased interest in understanding how key events turn the conflict, that is, increasing or decreasing it or shifting its direction (Kolb and Williams, 2002), or allowing disputes to become more or less ripe (amenable to dispute resolution techniques). New ideas from this area may be useful within organizations as practitioners seek to intervene in organizational conflict.

How Do Potential Ideas and Methods Get Translated into OD Practice?

Having described six areas of thinking and research that seem differentially ripe for conversion into new methods and practices in OD, we now turn to an analysis of how new methods get adopted and how new ideas move into currency *among practitioners*. This is a two-way process. Concepts more often come from academics, who are more interested in creating theory or testing the precise causal relationship between selected variables. (One wag has defined an academic as a person who is not interested in a practical idea unless he has demonstrated that it works in theory.) In contrast, implementation methods are usually created by practitioners in response to immediate and direct needs for improvement or change.

What does it take for a new concept, method, or idea to move from creation into the currency of use in practice? Why do some good concepts and methods remain marginal while other good ideas are picked up and widely adopted? Why was team building so popular in the 1970s? Why did quality circles become a 1980s fad? Clearly, it is not the case that only the best ideas become popular. For example, Barry Johnson's ideas and methods about polarity management (1997) are, in our view, enormously useful in consulting but have never achieved the level of adoption of many other methods.

Appreciative Inquiry

In the last fifteen years, a number of new methods have been at the top of the OD charts. Let us examine how they got there. Our first example is the current hot intervention, appreciative inquiry (AI), which was developed as an approach by David Cooperrider with

Suresh Srivastva (1987). The core of appreciative inquiry was a genuinely new approach to organizational change proposing that, rather than find and solve problems of organizational functioning, it might be better to focus on what was already in the organization that was life-giving and sustaining. Cooperrider and John Carter of the Gestalt Institute developed AI from a set of philosophical ideas into a change method. Carter used it extensively in numerous mergers in Canada and the United States with much success, but he did not publish or market his work. In the early 1990s, other people began to learn about, use, and develop the method. In 1990, Diane Whitney, one of the founders of the Taos Institute, began speaking and writing about AI and presenting training programs in the method. Books that described the method began to appear in 1996, but the most comprehensive in methodological detail is Watkins and Mohr (2001). Several major AI projects occurred internationally in the late 1990s as interest was created outside the United States. This culminated in 2001 in the First International Conference on Appreciative Inquiry: Accelerating Positive Change, a national meeting that focused on the AI method and what it could do for organizations. This history makes clear that even a good method needs sustained marketing to the OD community and good press in management circles in order to be widely accepted. When brought to people's attention, as in *The Tipping Point* (Gladwell, 2000), interest in this method increased exponentially.

Large Group Interventions

A second example is large group interventions, which are a collection of twelve methods for working with whole systems, each of which was developing at the same time. The history of large group interventions began in the mid-1980s when Kathy Dannemiller began doing work with very large groups at Ford Motor. These interventions signaled a basic paradigm shift in OD, from a training model that expected one training staff for every ten to twelve participants to one where a small group of staff could work with very large groups of people. Even survey feedback interventions had been based on this "one for twelve" algorithm. When Dannemiller began to work with systems of several hundred and only two consultants, this was indeed news. What was new about these methods was their ability to gather a whole system together to do whatever work needed to be done with all the relevant stakeholders in the same place at the same time. This meant that change could happen in a system immediately, not slowly over several months as had previously been the case.

In the early 1990s, we (Bunker and Alban, 1992) began to collect articles for a special issue of the *Journal of Applied Behavioral Science* about these new methods. This is an academic journal published by NTL Institute and Sage; the journal does not have a big circulation among practitioners. However, once it was published, the word spread and practitioners wanted copies. The special issue sold more than six thousand copies, requiring several printings and setting new records for the journal's circulation. We gave presentations at a number of national meetings drawing big crowds. This helped create demand as well as word of mouth. Then in 1995, 1996, 1997, and 1998, Tom Chase organized three national conferences on large group interventions in Dallas, where all the major practitioners made presentations. CEOs whose companies had used the methods spoke from their experience. Cases were presented by teams of consultants and clients about their experiences using the methods. Each of these conferences created more clients as well as practitioners who knew about these methods. Over the same time period, we were offering workshops several times a year on our framework, which helped people understand all twelve methods and their strengths and weaknesses. Individual developers of methods also began offering training workshops in the methods during the 1990s. Then in 1997, the first book that organized and created a framework for understanding these new methods, *Large Group Interventions* (Bunker and Alban, 1997), was published. Today, these methods are accepted as part of OD practice. In retrospect, it is clear that a sustained marketing effort occurred that informed practitioners and potential clients and created excitement about their potential. Gradually, these methods have become embedded in OD practice as one set of choices open to practitioners. For both appreciative inquiry and large group methods, the early faddist interest with overtones that these new methods are *the* answer has faded and been replaced by experience with what they can and cannot do and with experimentation in different settings.

In both of these cases, something genuinely new was being offered. But it is also the case that there was a clear, systematic, and explicit process that distributed information about these new methods and made them visible and available.

The Learning Organization

Another new idea that has come into currency during this time period is Peter Senge's notion of the "learning organization." When he started this work, Senge was very much aware that this kind of idea could become a fad. Of course, he wanted people to be excited and interested, but he particularly wanted to affect the decline-of-interest phase in the cycle of fads that usually occurs and leads to their abandonment. His strategy was to acquire an intellectually stimulating platform of ideas and tools early in the fad cycle—for example, systems thinking, mental models, personal mastery, shared vision, team learning, dialogue (Senge, 1990). He drew his ideas from a variety of sources, including Chris Argyris's concepts of single-loop and double-loop learning and interpersonal competence. Argyris is a very influential theorist and prolific writer whose ideas have affected OD since its inception. Yet, these very interesting and good ideas published in Argyris's many books and developed in practice by him and his students never became popular or entered practice in the sense that we are discussing here; they never took off. Initially, Senge promoted his ideas through workshops sponsored by Innovation Associates. With the publication of *The Fifth Discipline* (Senge, 1990), he organized the Center for Organizational

Learning at MIT's Sloan School of Management. (It did not hurt to have the name of a prestigious university associated with this work.) The center recruited corporate members, a consortium of well-known but diverse companies that both supported it and engaged in change efforts congruent with these ideas. Senge's approach was to create a system where ideas that needed more time to develop than the typical faddist cycle could do so. *The Fifth Discipline Fieldbook* (Senge and others, 1994) was a practical text on how to become an effective learning organization. Subsequent books on change in educational systems (Senge and others, 2000) and on sustaining momentum in learning organizations (Senge and others, 1999) have kept this work in front of the public. Senge continues to be a popular speaker who headlines conferences on organizational change. The learning organization as an idea has been an important concept in the management and consulting world for about fifteen years. Part of the sustaining power of Senge's work is that it was marketed not just to professional consultants and HR executives but also to managers, which was less true of either appreciative inquiry or large group interventions.

Implications and Conclusion

It is not the case that the well has gone dry! There are compelling ideas being developed in the academic community that need to engage practitioners and be promoted. As well, some new methods are being invented by practitioners. But in both cases more could be happening.

As we worked on this chapter, we debated why the breakdown between theory and practice continues to occur. There are numerous reasons, and many of them are rooted in the increasingly divergent subcultures of researchers and practitioners, who talk only to each other and are rewarded only for talking within their own groups. The differences between the cultures of academia and organizational consulting practice have been analyzed and described by a number of concerned writers (Amabile and others, 2001; Honeyman, McAdoo, and Welsh, 2001; Mohrman, Gibson, and Mohrman, 2001). These analyses make clear the differences in values, decision making, and ways of being in the world between the two groups. Authors such as Pfeffer and Sutton (2000), in their book *The Knowing-Doing Gap*, have shown that the problem is common in a number of academic and practice disciplines. What appears to *not* be happening is the exploration of shared or common ground that is often one of the first goals in bringing groups together (Bunker and Alban, 1997).

Rather than focusing only on why the problem continues to occur (the subject of a chapter itself), we chose to try to find examples of those working to create the necessary collaboration to allow better interchange to occur. One very interesting model is Chris Honeyman's work since 1995 in the domain of conflict resolution. With the support of the Hewlett Foundation, Honeyman has created a number of important projects that engage researchers and practitioners together and could be used as models for work with OD. For example, he suggests:

• Making research language practitioner-friendly. Have researchers write with more awareness of the practitioner. Even having practitioners translate research into their own language and then having the researchers react to the translation (like a version of "back translation" used in cross-cultural research) would create productive dialogue.

• Creating conversations between the two groups about what is known and what needs to be known. This has happened in several formats: freestanding conferences, short one-day encounters, or programs at national professional associations.

• Mixing groups of researchers, practitioners, and stakeholders (police, courts, social work) for talk about new ideas or ways to move existing ideas into practice.

• Publication of work stimulated by these conferences and gatherings, explicitly directed to practitioners.

- Creating support for multidisciplinary research in conflict resolution approaches.

Thus with financial support Honeyman has stimulated awareness and work on the gap. No one individual or group has taken on this role in the OD area, even though there is significant ongoing research about organizational change occurring mostly in business schools.

Partnerships between academics and consulting firms are another interesting possibility. Unfortunately, the norms of these two worlds are not well matched. The university has traditionally been a place where ideas were developed to be given away (though universities are more sophisticated about intellectual property now than they were). Consulting firms consider ideas a proprietary advantage and are usually quite unwilling to share them until they have generated a significant revenue stream.

Conferences and national meetings may create a neutral common ground where collaboration about these ideas can be openly explored. This, however, requires initiative on the part of the sponsoring bodies. The OD Network, ASTD, the Academy of Management OD division, and NTL Institute all could decide to take on the gap between research and practice and see what they could bring about to engage both parties. Only as the divide between research and practice is bridged will new ideas and methods flow into practice.

In conclusion, the field of organization development needs a continuous infusion of new ideas and approaches to practice. As we have tried to point out, there is no shortage of these ideas, but there may be a shortage of OD practitioners who are attempting to access this rich pool of ideas, and there clearly is a significant shortage of bridge builders or "translators" who can speak the language of both cultures and help to move these ideas into practice. Finding ways to productively reward these translators may be a highly productive investment for researchers and practitioners alike.

References

Amabile, T. M., and others. "Academic-Practitioner Collaboration in Management Research: A Case of Cross-Profession Collaboration." *Academy of Management Journal*, 2001, *44*(2), 418–431.

Austin, J., and Bartunek, J. G. "Theories and Practices of Organization Development." In W. Borman, D. Ilgen, and R. Klimoski (eds.), *The Handbook of Psychology*. New York: Wiley, 2003.

Bazerman, M., and Neale, M. *Negotiating Rationally*. New York: Free Press, 1992.

Bruhn, J. G. *Trust and the Health of Organizations*. New York: Kluwer Academic/Plenum, 2001.

Bunker, B. B., and Alban, B. (eds.). "Large Group Interventions." Special issue of *Journal of Applied Behavioral Science*, 1992, *28*, 4.

Bunker, B. B., and Alban, B. T. *Large Group Interventions: Engaging the Whole System for Rapid Change*. San Francisco: Jossey-Bass, 1997.

Coleman, P. "Characteristics of Protracted, Intractable Conflict: Toward the Development of a Meta-Framework-I." *Peace and Conflict: Journal of Peace Psychology*, 2003, *9*(1), 1–37.

Cooperrider, D. L., and Srivastva, S. "Appreciative Inquiry in Organizational Life." In W. A. Pasmore and R. W. Woodman (eds.), *Research in Organizational Change and Development* (Vol. 1). Greenwich, Conn.: JAI Press, 1987.

Cross, R., Baker, W., and Parker, A. "What Creates Energy in Organizations?" *Sloan Management Review*, 2003, *44*(4), 51–56.

Cross, R., Borgatti, S., and Parker, A. "Making Invisible Work Visible: Using Social Network Analysis to Support Networks." *California Management Review*, 2002, *44*(2), 25–46.

Cross, R., Nohria, N., and Parker, A. "Six Myths About Informal Networks—And How to Overcome Them." *Sloan Management Review*, 2002, *43*(3), 67–76.

Cross, R., Parker, A., Prusak, L., and Borgatti, S. "Knowing What We Know: Supporting Knowledge Creation in Social Networks." *Organizational Dynamics*, 2001, *3*(2), 100–120.

Dirks, K. "Fundamental Issues for Studying Trust." Paper presented at workshop on trust, Academy of Management Meetings, Seattle, Wash., Aug. 2003.

Druckman, D. "Stages, Turning Points and Crises: Negotiating Military Base Rights, Spain and the United States." *Journal of Conflict Resolution*, 1986, *30*(2), 327–360.

Duarte, D. L., and Snyder, N. T. *Mastering Virtual Teams: Strategies, Tools, and Techniques That Succeed*. San Francisco: Jossey-Bass, 1999.

Ferrin, D. "Research on Building Trust." Paper presented at workshop on trust, Academy of Management Meetings, Seattle, Wash., Aug. 2003.

Galford, R., and Drapeau, A. S. *The Trusted Leader*. New York: Free Press, 2002.

Gibson, C. B., and Cohen, S. G. (eds.). *Virtual Teams That Work: Creating Conditions for Virtual Team Effectiveness*. San Francisco: Jossey-Bass, 2003.

Gladwell, M. *The Tipping Point: How Little Things Can Make a Big Difference*. New York: Little, Brown, 2000.

Hackman, J. R. "The Design of Work Teams." In J. W. Lorsch (ed.), *The Handbook of Organizational Behavior*. Upper Saddle River, N.J.: Prentice Hall, 1987.

Hackman, J. R. (ed.). *Groups That Work (and Those That Don't)*. San Francisco: Jossey-Bass, 1990.

Hackman, J. R. *Leading Teams: Setting the Stage for Great Performances*. Boston: Harvard Business School Press, 2002.

Hackman, J. R., and Wageman, R. "A Theory of Team Coaching." *Academy of Management Review*, forthcoming.

Hackman, J. R., Wageman, R., Ruddy, T. M., and Ray, C. R. "Team Effectiveness in Theory and in Practice." In C. Cooper and E. A. Locke (eds.)

Hastings, W., and Potter, R. *Trust Me: Developing a Leadership Style People Will Follow*. Colorado Springs, Colo.: Waterbrook Press, 2003.

Honeyman, C. "Proven vs. Known: The Gap Between Research Findings and What Is Known in Practice." Symposium presented at International Association of Conflict Management Meetings, Paris, France, June 2001.

Honeyman, C., McAdoo, B., and Welsh, N. "Here There Be Monsters: At the Edge of the Map of Conflict Resolution." *Conflict Resolution Practitioner* (Office of Dispute Resolution, Georgia Supreme Court). www. convenor.com/madison/monsters.pdf. 2001.

Johnson, B. *Polarity Management: Identifying and Managing Unsolvable Problems*. Amherst, Mass.: HRD Press, 1997.

Kim, P. H., Ferrin, D. H., Cooper, C. D., and Dirks, K. T. "Removing the Shadow of Suspicion: The Effects of Apology Versus Denial for Repairing Competence Versus Integrity Based Trust." *Journal of Applied Psychology*, forthcoming.

Kolb, D., and Williams, J. *The Shadow Negotiation*. New York: Simon & Schuster, 2002.

Korsgaard, M. A., Brodt, S. E., and Whitener, E. M. "Trust in the Face of Conflict: The Role of Managerial Trustworthy Behavior and Organizational Context." *Journal of Applied Psychology*, 2002, 87, 312–319.

Kouzes, J., and Posner, B. *Credibility*. San Francisco: Jossey-Bass, 2003.

Krackhardt, D., and Hanson, J. R. "Informal Networks: The Company Behind the Chart." *Harvard Business Review*, 1993, *71*, 104–111.

Lane, C., and Bachmann, R. *Trust Within and Between Organizations*. New York: Oxford University Press, 1998.

Lederach, J. P. *Building Peace: Sustainable Reconciliation in Divided Societies*. Washington, D.C.: U.S. Institute of Peace Press, 1997.

Lewicki, R. J. "Issues in Trust Repair." Paper presented at workshop on trust, Academy of Management Meetings, Seattle, Wash., Aug. 2003.

Lewicki, R. J., Barry, B., Saunders, D., and Minton, J. *Negotiation*. (4th ed.) Burr Ridge, Ill.: Irwin/McGraw Hill, 2003.

Lewicki, R. J., and Bunker, B. B. "Trust in Relationships: A Model of Trust Development and Decline." In B. B. Bunker and J. Z. Rubin (eds.), *Conflict, Cooperation and Justice: A Tribute Volume to Morton Deutsch*. San Francisco: Jossey-Bass, 1995.

Lewicki, R. J., and Bunker, B. B. "Trust in Relationships: A Model of Trust Development and Decline." In R. Kramer and T. Tyler (eds.), *Trust in Organizations*. Thousand Oaks, Calif.: Sage, 1996.

Lewicki, R. J., Gray, B., and Elliott, M. (eds.). *Making Sense of Intractable Environmental Conflicts: Frames and Cases*. Washington, D.C.: Island Press, 2003.

Lewicki, R. J., McAllister, D., and Bies, R. H. "Trust and Distrust: New Relationships and Realities." *Academy of Management Review*, 1998, *23*(3), 438–458.

Mayer, R. C., and Davis, J. H. "The Effect of the Performance Appraisal System on Trust for Management: A Field Quasi-Experiment." *Journal of Applied Psychology*, 1999, *84*, 123–136.

Mayer, R. C., Davis, J. H., and Schoorman, F. D. "An Integrative Model of Organizational Trust." *Academy of Management Review*, 1985, *20*, 709–734.

McAllister, D. J. "Affect- and Cognition-Based Trust as Foundations for Interpersonal Cooperation in Organizations." *Academy of Management Journal*, 1995, *38*, 24–59.

McLean, B., and Elkind, P. *The Smartest Guys in the Room*. New York: Portfolio Books, 2003.

Mnookin, R. H., and Susskind, L. E. *Negotiating on Behalf of Others*. Thousand Oaks, Calif.: Sage, 1999.

Mohrman, S. A., Gibson, C. B., and Mohrman, A. M. "Doing Research That Is Useful to Practice: A Model and Empirical Exploration." *Academy of Management Journal*, 2001, *44*(2), 357–375.

Pfeffer, J., and Sutton, R. I. *The Knowing-Doing Gap: How Smart Companies Turn Knowledge into Action*. Boston: Harvard Business School Press, 2000.

Porras, J. I., and Robertson, P. J. "Organization Development Theory: A Typology and Evaluation." In W. A. Pasmore and R. W. Woodman (eds.), *Research in Organizational Change and Development* (Vol. 1). Greenwich, Conn.: JAI Press, 1987.

Pruitt, D. "Achieving Integrative Agreements." In M. Bazerman and R. J. Lewicki (eds.), *Negotiating in Organizations.* Thousand Oaks, Calif.: Sage, 1983.

Pruitt, D. G. "Process and Outcome in Community Mediation." *Negotiation Journal,* 1995, *11*(4), 365–377.

Pruitt, D., and Carnevale, P. *Negotiation in Social Conflict.* Pacific Grove, Calif.: Brooks-Cole, 1993.

Reynolds, L. *The Trust Effect.* London: Nicholas Brealey, 1997.

Robinson, R. J., Lewicki, R. J., and Donahue, E. "Extending and Testing a Five Factor Model of Ethical and Unethical Bargaining Tactics: The SINS Scale." *Journal of Organizational Behavior,* 2000, *21,* 649–664.

Senge, P. M. *The Fifth Discipline: The Art and Practice of the Learning Organization.* New York: Doubleday, 1990.

Senge, P. M., and others. *The Fifth Discipline Fieldbook: Strategies and Tools for Building a Learning Organization.* New York: Doubleday, 1994.

Senge, P. M., and others. *The Dance of Change: The Challenge of Sustaining Momentum in Learning Organizations.* New York: Doubleday, 1999.

Senge, P. M., and others. *Schools That Learn: A Fifth Discipline Fieldbook for Educators, Parents, and Everyone Who Cares About Education.* New York: Doubleday, 2000.

Simons, T. "Behavioral Integrity: The Perceived Alignment Between Managers' Words and Deeds as a Research Focus." *Organization Science,* 2002, *13,* 18–35.

Stevenson, W. B., Bartunek, J. M., and Borgatti, S. "Structural Autonomy and Planned Organizational Change." In J. M. Bartunek (chair), *Social Networks and Planned Organizational Change.* Symposium presented at annual meeting of Academy of Management, Washington, D.C., Aug. 2001.

Thompson, L. *The Mind and Heart of the Negotiator.* (2nd ed.) Upper Saddle River, N.J.: Prentice Hall, 2001.

Toeffler, B. L. *Final Accounting.* New York: Broadway Books, 2003.

Tracy, D., and Morin, W. *Truth, Trust and the Bottom Line.* Chicago: Dearborn Financial, 2001.

Tuckman, B. W. "Developmental Sequences in Small Groups." *Psychological Bulletin,* 1965, *63,* 384–399.

Wageman, R. "Interdependence and Group Effectiveness." *Administrative Science Quarterly*, 1995, *40*, 145–180.

Watkins, J. M., and Mohr, B. J. *Appreciative Inquiry: Change at the Speed of Imagination*. San Francisco: Pfeiffer, 2001.

Whitener, E. M. "Do 'High Commitment' Human Resource Practices Affect Employee Commitment? A Cross-Level Analysis Using Hierarchical Linear Modeling." *Journal of Management*, 2001, *27*, 515–535.

11

The Future of OD?

David L. Bradford and W. Warner Burke

What has happened to organization development? Is OD's heyday past? Should one pull the plug, as Jerry Harvey suggests in his chapter in this book, and let it die a graceful death? Is it barely kept alive by periodic transfusions of a new approach that rejuvenates the field for a short time, only then to relapse into a semicomatose state?

Or has it been so successful that it is firmly integrated into many other change approaches, as Tichy and DeRose (2003) suggest? They assert that, rather than dying, it has been reborn and currently widely used but without the OD label. One example they cite is the actions by Jack Welch in transforming GE with workout and other OD-like approaches. Is it time for the field to declare victory and move on?

Whether one takes the pessimistic or optimistic view, the implications are that we should acknowledge that OD is over. Long live the king; the king is dead. But in this chapter, we are going to suggest that such an announcement of the field's demise may be premature and that OD has the potential still to play a vital role in organizations. However, to do so requires some tough decisions about how it operates. Before exploring those requirements, a slight digression is necessary to place the role of OD within the larger field of organization change and development.

As has been discussed elsewhere (Burke, 2002), OD is a subset of the larger field of organization change, which includes directive change as well as collaborative change; change in structure and systems as well as culture, values, and norms; and change in purpose as well as process, technology as well as social factors. There is change constantly imposed by the organizational leaders, major consulting firms, and individual change agents.

This is not to minimize the potential importance of OD.

- In a world where change is constant, for organizations to be adaptive decisions must be pushed down the hierarchy and members must be aligned around the same strategic goals. OD practitioners know how to do this.

- This consistency of change means there is a decreasing probability that today's solutions will fit tomorrow's problems. Thus organizations need to learn how to learn. This is another area that OD practitioners have addressed.

- With organizations growing increasingly knowledge-based and staffed by employees with higher-level education and competence, OD practitioners can play a crucial role in knowing how to release and focus organizational members' abilities.

- With more than two-thirds of change efforts failing and an even greater number of mergers and acquisitions not achieving their financial promise, OD practitioners' expertise on implementation is crucial.

Mike Beer has made a persuasive argument about the importance of integrating the hard economic-based change strategies (E-change) with the softer organizational strategies (O-change) (Beer and Nohria, 2000). We fully subscribe to that proposition.

Not only is such an integration more effective, it also moves away from the trap of the present either-or modes of thinking ("Are we concerned for people or are we concerned for profits?" "Are we concerned about today or are we building for tomorrow?"). Or needs to be replaced with *and* to see if it is possible to have both.

Such exploration leads to a much more interesting set of questions than those presently being asked. With these two major change fields separated, much of the exploration is at best around new approaches (how-to issues). Though of use, these are more pedestrian and less exciting than the sort of fundamental "under what conditions" type of question that would arise if the two change approaches were integrated. "When should one involve people in the change effort, and what are the conditions in which such actions might not be useful?" "What are the conditions under which the process should be transparent, and when should information be withheld?" "What is the sort of information that is crucial to share?" "When should the change agents play the expert role, and when should they primarily focus on process (and under what the conditions can they be merged)?" Burke (2004b) has raised similar questions about what we need to know for the future.

It might appear that this integration would call for the end of OD as a separate field as it melds unobtrusively with other forms of organization change. But we suggest that taking this route is not advisable. Instead, there needs to be "differentiation before integration." *Hard drives out soft. Today's concerns drive out tomorrow's. What can be easily measured drives out what is more difficult to quantify.* A premature integration is likely to mean that E-change will overwhelm O-change approaches. Instead, OD practitioners need to work on developing their full voice before they can become an equal partner at the table with other forms of change. In doing so, their contributions are likely to be highly valued by organizational leaders who then will be more willing to include them when major change efforts are being developed.

How OD Needs to Change

If OD is to be a true partner with E-consulting and is to be listened to and respected by organizational leaders, OD practitioners must first confront and overcome its present barriers. Several authors in this volume have described various problems facing the field, and we have no argument with any of their points. However, there are three interrelated dimensions we wish to explore that are crucial to remedy if OD is to have a viable future:

1. Too little O in OD

2. Too exclusive an emphasis on *human* processes

3. The deleterious effects of humanistic values

Problem One: Where Is the O in OD?

"Where is the O in OD?" was a question that Richard Beckhard repeatedly asked. There is a difference between "using OD approaches" (for example, team building, survey research, appreciative inquiry) and "doing OD." We use this definition of OD: "Organization development is an effort (1) *planned*, (2) *organizationwide*, and (3) *managed from the top*, to (4) *increase organization effectiveness* and *health* through (5) *planned interventions* in the organization's 'processes,' using *behavioral-science* knowledge" (Beckhard, 1969, p. 9).

Chapter Five in this volume, by Tony Petrella, is one example of the component parts necessary to do OD. However, we assert that there are relatively few people who call themselves OD consultants who do OD as Beckhard and Petrella are defining it. Most OD consultants "use OD techniques." In doing so, they have minimal impact and are seen by executives (and E-consultants) as providing only marginal value.

There are multiple reasons why so few OD consultants do OD. For many, it is not having the comprehensive systems view that is necessary. For others, they are caught in a chicken-and-egg dilemma. Because they are not involved in systemwide change, they are not selected to help with the large-scale interventions. Instead, they are only brought in periodically to use some OD techniques or to clean up an "implementation mess." We want to examine four important causes that keep so many OD consultants stuck in their limited role and prevented from putting the O in OD.

The "Reductionist" Trap

In his interview in this volume, Jerry I. Porras talks about the assumptions made by the early leaders in the field. They held a reductionist notion that it was first important to develop healthy individuals who would then be able to have functional relationships that would in turn lead to high-performing teams that could produce beneficial organizations that would build a better society.

But this kind of thinking crosses levels of analysis. There can be excellence at one level without it existing at others. All of us have seen dysfunctional teams comprising healthy individuals as well as destructive organizations that contain functional teams. Conversely, it is possible to have effective organizations comprising poor functioning teams as well as functional teams with deeply flawed individuals (because the social system can control and compensate for dysfunction at a lower level of analysis).

This reductionist thinking has led many consultants to start with the individual, interpersonal, and team level and get no further. The present craze with executive coaching is one example of this orientation. Instead, as Petrella argues, one needs to take a total system orientation. Start with the system and, if necessary, move downward.

Lack of a Business Perspective

Any organizational consultant would agree that it is difficult to be effective if one doesn't understand and appreciate the client's concerns. But to what extent is this true for the OD practitioner? As a partner in an organization consulting firm put it: "The problem with too many OD folks is that they are *not business* people. They don't *think* like business people, they don't *talk* like business people, and they don't *behave* like business people. *E*-consultants always have the *business issue* front and center, and all work done in an organization is in service of addressing these business issues (such as *increasing profitability, opening new markets, developing competitive advantage* and so forth). In fact, not only are some OD consultants not business people, but they are proud of it! As though being a business person is somehow 'tainted'" (Carole Robin, personal communication, emphasis hers).

The need for a business perspective applies to the nonprofit sector as well. Museum directors, for example, need to be concerned about what "products" they offer, who their competitors are (in education or entertainment), and what value they are offering to justify grants and donations. Our point is that if OD consultants thought more like senior executives, they would then have to take on more of an organization perspective.

Failure to Integrate Social Systems with the Technical System

In the early years of OD, change work was done with a *sociotechnical systems* perspective. This perspective sees the interrelationship between the technical aspects of the organization and the social. But this orientation has been largely lost in present-day OD. Most OD consultants focus exclusively on the social system factors because few are knowledgeable about the technical. There is often the assumption that *what the organization does* isn't relevant ("It doesn't make a difference if we are dealing with computer chips or potato chips; interpersonal, group, and change dynamics are the same"). But if change agents do not take account of the uniqueness of the industry within which the organization operates (specific competitors, technology used, crucial skills required, and so on), then it is very difficult, if not impossible, to take a system perspective.

Structural Limitations

Most OD consultants work alone or with only a few colleagues. But it is not possible for two or three individuals, no matter how competent they are, to (1) understand the uniqueness of a particular industry; (2) be sufficiently knowledgeable about the company's technology; and (3) know enough about how IT, financial systems, strategic formulation, and other business processes affect the social system (and vice versa) to integrate these subsystems with the social change processes that they may be competent in. It is not by accident that the major consulting firms (who are able to gain the contracts to do systemwide change) are large enough to include these various competencies in a single consulting team.

There is a similar problem for the internal OD consultant. As Burke (2004a) points out, if one is stuck down in HR then one is structurally removed from the other central processes that are more likely to drive change in an organization.

Problem Two: Too Exclusive an Emphasis on *Human* Processes

Two of the mantras commonly heard from OD consultants are that "we never know the organization as well as the client does" and "if you have the right people at the table and the process is right, *they* will solve the problem; we don't have to be the task experts." This has led to an emphasis on *process consultation* (as contrasted with *expert consultation*; Schein, 1988), which has been one of the strengths of the field. This orientation has led to many useful ways to help clients feel empowered by discovering their own expertise without building dependency on the consultant. It has also led OD practitioners to avoid one of the common traps of the major consulting firms: an emphasis on *finding the solution* with less attention paid to *implementation*. But too rigid a focus on human processes has some significant costs and can seriously undermine the perceived value of the OD consultant in the client's eyes.

One of the problems with this focus is that it denies the possibility of task expertise (held by the OD consultant and *desired* by the client). A pure process stance might be appropriate for the neophyte starting out, but after years of experience the consultant will gradually acquire task expertise. Denying this knowledge can be extremely frustrating to the client, as illustrated in the example by Chris Argyris in his chapter, where the engineers kicked out the process consultant saying it was a case of the blind leading the blind.

Another problem with this emphasis on human processes is that it denies other forms of process expertise. As mentioned in the previous section, systemwide change can be successful only if *all* relevant systems are considered. This does not mean that OD practitioners must be fully qualified to design an IT intervention, revamp the financial or accounting systems, or be able to conduct a sophisticated strategic analysis. But OD practitioners need to know enough about these functions to be able to integrate relevant social processes. Most of the problems with mergers and acquisitions, for example, are not due to faulty initial financial analysis but to lack of integration of the two organizations' cultures. Difficulties with strategy are more likely to arise out of *implementation* than out of strategy formulation. But for OD consultants to be invited to the table when plans are being made in these areas, they have to be familiar enough with these processes to hold their own in the discussion.

Finally, such an exclusive focus on human processes distorts how situations are defined. Here is a story involving one of the authors that illustrates this problem.

If You Have Only a Hammer . . .

I was asked to teach a workshop on developing "high-performing teams" to a group of OD consultants who were presently enrolled or were alumni of a leading school that offers a master's in OD. Almost all of the participants were practicing consultants. As part of the program, I showed a video of a staff meeting. I told the participants, "Imagine that you are a consultant to Larry, the team leader. You have begun team building with that group and have built preliminary relationships with all the members. You are sitting in the corner of the room observing."

The video shows Larry starting the meeting by announcing that the only agenda item is whether the organization should purchase a new phone system. Dorothy, head of sales, knew about this plan and has come to the meeting prepared with a proposal. Hank, head of production, is surprised by this topic and raises all sorts of objections, saying that there is greater need for new machinery in the plant. Their argument escalates with some mutual name calling and ends with Dorothy rising from her seat and shouting, "With colleagues like you, who needs competitors!"

I then say to the participants, "Larry has now turned to you with the unspoken question, `What should I do now?' As the consultant, what would you do?"

"Clearly they are not aligned around the same goals," one person responded.

So what would you say as the consultant? I ask.

"I would lead a discussion about what was our vision and what should be our major goals."

"No, no," broke in a second participant. "The problem is that they haven't agreed on their norms of interaction. What the consultant should do is stop their discussion of the phone system and have them talk about what norms they want to operate under."

A third jumped in, disagreeing with the previous two. "The problem is the relationship between Dorothy and Hank. They aren't appreciating the other's point of view, so I would have each of them state what is valuable about the other's position."

This went on with a couple more suggestions of a similar nature, and finally one person tentatively raised his hand. "I'm new to this program and really don't know much about OD, but it seems to me that the team discussion is framed wrong. Shouldn't this be about what's the best ROI from various capital expenditures?"

Bingo.

Now, it is possible that members of this team aren't aligned around the same goals, that they aren't in full agreement as to their norms, and that Dorothy and Hank have a strained relationship. *But those aren't the present problem.* If they are frustrated because the agenda has been defined in a way that prevents them from having an objective discussion about the best payoff for a major capital expenditure, then they will be even more frustrated by our consultant doing the touchy-feely thing. Imagine the eye-rolling if our consultant makes any of the first three interventions. No wonder the field gets described as soft and irrelevant.

Problem Three: Deleterious Effects of Rigid Adherence to Humanistic Values

Again, one of OD's strengths is also a major weakness. A valuable contribution that OD has made is "democratizing" organizations and stressing the inherent value of the human component. The field has amounted to a useful counterbalance to overreliance on "experts," be they from outside the organization or represented by the top leadership. OD has pioneered numerous approaches that tap into the knowledge and competence that exist throughout the institution.

Another benefit from humanistic values is the emphasis on multiple *stakeholders* that an organization should respond to, rather than a sole focus on *shareholders* with their economic priority. Many, if not most, organizations have a culture that ignores the human side of the enterprise. Recently a client of ours described his company's culture as "hard and spikey." OD practitioners with a humanistic bias have confronted these attitudes, thereby making a significant contribution to organizational effectiveness and change.

However, there is a difference between having a humanistic bias and deifying these values as the only way to be. The latter can produce a limited mind-set that focuses only on human factors and is blind to a broader perspective that considers the needs of both the organization *as well* as the members. This emphasis on humanistic values has produced a series of negative consequences.

Which Values?

OD practitioners also claim that they are applied behavioral scientists. (Note the definition of the field given earlier and the admonition by Schein in his chapter in this volume that consultants be anthropologists—a behavioral science.) But what happens when research findings from the behavioral sciences contradict the beliefs they hold from their humanistic values? For example, research shows that commitment can be built *without* involving people in the decision-making process, that there are times when coercive change is more effective (in the long run as well as the short) than collaboration, that under some conditions individuals make superior decisions to groups, and that cohesive groups can hold down the high performers. (See the chapter by Bunker, Alban, and Lewicki in this volume.)

When such a contradiction occurs, it is the humanistic values that tend to trump the research findings. Recently in conversation a respected senior OD consultant made the astonishing claim that "there has been no successful change that hasn't been collaborative." Such a value-driven belief not only distorts reality and decreases the consultant's effectiveness but also opens that person (and the field) to the charge of pseudoscience—of using only those results that fit their preconceptions.

Whose Values?

When there is a strong belief that humanistic values are the "right ones," then the consultant moves from a helping role into an advocacy position. The goal shifts from helping the client achieve *their* goals to the client being the site for the consultant's need "to make a better world" *as the consultant has defined it*. When this is the case, OD changes from organization consulting to being on a social mission. As Tony Petrella stressed in his chapter, the consultant has to accept the goals and purpose of the organization. Yet in a recent book by OD consultants, Meg Wheatley writes, "I believe that in the war of values, there has been a victory. Market values have won: individualism, competition, speed, and greed" (Wheatley and others, 2003, p. 9).

The Client as Enemy

There is a strong antileadership streak that runs through much of the OD community. It is unclear whether this comes from the humanistic values, counterdependency on the part of the practitioners, or carryover from the culture of the 1960s when the field was emerging. But one has only to overhear conversation at meetings or read e-mail in OD chatrooms to pick up the notion that it is the CEOs and senior executives who are the bad guys. They are charged with being concerned only with achieving quarterly results, propping up the stock price, and acquiescing to the Wall Street analysts. In doing so, they are willing to exploit employees and fire at will.

Several years ago at an annual OD Network meeting, there was a special one-day session where the leading OD consultants were invited to discuss how the field was doing. Much of the conversation was self-congratulatory, but there was a fair amount of criticism about the myopic economic focus of business leaders and their lack of concern for "human factors." One of us mused, "I wonder how CEO's would feel, listening to our conversation?" A leading OD consultant snapped back, "Why should we care what CEOs think!" Nobody else in the room expressed any dissent to that opinion.

In a recent article, Burke (2004b) raised the question, "Why is it that OD practitioners do not have a seat at the executive table in the organizations they work for or consult with as an external?" Fred Nichols, in an e-mail to the OD Network, gave two answers.

> For some ODers, OD is a social movement, aimed at changing the world around them. More important, it aims to change the world in ways that ODers value and approve of. Instead of helping execs and managers with the issues the managers and execs care about, the managers and execs become the bad guys and ODers draw a

bead on them and their systems. In short, some ODers are working their own agenda through OD.

[Second,] some ODers belong to what I call the "warm and fuzzy" school of OD, the "soft side" of OD. They seem convinced that improving interpersonal and intergroup relations, for example, will improve organizational performance. Like much of training, "warm and fuzzy" OD work is often an act of faith.

Neither set of OD folks I've just stereotyped is likely to get a seat at the table.

What's a Given, and What's Up for Examination?

When one holds a certain value position, it is difficult to question the underlying assumptions behind the belief system (the challenge of double-loop learning). If there is the belief that collaboration is always best, then the question is not asked, Under what conditions is that true and not true? Unfortunately, adherence to humanistic values has meant there are a range of issues that are not up for exploration. If it is true that the earth is the center of the universe, what is the use of looking through Galileo's telescope?

Unexplored "Dark Side"

Any approach has a dark side: unintended negative effects. In his article in this volume, Argyris charges that one consequence of how humanistic values are used in OD is that it denies the ability to objectively assess the impact of an intervention. We would suggest that there is reticence among OD consultants to look at the dysfunctional effects of their interventions. For example, in the 1990s Levi Strauss made extensive use of OD throughout the organization. The activities did much to increase members' willingness to take initiative and feel empowered. However, one of the unintended consequences of the belief that "those affected by a decision should be involved in making it" was that members who weren't involved sometimes refused to abide by the decision, leading to significant barriers to producing change.

Devaluating Organizational Politics

OD has often been accused of naïveté. Does the emphasis on open-ness, trust, self-disclosure, and the like lead to denial that organizations are basically political systems? We are not talking about sliminess, deception, and behind-the-back attacks but instead about the recognition that every organization has a history and an informal system. It is the realization that:

- There are historic events in the organization that stigmatize certain approaches and support others.

- There are sacred cows that must be taken account of if any change is to be successful.

- There are some people who have more influence than their position on the organization chart would suggest and others who have less.

- There are some people who must be included in any change and others who can be ignored.

- There are some people who are the "rainmakers"; their approval will have a significant impact on other's acceptance.

The preceding section sounds as if we are opposed to humanistic values. That is not the case. As individuals, we subscribe to most of them. The distinction we are making is between *values that individuals hold for themselves* and *values that underlie the field*. All conceptual systems have underlying values, including the applied behavioral sciences (for example, the importance of data that can be objectively verified).

We are in support of individual consultants being clear on their own personal values and using them to determine which clients they work with and the nature of the consulting they do. Our concern is when these values are used to define the field itself. OD practitioners can't claim to be applied behavioral scientists *and* treat humanistic values as the underlying belief system of the field. They have to decide which is dominant.

What OD Could Become

We first need to clarify that this discussion does not apply to *all* OD consultants. There are some who do take an open systems approach, support the organization's goals, and integrate technical with social systems. But we argue they are a small minority. What we are discussing is the field as a whole. Nor are these concerns ours alone; recently the major OD organizations (OD Network, the OD Institute, and the International Organization Development Association) sponsored a study of the field. In a preliminary survey involving more than nine hundred OD consultants, many of the respondents expressed the same issues we have stated (Wirtenberg, Abrams, and Ott, 2004).

The premise of this book is that OD has much to offer today's organizations. Maybe the field is stuck in the mind-set of the late 1950s, when OD started. At that time, much work was routine, compliance was stressed, and initiative was frequently punished. It is not surprising that OD folks felt in moral combat to "humanize the organization" and saw themselves at odds with the existing leadership.

But much has changed in the past half-century. Computers, IT, and automation have replaced much of the routine work done before. The knowledge economy has become central, and the battle between centralized planning and market economy is over. Rather than bemoaning the values of "individualism, competition, speed and greed," why not embrace them? Does OD really want to be seen as the bastion of "sameness, routine, slowness, and failure?"

With this new orientation, couldn't OD practitioners say:

- "We believe in competing against one's own past performance, against standards of excellence, and against the market competitor. We have approaches that help you achieve that by learning how to cooperate with colleagues so all can compete better and so we hold each other accountable for high performance."

• "In your consideration of which company to acquire, we can help not only in assessing the cultural fit of the various possibilities but in assisting with the acquisition process itself to speed up integration and maximize profits. We agree that the acquisition will lead to layoffs, and we have approaches that can make that process fair and objective."

• "We know that organizations can't guarantee lifetime employment. But you can build employee loyalty and commitment through increasing their *employability*. We know how to build learning systems so that your people can perform better while increasing their competencies."

• "Given your thoughts about [moving into new markets, providing other products and services], we can help you develop the appropriate structures and systems. To do that, we need to be involved in the strategic planning process."

• "Time, not money, is the scarce resource today. Organizations waste incredible amounts of time avoiding issues and being indirect. We have approaches that will save you time and money by building organizations where directness is the norm."

• "You are losing time and money in your change efforts largely because differences and disagreements can't be productively raised and resolved. We know how to make yours a conflict-positive organization."

• "In the new IT system that you want to introduce, we can help in developing the process for determining the specific needs of the various divisions in a way that will produce the most valid data and decrease resistance."

• "The trouble is that your managers aren't tough enough. They either won't make the difficult decisions or they confuse toughness with punitiveness, but they aren't the same. Being tough is being willing to give honest feedback, confront issues rather than manage around them, and make the hard decisions. We have approaches that can build that sort of toughness in your organizational culture."

With these changes in mind-set, OD practitioners will be better able to align their skills with the organization's goals (economic and developmental). Doing so increases the chance of the OD practitioner being included in the planning process in the business development, IT, and strategy departments as well as being invited to the executive table, where the crucial change decisions are made. This orientation can also build bridges to E-consultants because both groups now have complementary ways to reach the same objectives—a more developed organization better skilled in achieving its core performance and economic goals.

Will the Promise Be Achieved?

When we started this project, we were relatively optimistic that OD could reinvent itself and be a major player in the change world. After eighteen months of work, discussions with colleagues, and our own reflection, we are less sanguine about this occurring. We see formidable barriers:

- *Few organizations can reinvent themselves.* The success rate of organizations basically changing their orientation is very low, be it in the profit or nonprofit sector. Just because OD deals with change doesn't mean it can apply those skills to itself. Too often the cobbler's children go without shoes.
- *Requirement of new competencies.* What has been laid out is not just a change in mind-set, which is challenging enough. But it demands learning new competencies. This may not require going back for an MBA, but it does require learning the various business functions that the degree covers. How many OD consultants will retool themselves? Also, how many will put in the effort to become competent in IT technology, finance, and strategy?
- *Needs presently being fulfilled.* When OD consultants talk about where they find personal satisfaction, it is rarely about how they increased ROI, cut cycle time, or reengineered the work flow. Instead, it tends to be around personal transformation on the part

of the client or incidents of high self-disclosure and vulnerability in a team interaction. *Developing the organization* might actually be a secondary goal for most OD practitioners!

• *The hold of humanistic values.* A common lament when OD practitioners assemble is, "Have we lost our values?" (There is no corresponding worry of "Have we lost our relevance?") Will they be willing to objectively assess the situation and, when necessary, embrace downsizing, cost-cutting, reengineering, and the like?

• *Changes required in supporting systems.* For the changes that we (and the other authors in this volume) have suggested, there has to be change in the role of the supporting systems. Books and articles on OD must become cross-disciplinary and deal with issues of technology, strategy, and the like. OD master's programs should modify their curriculum to be more concerned with *organization change* (as contrasted with the more limited *organization development*) and bring in other business functions now typically covered in a standard MBA program. The OD Network presently appears to be primarily concerned at its annual meeting with giving members what they want (tools, reassurance they are doing the right thing, and a chance for socioemotional bonding). Instead, will it be willing to build those sessions around what the members *need* (which may include confronting present complacency and lack of relevant competencies)?

• *The leadership void.* Most fundamental change requires a strong leader who is willing to wrench the organization in a new direction. The decision to change is rarely or ever produced by a committee. Yet this is where OD gets hoisted on its own petard. Being an advocate of inclusion (and dubious about directive leadership), will it tolerate a leader (or leaders) who demand this necessary change? (It is interesting to note that the change study referred to that was sponsored by the various OD organizations has set up an advisory committee of two hundred members!)

Our hope is that the field of OD will rise to the challenge and reinvent itself. One positive sign is the previously mentioned study sponsored by the major OD organizations. That they are willing to look at themselves is a hopeful sign. But are they willing to act on it? Our fear is that they will not, and that the future of OD will be just more of how it has been in the past. It will not change its basic orientation, and the field will comprise people who largely *use* OD tools and techniques but don't *do* OD. The consequences are that they will not be at the table where the significant change decisions are made. Instead, at that table will be representatives from the major consulting firms. Only the crumbs will be left for the OD practitioner.

Instead, what will emerge is a new field of *organization change and development* that will integrate the E and the O consulting that Beer discusses. This will likely be housed in schools of business and see an integration of strategy with change theory. It would include imposed change with collaborative change, and it would truly be concerned with development of the organization's competencies, not just those of the individual members.

This new field will not be as strong as it could be because it will not have much substantive input from OD. Instead, there is the danger of pseudo-OD, where organization members are involved in change projects, *not* to tap into their knowledge but to gain their compliance. Furthermore, any member involvement will be on the safe, "cosmetic" issues, not on the crucial ones where their knowledge could make a significant difference. This would be a loss—to the development of an integrative theory of organizational change and to OD. Instead, let us hope that the leaders in the field will be willing to face this present crisis in OD so that its potential can be fully realized.

References

Beckhard, R. *Organization Development: Strategies and Models.* Reading, Mass.: Addison-Wesley, 1969.

Beer, M., and Nohria, N. "Cracking the Code of Change." *Harvard Business Review*, 2000, 78(3), 133–141.

Burke, W. W. *Organization Change: Theory and Practice.* Thousand Oaks, Calif.: Sage, 2002.

Burke, W. W. "Internal Organization Development Practitioners: Where Do They Belong?" *Journal of Applied Behavioral Science*, 2004a, 40(4), 423-431.

Burke, W. W. "Organization Development: What We Know and What We Need to Know Going Forward." *OD Practitioner*, 2004b, 36(3), 4–8.

Schein, E. H. *Process Consultation*. Vol. 1: *Its Role in Organization Development* (2nd ed.). Reading, Mass.: Addison-Wesley, 1988.

Tichy, N. M., and DeRose, C. "The Death and Rebirth of Organizational Development." In S. Chowdhury (ed.), *Organization 21C: Someday All Organizations Will Lead This Way*. Upper Saddle River, N.J.: Financial Times Prentice Hall, 2003.

Wheatley, M., Tannenbaum, R., Griffin, P. Y., Quade, K., and Organization Development Network. *Organization Development at Work*. San Francisco: Pfeiffer, 2003.

Wirtenberg, J., Abrams, L., and Ott, C. "Assessing the Field of Organization Development." *Journal of Applied Behavioral Science*, 40(4), 2004.

About the Editors

David L. Bradford is Senior Lecturer in Organizational Behavior in the Graduate School of Business at Stanford University. He has consulted with a variety of organizations in the nonprofit and for-profit sector and is a member of the American Psychological Association, the Academy of Management, and the Organizational Behavior Teaching Society (being the founder and first editor of that society's journal). His publications have focused on leadership and influence; he is the coauthor of *Managing for Excellence* (1997), *Influence Without Authority* (2005), and *Power Up: Transforming Organizations Through Shared Leadership* (1998). He is dean of the Stanford Executive Program on Leadership.

W. Warner Burke is the Edward Lee Thorndike Professor of Psychology and Education and coordinator for the graduate programs in social-organizational psychology in the Department of Organization and Leadership at Teachers College, Columbia University in New York City. He was the first executive director of the OD Network. His consulting experience has been with a variety of organizations in business and industry, education, government, religion, and medical systems. A diplomate in I/O psychology from the American Board of Professional Psychology, he is also a Fellow of the Academy of Management, the American Psychological Society, and the Society of Industrial and Organizational Psychology, and past editor of both *Organizational Dynamics* and the *Academy of Management Executive*. His publications number more than 150, and among his awards are the Public Service Medal from the National Aeronautics and Space Administration and, most recently, the Distinguished Scholar-Practitioner Award from the Academy of Management. His latest book is *Organization Change: Theory and Practice* (2002).

About the Contributors

Billie T. Alban is president of Alban and Williams, Ltd., consultants to organizations. From 1960 to 1965, she was vice president and general manager of Transpetroleo Corporation in South America. She has consulted extensively in the for-profit sector with such organizations as General Electric, Bankers Trust, Johnson and Johnson, National Health Service UK, and British Airways. She has also consulted to nonprofit and government organizations that include NASA, the Department of Social Welfare in New Zealand, and the IRS. Some of her activities include strategic planning and organizational redesign. In recent years, her practice has been focused on working with organizations and communities on large-scale change efforts, using highly participative methods, which increase the ownership of the new strategies, direction, and structure. She edited with Barbara Bunker a special edition of the *Journal of Applied Behavioral Science* on large group interventions, now in its fifth printing. Her most recent book with Barbara Bunker is *Large Group Interventions: Engaging the Whole System for Rapid Change* (Jossey-Bass, 1996).

Chris Argyris is the James Conant Professor of Education and Organizational Behavior emeritus at Harvard University. He has consulted to numerous private and governmental organizations. He has received many awards, among them eleven honorary degrees and lifetime contribution awards from the Academy of Management, American Psychological Association, and American Society of Training and Development. His most recent books are *Reasons and Rationalizations: The Limits to Organizational Knowledge, Flawed Advice,* and *On Organizational Learning.* He is a director of Monitor Group.

Barbara Benedict Bunker is professor of psychology emeritus at the University of Buffalo. Her activities in the area of planned organizational change span more than thirty years. As an organizational consultant, she has assisted a range of clients in business, education, health care, and government, both in the United States and abroad. She is a frequent lecturer at university executive development programs. In 1984 and again in 1990, she was a Fulbright lecturer in Japan, where she taught at Keio University and Kobe University. In 1998, she was exchange professor at Konan University in Kobe and at Hangzhou University in China. During these exchanges, she had the opportunity to study Asian organizations and senior Japanese women executives. Her research and writing include *Conflict, Cooperation, and Justice* with Jeffrey Rubin; and *Large Group Interventions: Engaging the Whole System for Rapid Change* (Jossey-Bass, 1996) with Billie T. Alban. She has just completed editing a special issue of the *Journal of Applied Behavioral Science* on current developments in large group methods.

Thomas G. Cummings is professor and chair of the Department of Management and Organization at the Marshall School of Business, University of Southern California. His pioneering work in sociotechnical systems led the way for many current applications of self-managed work teams in companies throughout the United States. During the past thirty years, he has served as a senior consultant to numerous Fortune 100 companies in managing strategic change. He has authored more than sixty articles and nineteen books, including the critically acclaimed *Self-Designing Organizations: Learning How to Create High Performance* (with Susan Mohrman) and

Organization Development and Change, 8th Edition (with Christopher Worley). Cummings is formerly president of the Western Academy of Management, chair of the Organization Development and Change Division of the Academy of Management, and editor-in-chief of the *Journal of Management Inquiry*. He is associate editor of the *Journal of Organizational Behavior* and president-elect of the Academy of Management.

Larry E. Greiner is professor of management and organization in the Marshall School of Business, University of Southern California. He currently serves as academic director of the school's Global Executive MBA Program. He is former chairperson of the Management Department at USC, as well as chairperson of the Organization Development Division and the Managerial Consultation Divisions of the Academy of Management. Greiner is the author of numerous publications on the subjects of organization growth and development, management consulting, and strategic change. His most recent book, *The Contemporary Consultant* (with Flemming Poulfelt), has been widely recognized as a major contribution to the field. Among his many articles is the *Harvard Business Review* classic "Evolution and Revolution as Organizations Grow." In 1999, he and Arvind Bhambri won the McKinsey Prize from the Strategic Management Society for their paper "New CEOs and Strategic Change Across Industries." Greiner has served on numerous editorial and corporate boards and has consulted with many companies and government agencies.

Jerry B. Harvey is professor emeritus of management science at George Washington University. He is best known for "The Abilene Paradox," which began with an article in 1974 published in *Organizational Dynamics* and is now published in a book and in a recent second edition of a film. Harvey has consulted with businesses, government, and in the nonprofit sector. He received his Ph.D. in social psychology from the University of Texas, Austin.

Roy J. Lewicki is the Dean's Distinguished Teaching Professor and professor of management and human resources at the Max M. Fisher College of Business, Ohio State University. He was the founding editor of the *Academy of Management Learning and Education Journal*, has served as program chair and president of the International Association of Conflict Management, and is chair of the board of trustees of the Columbus Council for Ethics in Economics. He was named a Fellow of the Academy of Management in 2003. Lewicki has extensive experience in designing and teaching executive education programs and in business consultation. His areas of specialization include executive negotiation skills, conflict management, the use of power and influence in organizations, executive leadership, and management of change. He is an author or editor of twenty-eight books, notably *Negotiation*; *Negotiation: Readings, Exercises and Cases*; *Essentials of Negotiation*; and *Making Sense of Intractable Environmental Conflicts: Frames and Cases*.

Robert J. Marshak is an organizational consultant and educator with a global practice. In addition to his work with corporations, government agencies, and nonprofit associations, he is adjunct professor-in-residence at American University, Washington, D.C., where he teaches in the AU/NTL master of OD program. Marshak also maintains affiliations with other universities and institutes in North America, Europe, and Asia, where he leads courses in OD and change leadership. Among his more than forty publications, his articles on East Asian change philosophy and the role of metaphor and language in organizational consulting and change are considered classics in the field. He has served on the board of directors of the NTL Institute, cochaired the 1984 National OD Network Conference, served as acting editor of the *Journal of Applied Behavioral Science*, and is currently a trustee of the OD Network. He was awarded the OD Network's Lifetime Achievement Award in 2000.

Tony Petrella has consulted to key executives in the United States and internationally for more than forty years. He works with executives on leadership effectiveness and organizational improvement. In 1968, he cofounded Block Petrella Weisbord and was its managing partner until 1995. From 1975 to 1985, he was executive director of the National Organization Development Network. He is a guest lecturer at the Brookings Institution, Columbia University, George Washington University, Pepperdine University's MSOD program, and Queen's University.

Jerry I. Porras is the Lane Professor of Organizational Behavior and Change emeritus at Stanford University's Graduate School of Business. He taught courses in leadership, interpersonal dynamics, and organization development and change in its MBA and executive programs and directed the school's Executive Program on Leading and Managing Change for sixteen years. From 1991 to 1994, he was an associate dean for academic affairs in the GSB. He has consulted with a variety of organizations in the United States, Mexico, and Argentina and has presented his work to more than two hundred senior management audiences. Porras is the coauthor of the global bestseller *Built to Last: Successful Habits of Visionary Companies* (translated into twenty-six languages); the author of *Stream Analysis: A Powerful New Way to Diagnose and Manage Organizational Change*, which has since been converted into a software tool; and numerous articles on the dynamics of organizational change. He currently serves on the board of directors of State Farm Automobile Insurance, State Farm Life Insurance, State Farm General Insurance, and Quaker Fabrics.

Edgar H. Schein is the Sloan Fellows Professor of Management emeritus at the MIT Sloan School of Management, where he taught from 1956 until 2004. Considered one of the pioneers of organizational psychology and OD, he has published extensively, including such titles as *Organizational Psychology* (1965, 1980), *Process Consultation* (1969, 1999), *Career Dynamics* (1978), and *Organizational Culture and Leadership* (1985, second and third editions Jossey-Bass, 1992, 2004). His book *Career Anchors: Discovering Your Real Values* (Jossey-Bass, 1985) is widely used for career counseling and career self-development. He has written two organizational "historical cases," on the Singapore Economic Development Board (1996) and Digital Equipment Corporation (2003).

Peter P. Vaill is university professor of management in the Ph.D. program in leadership and change of Antioch University. Prior to joining the Antioch faculty, he held the Distinguished Endowed Chair in Management Education at the University of St. Thomas and before that was for many years professor of human systems at George Washington University. He has consulted widely with corporations and nonprofits as well as with most of the departments of the federal government. His publications deal principally with the extremely turbulent and unstable environments within which all organizations are functioning and with the implications of these conditions for managerial leaders. His most recent books are *Learning as a Way of Being* (Jossey-Bass, 1996) and *Spirited Leading and Learning* (Jossey-Bass, 1998). He is a member of the Academy of Management, the Organizational Behavior Teaching Society, the Organization Development Network, and the International Leadership Association.

Index

A

Abrams, L., 5, 209
Academy of Management, 166
Academy of Management Executive, 166
Academy of Management Journal, 166
Accenture (formerly Andersen Consulting), 20
Ackoff, R. L., 68, 127
Addison Wesley OD series, 92, 98
Alban, B. T., 4, 163, 185, 188, 205
Amabile, T. M., 165, 188
American Society for Training and Development, 92
Ansbacher, H. L., 73
Ansbacher, R. R., 73
Appreciative inquiry (AI), 31, 101, 184
Argyris, C., 3, 7, 13, 21, 89, 91, 101, 113, 115, 116, 120, 121, 126, 159, 186
Armenakis, A., 92
Arthur Andersen, 115
Association for Conflict Resolution, 170
Austin, J., 166
Authority, for conflict management/resolution, 74–75

B

Bachmann, R., 178
Baker, W., 177
Barnard, C., 40
Barnes, L., 91
Barry, B., 171
Bartunek, J. M., 166, 177

Bazerman, M., 171
BearingPoint (formerly KPMG), 20
Beauvais, J., 97
Beckhard, D., 52
Beckhard, R., 13, 66, 102
Beer, M., 102, 196
Behavioral integrity research, 179
Belcher, J., 100
Bell, C., 88
Benedictine, 87
Benne, K. D., 23, 90
Bennis, W. G., 13, 23, 90, 102, 132
Berg, P. O., 92
Bergquist, W., 31
Bhambri, A., 105
Bies, R. H., 179
Blake, B., 133
Blake, R. R., 13, 91, 133
Bob & Carol & Ted & Alice (film), 94
Boeing, 62
Borgatti, S., 175, 176, 177
Boris, S., 92
Boscolo, L., 134
Bradford, D. L., 7, 43, 195. *See also* Porras interview
Brigham Young University, 87–88
Brodt, S. E., 180
Bruhn, J. G., 178
Buchanan, P., 9, 13
Built to Last (Porras and Collins), 55, 56, 61, 62
Bunker, B. B., 4, 163, 179, 185, 188, 205

Buono, A. P., 105
Burke, W. W., 7, 21, 102, 145, 149, 195, 196, 197, 201, 206
Business perspective, 199–200
"Business process reengineering" services, 21

C

Cameron, K., 102
Campbell, D., 134
Cap Gemini Ernst and Young, 20
Carnevale, P., 171
Carter, J., 184
Case Western Reserve, 13, 88, 145, 159
Catholic Church, 115
Cecchin, G., 134
Center for Organizational Learning (MIT's Sloan School of Management), 186–187
Champy, J., 100
Change: axiom of participation in, 90; creation metaphor of, 81; O-change and e-change approaches to, 196–197; OD assumption regarding, 22–23; OD practitioner's marginalization during, 19–20; OD role during worldwide organization, 19; OD work relating to reaction to, 10; organizational values linked to, 62; orientation of companies to, 61; process and implementation theories of, 166–167; required of OD to have viable future, 198–209; social network analysis to study, 177–178; traditional vs. newer OD perceptions of, 100–101
Change management: assumptions of, 22; comparing OD and, 22–23, 24t, 157; described, 21–22; leading creative and constructive, 81–83; as OD challenge, 28–29; values of, 23, 24t
Change process theory, 166
Chase, T., 185
Chin, R., 23, 90
Classical OD, 37t, 38–39, 41
Clegg, C., 100
Clients: explaining change management to, 21–22; organizations as "ultimate," 141; perceived as the enemy, 206–207; systemic point of view on concept of, 141. See also Organizations
Clinical inquiry method, 136–137
Coghlan, D., 141
Cohen, S. G., 100, 168

Coldicott, T., 134
Coleman, P., 181
Collins, J., 55
Columbia disaster, 115
Columbia Teachers College, 88
Commitment-involvement relationship, 8
Conflict: anxiety and fear over power and, 75; managing intractable, 181–183; over exploitation of employees, 75–76
Conflict resolution: legitimate authority for, 74–75; performance and importance of, 74–77; research on, 169–172, 181–183
Cooper, C. D., 180
Cooperrider, D. L., 101, 159, 184
Corey, K. E., 23
Corporate culture: anthropological approach to understanding, 137–140, 142; clinical inquiry approach to data of, 136–137; cultural naïveté issue and, 135–137; importance of, 80–81; M&M Mars, 77–79; observations about, 79–80. See also Organizations; Value system
Cross, R., 175, 176, 177
Cultural issues, 135–137
Cultural naïveté issue, 135–137
Cummings, T. G., 2, 21, 87, 88, 100, 105

D

Dannemiller, K., 184–185
Davenport, T., 97, 101
Davis, J. H., 178, 180
Davis, S., 9, 13, 107
DEC (Digital Equipment Corporation), 140–141
Defensive reasoning: contradictions between productive and, 115–116; described, 114–115; OD turning from productive to, 116–117
Deming, W. E., 159
DeRose, C., 195
DeVogel, S. H., 107
Dirks, K. T., 179, 180
Donahue, E., 171
Double-loop learning, 115, 127
Dow Chemical, 13
Downsizing, 26–27
Drapeau, A. S., 179, 180
Drexler, A., 148, 154
Drucker, P., 97
Druckman, D., 182

Duarte, D. L., 169
Dunlap, J., 13
Dutton, J., 102

E

E-change, 196, 197
Elkind, P., 178
Elliott, M., 182
Emery, F., 12
Emotional-subjective reasoning, 117–120
Employees: better educated and more demanding, 96–97; calculating contribution/values of, 60–61; downsizing, 26–27; exploitation of, 75–76; increasing diversity of, 96; laying off, 58–60. *See also* Organizations
Enfield case study, 120–121
Enron, 115
Episcopal Church, 13
Esso (now Exxon Mobil), 13, 133
Executive coaching, 30
Expert consultation, 201
Expertise (organization), 120–121

F

Feedback loop, 10–11
Ferguson, C., 13
Ferrin, D. H., 179, 180
Feyerherm, A. E., 27, 38
Field, H. S., 92
The Fifth Discipline Field Book (Senge and others), 187
The Fifth Discipline (Senge), 186
First International Conference on Appreciative Inquiry (2001), 184
Fisher, D., 100
French, W., 88, 102
The Functions of the Executive (Barnard), 40
"Future search conferences," 159

G

Galbraith, J., 97
Galford, M., 179
Galford, R., 181
Gandhi, M., 83
Gant, J., 148, 154
GE (General Electric), 62
General Mills, 13
Gestalt Institute, 184
Gibson, C. B., 165, 168, 188

Gladwell, M., 184
GM (General Motors), 75
Goggin, W. C., 127
Grandma metaphor, 15–18
Gray, B., 182
Greiner, L. E., 2, 87, 91, 92, 93, 104, 105

H

Hackman, R., 172, 173, 174
Hammer, M., 100
The Handbook of Psychology, 166
Hanson, J. R., 175
Harvey, J. B., 2, 6, 15, 62, 145
Harwood-Weldon Manufacturing, 13
Hastings, 180
Herzberg, F., 94
Hewlett Foundation, 169, 188
"High-involvement organizations," 101
Honeyman, C., 170, 188
HP (Hewlett Packard), 62
Human actions: behavioral integrity, 179; corporate culture influence on, 77–81; reasoning mind-sets dominating, 114–115; too much OD emphasis on processes of, 201–204. *See also* Value systems
Human Resources: assumptions on learning held by, 125; case of Tom and, 125–127; OD functions practiced by, 29–30
Hutton, C., 33

I

IBM Business Consulting Services, 20
"If You Have Only a Hammer. . ." story, 202–204
Implementation theory, 166
Incremental degradation, 78
Industrial Network, 145
International Association of Conflict Management, 170
Intractable conflict, 181–183
Involvement-commitment relationship, 8

J

Jackson, P., 100
Jensen, M., 114
John's case study, 117–121
Johnson, B., 183
Journal of Applied Behavioral Science, 185

K

Kanter, R. M., 8
Kaplan, M., 33
Kemp, N., 100
Kim, P. H., 180
King, M. L., Jr., 83
Kinsella, K., 134
The Knowing-Doing Gap (Pfeffer and
    Sutton), 188
Kolb, D., 182
Kolb, H., 9, 13
Koon, E., 97
Korsgaard, M. A., 180
Korten, D., 96
Kouzes, J., 180
Krackhardt, D., 175
Kristoff, A., 100

L

"Laboratory education," 150
Lane, C., 178
Large group interventions, 184–186
Large Group Interventions (Bunker and
    Alban), 185
Lawler, E. E., 97, 100, 101, 104
Lawrence, P. A., 13, 101, 107
Leadership: moral, 76–77; vital, 83–85
Leadership (MacGregor Burns), 76
Leading Teams (Hackman), 173
Learning: double-loop, 115, 127; felt
    directly and unequivocally, 147; HR
    assumptions about, 125; single-loop,
    115; T-group production of uncon-
    scious, 149–151. *See also* Organizational
    learning movement
Learning organizations, 186–187
Lederach, J. P., 181
Ledford, G., 100
Legal Educators Section of the American
    Bar Association, 170
Lehner, G., 13
Levy, S., 9, 13
Lewicki, R. J., 4, 163, 171, 179, 180,
    182, 205
Lewin, K., 21, 89, 90, 132, 164
Likert, R., 89

M

M&M Mars, 77–79
McAdoo, B., 188
McAllister, D. J., 179

McGill, M., 97
MacGregor Burns, J., 76
MacGregor, D., 13, 21
McGregor, D., 90, 134
McLean, B., 178
McLean, G. N., 107
Maister, D., 107
Management: conflict resolution by,
    74–77, 169–172; executive coaching of,
    30; moral leadership of, 76–77; OD
    reeducation activities for, 92; vital lead-
    ership by, 83–85. *See also* Power
Managerial Grid, 91, 133
Mao Tse-Tung, 83
Marrow, A., 132
Marshak, R. J., 2, 19
Maslow, A., 21, 89, 134
Mastering Virtual Teams: (Duarte and
    Snyder), 169
Mayer, R. C., 178, 180
Mediation research, 172
Mega case series, 105
Melchionno, R., 97
Mencken, H. L., 65
Minahan, M., 33
Minton, J., 171
Misciagna, M., 17
Mnookin, R. H., 171
Mohr, B. J., 184
Mohrman, A. M., 165, 188
Mohrman, S. A., 97, 100, 104, 165, 188
Moore, K., 22
Moral leadership, 76–77
Morrison, P., 92
Mouton, J., 13, 91, 133

N

Nadler, D., 107
National Institute for Dispute Resolution,
    169–170
Neale, M., 171
Negotiation research, 170–171
Neoclassical OD, 37t, 38, 39–40
Network theory, 174–175
Networks: research on energy, 176–177;
    types of, 176
New OD (or social interaction OD), 37t,
    39, 40–41
New red flags. *See* Red flags
Nichols, F., 206–207
Nohria, N., 175, 196

NTL (National Training Laboratories), 12, 14, 21, 88, 91, 131–132, 145, 152, 189

NTL's Program for Specialists in Organization Training and Development, 14

O

O-change, 196, 197

OD adapters, 98–99t, 100–102

OD demise: current marginalization of OD leading to, 19–20, 25–26; fragmentation and loss of direction leading to, 154–159; Grandma metaphor of, 15–18; historic biases toward OD and, 34–35; inefficient organizational use of OD and, 1; Jerry Porras's interview on the, 43–64; new red flags facing today's OD, 103–108; observations about OD and, 1, 113; organizational inner contradictions and, 115–116; problems of humanistic thinking and, 116–127; reasoning mind-sets reliance and, 114–115; six red flags warning of, 93–94, 95; summarizing reasons for, 137

OD future: challenges and controversies over, 20–33, 211–212; Grandma metaphor of, 15–18; Jerry Porras's interview on the, 43–64; new red flags facing, 103–108; paths forward for, 36–41, 108; potential relevance of OD, 7–10, 196, 209–211

OD future challenges: barriers to reaching potential, 211–212; changing organizational conditions as, 95–98, 96t; from change management, 28–29; from downsizing, 26–27; from executive coaching, 30; from human resources, 29–30; from lean organization trend, 29–30; from reengineering, 27–28

OD future controversies: humanistic or business orientation of, 21–25, 24t; modern to postmodern OD, 31–33, 32t; touchy-feely or bottom-line orientation, 25–26

OD history: change management role in, 21–22; early OD scholars contributing to, 21, 88–90, 131–135; evolution of OD leading to loss skills, 134–135; historical roots and development (1960s-1980s) of, 87–88; internal professionals contributing to, 13–14; "micro" psychological approach to early OD, 21, 89;

NTL role in early, 12, 14; OD adapters vs. OD holdouts responses to changes, 98–102; OD development as movement, 90–93; OD Network formation, 14; organizational approach to OD, 89–90; sensitivity training focus by OD practitioners, 92–93; summarizing OD trends, 99t; transformation of OD (1970s-present), 95–96. See also OD profession; T-group (sensitivity training)

OD holdouts, 98–99t, 100–102

OD movement: development of OD into, 90–93; media attacks on the, 94–95; six flags criticisms of OD and, 93–95

OD Network, 14, 33t, 34, 88, 92, 152, 153, 206

OD (organizational development): assumption regarding change in, 22–23; barriers to potential of, 211–212; changes required to remain viable, 198–209; comparing change management and, 22–23, 24t, 157; confident professional culture of, 147; content and process of, 10; cultural issues facing, 135–137; definitions of the new, 102; definitions of, 10–12, 23; potential relevance of, 7–10, 196, 209–211; reflecting on the new form of, 102–108; as subset of organizational change field, 196; three types of, 37t–41. See also Theories

OD practice: bridging the theory-practice gap, 165–167; getting potential ideas/methods translated into, 183–187; new ideas for renewing, 163; recommendations for renewing, 187–189; tracing gap between theory and, 164–165; translating promising research into, 167–183

OD practitioners: comparing "holdouts" and "adaptors" among, 98–102; current marginalization of, 19–20, 25–26; decrease in doctoral-level, 35; developing organizational therapist skills, 140–142; lack of business perspective by, 199–200; learning to think more like anthropologists, 137–140, 142; multiple roles played by, 5, 9; new roles taken by adaptive, 100–101; ongoing differentiation between OD scholars and, 35–36; performance principles for, 66–86;

sensitivity training focus by, 92–93; shifting demographics of, 33t–36; structural limitations of, 200–201; STS principles used by, 27–28; types of interventions by, 155–157; values representative of, 11; working conditions of, 8–9

OD problems: 1: where is the O in OD?, 198–201; 2: too exclusive an emphasis on human processes, 201–204; 3: deleterious effects of rigid adherence to humanistic values, 204–209

OD profession: confident, dynamic culture of, 151–153; conscious learning and laboratory education using, 149–151; early promise of, 152–153; fragmentation and loss of direction by, 154–159; Grandma metaphor of, 15–18; new red flags facing, 103–108; paradigm of vitality and mission for the, 153; rapid growth (1960s-1970s) of, 145–146; sensitivity to process development of, 147–149. See also OD history; T-group (sensitivity training)

Old Network, 14

Open systems theory: definition of total system under, 68–69; as underlying OD practice, 10–11; to understand organizations, 68–71

Organization Development and Change Division (Academy of Management), 19, 88

Organizational effectiveness, 21

Organizational learning movement, 159–160. See also Learning

Organizations: cultural issues facing, 135–137; economic, workforce, technical forces demands on, 95–98, 96t, 155; expertise found within, 120–121; function of purpose in, 58; inefficient use of OD by, 1; learning, 186–187; new roles by adaptive OD practitioners in, 100–102; OD thinking toward "high-involvement," 101; open systems framework to understand, 68–71; politics within, 75, 208; as sociotechnical systems, 134; trend toward lean, 29–30; trends and contexts facing modern, 95–97, 96t; as "ultimate" client, 141. See also Clients; Corporate culture; Employees; Value system

Ott, C., 5, 209

Owen, H., 159

P

P&G (Proctor and Gamble), 13, 54–55

Palazzoli, M. S., 134

Parker, A., 175, 176, 177

Pepperdine University, 88

Performance principles: conflict management/resolution importance, 74–77; constructive and creative change transition, 81–83; listed, 66–67; use of open systems framework, 68–71; people create value, 72–74; purpose comes first, 67–68; three perspectives used to examine, 67; on vital leadership, 83–85

Personal integrity issue, 107–108

Peters, T., 158–159

Petrella, T., 2, 65

Pfeffer, J., 188

Pfeiffer, 133

Pillsbury, 13

The Planning of Change (Bennis, Benne, and Chin), 90

Politics, 75, 208

Porras interview: on calculating individual's contribution/values, 60–61; on function of purpose in organizations, 58; on future of OD, 62–63; on his early OD research, 48–50; on his long involvement in OD, 43–45; on historic view of OD as organizational tool, 46; on irrelevancy of OD, 50, 51; on lack of OD group accomplishments, 51–52; on letting employees go, 58–60; on OD master's programs, 64; on OD rejection of reengineering movement, 52–54; on OD values, 50, 56–57; on P&G example of OD benefits, 54–55; on primary focus of OD analysis, 46–48; on reasons for OD ineffectiveness, 52; on stream analysis approach, 55–56. See also Bradford, D. L

Porras, J. I., 2, 43, 92, 166, 199

Positive organizational scholarship, 101–102

Posner, B., 180

Potter, 180

Power: anxiety and fear over conflict and, 75–76; based on set of values, 76–77; OD consultant role in legitimate use of, 76. See also Management

PPV (paradigm of professional vitality), 157–159

Prata, G., 134

PriceWaterhouseCoopers Consulting, 20

Process consultation, 173, 174, 201
Productive reasoning: described, 114; inner contradiction of defensive and, 115–116; OD professional's promotion of, 126; OD turning to defensive reasoning from, 116–117
Program for Specialists in Organization Training and Development (NTL), 14
Pruitt, D., 171, 172
Prusak, L., 101, 176
Pseudo-OD, 213
PSOTD (later PSOD), 14
Purpose: function of, 58; as performance principle, 67–68
Putnam, R., 115

Q
Quinn, R. E., 19, 102

R
Rashford, N. S., 141
Rational-objective reasoning, 117–120
Reasoning mind-set case studies: case of John, 117–121; case of Tom, 122–127; Enfield case, 120–121
Reasoning mind-sets: defensive, 114–117; emotional-subjective/rational-objective, 117–120; productive, 114, 115–117, 126
Red flags: 1: neglected involvement in management decision making, 104; 2: neglected involvement in strategy formulation, 104–105; 3: neglected involvement in mergers and acquisitions, 105–106; 4: neglected involvement in globalization, 106; 5: neglected involvement in alliances/virtual organizations, 106–107; 6: neglected involvement in corporate governance/personal integrity, 107–108; Greiner's six warnings of OD demise (1972), 93–94, 95
"Red Flags in Organization Development" (Greiner), 93
Reductionist thinking trap, 199
"Reeducation" activities, 92
Reegineering: as early OD service, 21; as OD challenge, 27–28; OD rejection of, 52–54
Research areas: conflict resolution, 169–172; intractable conflict, 181–183; SNA (social network analysis), 174–178; three degrees of applicability of, 167, 168fig; trust, 178–181; virtual

teams, 167–169; work group effectiveness, 172–174. See also Theories
Reynolds, L., 179
"Ripeness" concept, 182–183
Robertson, P. J., 166
Robinson, R. J., 171
Rogers, C., 89
Rothwell, W. J., 107
Ruddle, K., 22

S
Saunders, D., 171
Schein, E. H., 3, 13, 104, 131, 132, 136, 138, 139, 141, 142, 201, 205
Schmidt, W., 13
Schön, D., 101, 115, 126, 159
Schoorman, F. D., 178
Scientific Methods, 91
"Self-actualization," 89
Senge, P., 101, 186, 187
Shepard, H., 13, 133
Sherif, M., 132
Sikes, W., 148, 154
Simons, T., 179
Single-loop learning, 115
Six red flag warnings, 93–94, 95
Six Sigma, 62
Sloan, A. P., 73
Slocum, J., 97
Smith, D., 115
SNA (social network analysis) research, 174–178
Snyder, N. T., 169
Social interaction OD (or New OD), 37t, 39
Social network analysis, 177–178
Society for Professionals in Dispute Resolution, 170
Sorenson, P., 101
Srivastva, S., 159, 184
Stavros, J. M., 159
Stevenson, W. B., 177
Strauss, L., 207
Stream analysis approach, 55–56
STS (sociotechnical systems) principles, 27–28
Sullivan, R., 107
Susskind, L. E., 171
Sutton, R. I., 188

T
T-group (sensitivity training): conscious learning produced by, 149–151; contributions to

OD work, 148–149; OD historic roots in, 12, 13, 91, 128, 132, 146–147; OD sensitivity to group processes and, 147–149; paradigm of learning leading to vitality lesson of, 153; research translated into practice through, 164. *See also* OD history; OD profession
Tannenbaum, B., 13
Taos Institute, 184
Tavistock Institute (London), 12, 131, 132
Taylor, F., 121
Team building, 133, 173
Theories: change process, 166; gap between practice and, 164–183; implementation, 166; network, 174–175; open systems, 10–11, 68–71; X and Y, 90. *See also* OD (organizational development); Research areas
"Theories and Practices of Organization Development" (Austin and Bartunek), 166
Theory X, 90
Theory Y, 90
Theory-practice gap: bridging the, 165–167; tracing evolution of, 164–165; translating promising research into practice, 167–183
"Therapy for normals," 132–133
Thomas, R., 96
Thompson, C., 97
Thompson, L., 171
3M, 62
360 degree feedback, 135–136
Thurow, L., 96
Tichy, N. M., 195
The Tipping Point (Gladwell), 184
Toeffler, B. L., 178
Tolbert, W., 100
Tom's case study, 121–127
Topeka dog food plant experiment (1960s), 13
Trist, E., 12
Trust: defining, 178–179; repairing, 179–181; understanding how it is built, 179
TRW Systems (Los Angeles), 13
Tuckman, B. W., 174

U
Union Carbide, 13
United Kingdom: early days of OD in the, 12–13; Tavistock Institute of, 12, 131, 132

University Associates (later Pfeiffer), 133
U.S. State Department, 13

V
Vaill, P. P., 3–4, 145
Value: calculating employee contribution and individual, 60–61; collective work producing, 73; people as creating, 72–74
Value system: comparing change management and, OD, 24t; corporate culture and, 77–81; OD (organizational development), 11, 23, 50, 56–57; OD's rigid adherence to humanistic, 204–209; personal integrity, 107–108; power based on, 76–77; relationship between change and organizational, 62. *See also* Corporate culture; Organizations
Virtual teams research, 167–169
Virtual Teams That Work: Creating Conditions for Virtual Team Effectiveness (Gibson and Cohen), 168
Vital leadership, 83–85

W
Wageman, R., 174
Wall, T., 100
Watkins, J. M., 184
Weisbord, M., 159
Welch, J., 59, 60, 195
Welsh, N., 188
Wheatley, M. J., 31, 205–206
Whitener, E. M., 180
Whitney, D., 101, 159, 184
Williams, J., 182
Wirtenberg, J., 5, 209
Woodwell, W., 97
Work group effectiveness research, 172–174
Workout, 62
World Bank, 175–176
Worley, C. G., 21, 27, 38, 88
Worren, N.A.M., 22

Y
Yaeger, T., 101

Z
Zautra, A., 94
Zawacki, R., 88

Pfeiffer Publications Guide

This guide is designed to familiarize you with the various types of Pfeiffer publications. The formats section describes the various types of products that we publish; the methodologies section describes the many different ways that content might be provided within a product. We also provide a list of the topic areas in which we publish.

FORMATS

In addition to its extensive book-publishing program, Pfeiffer offers content in an array of formats, from fieldbooks for the practitioner to complete, ready-to-use training packages that support group learning.

FIELDBOOK Designed to provide information and guidance to practitioners in the midst of action. Most fieldbooks are companions to another, sometimes earlier, work, from which its ideas are derived; the fieldbook makes practical what was theoretical in the original text. Fieldbooks can certainly be read from cover to cover. More likely, though, you'll find yourself bouncing around following a particular theme, or dipping in as the mood, and the situation, dictate.

HANDBOOK A contributed volume of work on a single topic, comprising an eclectic mix of ideas, case studies, and best practices sourced by practitioners and experts in the field.

An editor or team of editors usually is appointed to seek out contributors and to evaluate content for relevance to the topic. Think of a handbook not as a ready-to-eat meal, but as a cookbook of ingredients that enables you to create the most fitting experience for the occasion.

RESOURCE Materials designed to support group learning. They come in many forms: a complete, ready-to-use exercise (such as a game); a comprehensive resource on one topic (such as conflict management) containing a variety of methods and approaches; or a collection of like-minded activities (such as icebreakers) on multiple subjects and situations.

TRAINING PACKAGE An entire, ready-to-use learning program that focuses on a particular topic or skill. All packages comprise a guide for the facilitator/trainer and a workbook for the participants. Some packages are supported with additional media—such as video—or learning aids, instruments, or other devices to help participants understand concepts or practice and develop skills.

- *Facilitator/trainer's guide* Contains an introduction to the program, advice on how to organize and facilitate the learning event, and step-by-step instructor notes. The guide also contains copies of presentation materials—handouts, presentations, and overhead designs, for example—used in the program.

- *Participant's workbook* Contains exercises and reading materials that support the learning goal and serves as a valuable reference and support guide for participants in the weeks and months that follow the learning event. Typically, each participant will require his or her own workbook.

ELECTRONIC CD-ROMs and web-based products transform static Pfeiffer content into dynamic, interactive experiences. Designed to take advantage of the searchability, automation, and ease-of-use that technology provides, our e-products bring convenience and immediate accessibility to your workspace.

METHODOLOGIES

CASE STUDY A presentation, in narrative form, of an actual event that has occurred inside an organization. Case studies are not prescriptive, nor are they used to prove a point; they are designed to develop critical analysis and decision-making skills. A case study has a specific time frame, specifies a sequence of events, is narrative in structure, and contains a plot structure—an issue (what should be/have been done?). Use case studies when the goal is to enable participants to apply previously learned theories to the circumstances in the case, decide what is pertinent, identify the real issues, decide what should have been done, and develop a plan of action.

ENERGIZER A short activity that develops readiness for the next session or learning event. Energizers are most commonly used after a break or lunch to stimulate or refocus the group. Many involve some form of physical activity, so they are a useful way to counter post-lunch lethargy. Other uses include transitioning from one topic to another, where "mental" distancing is important.

EXPERIENTIAL LEARNING ACTIVITY (ELA) A facilitator-led intervention that moves participants through the learning cycle from experience to application (also known as a Structured Experience). ELAs are carefully thought-out designs in which there is a definite learning purpose and intended outcome. Each step—everything that participants do during the activity—facilitates the accomplishment of the stated goal. Each ELA includes complete instructions for facilitating the intervention and a clear statement of goals, suggested group size and timing, materials required, an explanation of the process, and, where appropriate, possible variations to the activity. (For more detail on Experiential Learning Activities, see the Introduction to the *Reference Guide to Handbooks and Annuals*, 1999 edition, Pfeiffer, San Francisco.)

GAME A group activity that has the purpose of fostering team spirit and togetherness in addition to the achievement of a pre-stated goal. Usually contrived—undertaking a desert expedition, for example—this type of learning method offers an engaging means for participants to demonstrate and practice business and interpersonal skills. Games are effective for team building and personal development mainly because the goal is subordinate to the process—the means through which participants reach decisions, collaborate, communicate, and generate trust and understanding. Games often engage teams in "friendly" competition.

ICEBREAKER A (usually) short activity designed to help participants overcome initial anxiety in a training session and/or to acquaint the participants with one another. An icebreaker can be a fun activity or can be tied to specific topics or training goals. While a useful tool in itself, the icebreaker comes into its own in situations where tension or resistance exists within a group.

INSTRUMENT A device used to assess, appraise, evaluate, describe, classify, and summarize various aspects of human behavior. The term used to describe an instrument depends primarily on its format and purpose. These terms include survey, questionnaire, inventory, diagnostic, survey, and poll. Some uses of instruments include providing instrumental feedback to group members, studying here-and-now processes or functioning within a group, manipulating group composition, and evaluating outcomes of training and other interventions.

Instruments are popular in the training and HR field because, in general, more growth can occur if an individual is provided with a method for focusing specifically on his or her own behavior. Instruments also are used to obtain information that will serve as a basis for change and to assist in workforce planning efforts.

Paper-and-pencil tests still dominate the instrument landscape with a typical package comprising a facilitator's guide, which offers advice on administering the instrument and interpreting the collected data, and an initial set of instruments. Additional instruments are available separately. Pfeiffer, though, is investing heavily in e-instruments. Electronic instrumentation provides effortless distribution and, for larger groups particularly, offers advantages over paper-and-pencil tests in the time it takes to analyze data and provide feedback.

LECTURETTE A short talk that provides an explanation of a principle, model, or process that is pertinent to the participants' current learning needs. A lecturette is intended to establish a common language bond between the trainer and the participants by providing a mutual frame of reference. Use a lecturette as an introduction to a group activity or event, as an interjection during an event, or as a handout.

MODEL A graphic depiction of a system or process and the relationship among its elements. Models provide a frame of reference and something more tangible, and more easily remembered, than a verbal explanation. They also give participants something to "go on," enabling them to track their own progress as they experience the dynamics, processes, and relationships being depicted in the model.

ROLE PLAY A technique in which people assume a role in a situation/ scenario: a customer service rep in an angry-customer exchange, for example. The way in which the role is approached is then discussed and feedback is offered. The role play is often repeated using a different approach and/or incorporating changes made based on feedback received. In other words, role playing is a spontaneous interaction involving realistic behavior under artificial (and safe) conditions.

SIMULATION A methodology for understanding the interrelationships among components of a system or process. Simulations differ from games in that they test or use a model that depicts or mirrors some aspect of reality in form, if not necessarily in content. Learning occurs by studying the effects of change on one or more factors of the model. Simulations are commonly used to test hypotheses about what happens in a system—often referred to as "what if?" analysis—or to examine best-case/worst-case scenarios.

THEORY A presentation of an idea from a conjectural perspective. Theories are useful because they encourage us to examine behavior and phenomena through a different lens.

TOPICS

The twin goals of providing effective and practical solutions for workforce training and organization development and meeting the educational needs of training and human resource professionals shape Pfeiffer's publishing program. Core topics include the following:

Leadership & Management

Communication & Presentation

Coaching & Mentoring

Training & Development

E-Learning

Teams & Collaboration

OD & Strategic Planning

Human Resources

Consulting

What will you find on pfeiffer.com?

- The best in workplace performance solutions for training and HR professionals

- Downloadable training tools, exercises, and content

- Web-exclusive offers

- Training tips, articles, and news

- Seamless on-line ordering

- Author guidelines, information on becoming a Pfeiffer Affiliate, and much more

Discover more at www.pfeiffer.com

Customer Care

Have a question, comment, or suggestion? Contact us! We value your feedback and we want to hear from you.

For questions about this or other Pfeiffer products, you may contact us by:

E-mail: **customer@wiley.com**

Mail: **Customer Care Wiley/Pfeiffer**
10475 Crosspoint Blvd.
Indianapolis, IN 46256

Phone: **(US) 800-274-4434** (Outside the US: 317-572-3985)

Fax: **(US) 800-569-0443** (Outside the US: 317-572-4002)

To order additional copies of this title or to browse other Pfeiffer products, visit us online at **www.pfeiffer.com**.

For **Technical Support** questions call **(800) 274-4434**.

For authors guidelines, log on to www.pfeiffer.com and click on "Resources for Authors."

If you are . . .

A **college bookstore, a professor, an instructor, or work in higher education** and you'd like to place an order or request an exam copy, please contact jbreview@wiley.com.

A **general retail bookseller** and you'd like to establish an account or speak to a local sales representative, contact Melissa Grecco at 201-748-6267 or mgrecco@wiley.com.

An **exclusively on-line bookseller**, contact Amy Blanchard at 530-756-9456 or ablanchard@wiley.com or Jennifer Johnson at 206-568-3883 or jjohnson@wiley.com, both of our Online Sales department.

A **librarian or library representative**, contact John Chambers in our Library Sales department at 201-748-6291 or jchamber@wiley.com.

A **reseller, training company/consultant, or corporate trainer**, contact Charles Regan in our Special Sales department at 201-748-6553 or cregan@wiley.com.

A **specialty retail distributor** (includes specialty gift stores, museum shops, and corporate bulk sales), contact Kim Hendrickson in our Special Sales department at 201-748-6037 or khendric@wiley.com.

Purchasing for the **Federal government**, contact Ron Cunningham in our Special Sales department at 317-572-3053 or rcunning@wiley.com.

Purchasing for a **State or Local government**, contact Charles Regan in our Special Sales department at 201-748-6553 or cregan@wiley.com.